A CUTTING GARDEN FOR FLORIDA

Third Edition
Revised and Expanded

Grow marvelous flowers for bouquets in your Florida home landscape!

By Betty Barr Mackey and
Monica Moran Brandies

B. B. Mackey Books
P. O. Box 475
Wayne, PA 19087

A Cutting Garden For Florida

Third edition, revised and expanded. A CUTTING GARDEN FOR FLORIDA

© Copyright 2001, 1992, 1985, by Betty Barr Mackey and Monica Moran Brandies. First edition © 1985 by Betty Barr Mackey. Second edition © 1992 by Betty Barr Mackey and Monica Moran Brandies.

Pen and ink illustrations © 2001 and 1992 by Betty Mackey. Page 4 © by Heather Lovett, 1992.

Front cover photo by Betty Mackey. Back cover photo by Alan Mackey. Lithographs and art from antique and copyright-free sources. Computer graphics by Betty Mackey.

ISBN 0-9616338-9-1

Library of Congress Catalog Card Number 92-93264

All rights reserved, including the right of reproduction in whole or in part.

ACKNOWLEDGMENTS

Special thanks to my husband David who puts up with my leaf gathering and supports my writing and to all the Florida gardeners who have shared their knowledge, plants, and time with me, especially the people at the Hillsborough County Extenion Service. And to Betty Mackey, who started me on great adventures with the last edition of this book. —Monica Brandies

I thank all the readers of the first and second editions, whose encouragement inspired this volume. Many wrote that they wanted their own copy after borrowing one from the library—the ultimate compliment. One herb store owner threatened to spank me if I didn't bring out edition three! And special thanks to Monica Brandies, without whose years of participation, support, friendship, and contributions I would be lost. Thanks to author Pat Kite, too. I thank my family for their help and understanding, my friends Cissy Barrows, Jean Mansmann, Laura Botte, Heather Lovett, Caroline Tumola, David Brandies, Helene Friedman, Jan Allyn, Joyce Allyn, Marian van Atta, Tom MacCubbin, Vince Sims, and Kathy and Wae Nelson. My very special thanks to Sylvester Rose for well-thought out improvements to this edition. —Betty Mackey

B. B. Mackey Books is an award-winning independent publisher with several titles for Florida gardeners, garden notebooks, and books on other special garden topics. Their recent title *Creating and Planting Garden Troughs* won a Book of the Year 2000 award from the American Horticultural Society.

Books may be ordered from any full service bookstore, or by mail from **B. B. Mackey Books**, P. O. Box 475, Wayne, PA 19087. Please write to that address or send email to bbmackey@prodigy.net for a free booklist and order form.

Books are available at wholesale terms: contact **Great Outdoors Publishing** in St. Petersburg at **1-800-869-6609** for information about wholesale and retail purchases of this and many other fine books.

DEDICATION

To my daughters Mary and Brigid and their families, Elizabeth, Jason, Ethan, Amy, Darcie, and Jacob. Also for daughter-in-law Susan, and John's Dawn, Meranda, and Daron, and for son-in-law Tony who grows Florida flowers. In memory of my Aunt Joan, who won ribbons at the Xenia fair and always kept the house full of flowers.

* Monica

To Tom, Ed, and Al, above all. And to all the Barrs whose unique outlook on life keeps me happy: Dot, Dad, Mary, Joan, and Al, plus Octavio, Roberto, and Virgilio, who put up with us all, especially at Thanksgiving. And to the memory of my mother.

* Betty

Contents

Introduction..... 5

Chapter One: Cut Flowers in Florida Landscapes.....7

Chapter Two: Making a Cutting Garden..... 9

Chapter Three: A Seasonal Guide..... 19

Chapter Four: Nursing Your Seedlings..... 23

Chapter Five: Propagating Plants from Cuttings and Divisions..... 29

Chapter Six: Cut Flower Choices; Tender Annuals..... 35

Chapter Seven: Cut Flower Choices; Hardy Annuals and Biennials..... 47

Chapter Eight: Cut Flower Choices; Perennials..... 59

Chapter Nine: Cut Flower Choices; Bulbs..... 79

Chapter Ten: Cut Flower Choices; Trees and Shrubs..... 89

Chapter Eleven: Beauty From Everlastings..... 105

Chapter Twelve: Arranging the Bounty..... 115

About the Authors..... 129

Bibliography..... 131

Suppliers and Resources..... 133

Garden Visits..... 135

Index..... 138

A Cutting Garden For Florida

INTRODUCTION

Like so many fellow gardeners, Monica Brandies and I believe that a garden should be a beautiful and friendly place around the home, not too formal and untouchable. We'd rather have freely blooming masses of flowers, enough to cut abundantly for indoor bouquets without spoiling the landscape.

However, in Florida, which was named for this kind of abundance, such a garden is too rarely seen. It takes special knowledge to help flowering plants thrive in our Florida soils and climate. Gardening here is remarkably different from gardening in the rest of the country.

In spite of the obstacles, it is not difficult to have a succession of year-round bloom. In this book we hope to help Floridians create lovely and enjoyable home cutting gardens. In this, the third edition of our book on cutting gardens for Florida, we hope to continue to encourage people to grow a wide array of flowers and expand on the information we have presented in the previous editions of this book.

Both of us arrived in Florida with our husbands, who were transferred. We know the confusion of trying to garden here with skills learned elsewhere. Florida gardening is not the same as in more typical regions of the United States, and too many people give up at the first barrier.

If you have recently moved in or have not yet gardened in Florida, the information we present is a shortcut to understanding conditions and requirements here. You'll be able to grow all the flowers you want, and apply the same principles to growing better vegetables, herbs, and fruits as well. Understanding the realistic possibilities will help you create a garden that will be truly satisfying and personal.

Back in 1985, after learning how to make my new Florida garden grow my favorite flowers, I wrote the first edition of this book to keep others from repeating my early mistakes, and to show the wide range of flowers that can be part of any home gardener's landscape. Many readers wrote to say how much they enjoyed it. Two years later, when my husband was transferred to Philadelphia, I had to leave my new state. I was sure that it would be the end of this cutting garden book.

Then I learned that Monica had moved from Iowa to the Tampa area. We had never met, but I had always particularly liked her magazine articles. So I wrote to her with my good wishes and a bit of advice about gardening in Florida, and sent her a copy of the book. She wrote back and sent one she had written (*Sprouts and Saplings, 1986*). We have been friends ever since.

Meanwhile demand for the original edition of *A Cutting Garden for Florida* continued until it was sold out. So it seemed entirely natural that I would enlist Monica, now acclimatized to Florida and its garden ways, to coauthor a second edition, released in 1992. Without her it would not have been possible. In the years since, we've done many books together.

We are now expanding and reprinting this one. We've updated the original list of sources and added many new plants, tips, charts, and techniques. But not everything has changed: you'll find the same comfortable, concise instructions for growing, harvesting, conditioning, and arranging flowers and practicing environmentally friendly pest control. We have expanded the list of public gardens to visit for inspiration.

Monica and I hope you'll enjoy reading and using our book as much as we have enjoyed sharing garden experiences and working together. Happy gardening!

– Betty Mackey

A Cutting Garden For Florida

Chapter One
CUT FLOWERS IN FLORIDA LANDSCAPES

Have you ever driven through some of the older, quieter neighborhoods in Florida's small towns? Places like Mount Dora, Sanford, Winter Park, Fort Myers, Ocala, and Coral Gables? Whether the homes are cottages, mobile homes, or stately dwellings, they often are surrounded by breathtaking foliage, fruit, and flowers. As the seasons change, so do these lovely old-fashioned gardens.

In these homes are the old-timers of Florida who have mastered the unusual garden calender, and their new neighbors who have learned from them. In contrast, many homes in newer suburbs feature a limited blend of rugged landscape shrubs around the foundation. Often enough, this is not what they want, but what they have settled for after their garden skills, transplanted from states farther north, have failed to work against Florida sand, bugs, and weather. Fortunately, special gardening techniques and a different garden calendar are all it takes to turn frustration into garden success.

If you are interested in growing a wide range of flowers and foliage to bring indoors for bouquets, it is important to experiment, as we did when we arrived. In your first year you may make more than the usual number of mistakes, but you will also have many unexpected successes and delights. After that you are on your way to becoming an outstanding Florida gardener.

For it is quite possible—even easy—to grow a wide assortment of beautiful flowers for cutting in all parts of Florida, in all seasons. Lots of people do. With appropriate timing and techniques, you will soon enjoy similar abundance.

UNDERSTANDING FLORIDA CONDITIONS

Soil in Florida tends to be very sandy and infertile, but it can be corrected. The main difference between Florida and more northerly states is the weather and how it affects planting time. You can't change it, but you can time your garden activities for best success. Though many Florida gardeners are not aware of it, gorgeous bunches of baby's breath, sweet peas, nasturtiums, shirley poppies, carnations, and phlox grow readily here, even though they are thought of as northern flowers. The secret of growing them well is cool weather planting. Almost any known annual or biennial flower will grow in Florida if planted at the right time of year.

Perennial flowers point up differences between northern, central, and southern Florida (see USDA zone map, page 18). Northern Florida is the southernmost limit for many favorite perennials. Gardeners there enjoy such cut flower classics as peonies, hosta, shasta daisies, bearded iris, and columbine. The rest of us must get along without them or expect results from so-so to disastrous, depending on the weather.

Perennials for northern and central parts of the state include African daisy, gaillardia, daylily, chrysanthemum, oxalis, yucca, calla lily, amaryllis, canna lily, agapanthus, impatiens, and gladiolus. South Florida has these plus tropicals: orchid, bird-of-paradise, anthurium, poinsettia, bougainvillea, kalanchoe, allamanda, pentas, frangipani, and more, all of which need protection from frost.

Biennial flowers do well in Florida if planted after the worst heat of summer passes. September/October is their best planting time in northern Florida; late

A Cutting Garden For Florida

October through early December is the best period in the rest of the state. Some kinds will bloom only a few months later in the early spring. Annual phlox, *Phlox drummondii*, is best treated as a biennial. It grows wild in many parts of the state. Pansies, California and shirley poppies, some types of foxglove, lupine, and gloriosa daisies do well if grown as biennials.

Some annuals are grown like biennials, and some tender perennials like impatiens are usually called annuals because they freeze in northern states and are used annually. Other perennials are more like biennials here, and some plants behave one way one year and another way the next because the weather pattern changed. The terms can be very confusing, but in our chapters, we made final placement of plants in categories according to the British classification system used in Thompson and Morgan's seed catalog. It seemed best, in light of our experience.

Besides flowers, the home landscape for cutting can include palms, leatherleaf fern, asparagus fern, lemon leaves, magnolia leaves, nandina, pittosporum, silver dollar eucalyptus, dracena, podocarpus, and other greenery for adding to fresh bouquets. Many of these are used in flower shops. For dried arrangements, our native grasses are lovely.

The trees, shrubs, ground covers, and other plants that frame and form your landscape can be selected to include desired blooms, berries, and foliage for arrangements. When you cut for bouquets, prune for shape.

Even yards that were not landscaped with bouquets in mind often yield pleasant surprises. "Snowbird" friends who winter in Florida taught Monica to display hibiscus flowers without water in star-shaped hibiscus holders. A single flower plucked on a morning's walk can grace a table all day, lasting as long as it would on the bush. Pyracantha, East Palatka holly, bougainvillea, ginger lilies, the weedy vine, mordica, and the Virginia creeper that shades the screened porch can be used for attractive indoor accents.

Growing plants from seed yields many beautiful, unusual cut flowers. Seed catalogs offer a wide variety. Because they provide photographs, descriptions, and advice, the catalogs are great aids in planning. Most are mailed free on request and you should keep them in a special place for ready reference. However, information must be adjusted for Florida conditions and timing.

Without a garden rest period enforced by winter, we Florida gardeners must make time for the "armchair" phase, the time spent browsing through catalogs and dreaming of next season's garden, always the best. We like to review the catalogs in winter when they arrive and again during the hot part of summer, when it is too hot for most seeds or small plants to grow, but time to plan for the autumn planting season which lies ahead.

Chapter Two
MAKING A CUTTING GARDEN

FINDING ROOM FOR CUT FLOWERS

Plants placed in the most visible parts of your home landscape ought to look presentable during all phases of their growth. With planning, you can make selections for your landscape which serve just as well as sources of flowers, berries, and greens for cutting, and have all you like.

For multi-purpose groundcover, choose ivy, leatherleaf, or wandering jew rather than border grass. Flowering shrubs and trees such as hibiscus, camellia, azalea, crape myrtle, buddleia, gardenia, viburnum, and hydrangea look wonderful in the landscape and provide generously for bouquets. So do foliage plants like pittosporum and nandina. Flowerbeds can be planted so thickly that a few African daisies, dianthus blooms, or snapdragons can be cut without leaving a bare spot. A bed of roses can have a wonderful effect on the landscape, and so can a row of sunflowers along a fence.

But for the most flexibility in what you grow and cut, we recommend planting a separate cutting garden, remote from view if possible, like a vegetable garden. In fact, if you have a vegetable garden already, the easiest thing to do is set aside several rows and lavishly plant flowers along with the vegetables. Here, annual flowers in their early stages of growth offend no eye with bare spots. If you need lots of pink cosmos and baby's breath to make a special arrangement, there is nothing to prevent you from cutting it all.

In a cutting garden you can try planting a packaged mixture of annual flower seeds. This is an inexpensive way to experiment and find flowers that suit your conditions. A mix of California wild flowers is fun—plant it in January or February in southern or central Florida, in March farther north. There are all different kinds of mixtures, with the species included grouped by height, color, climate preference, or other criteria (Many kinds of white flowers, for instance, or long-stemmed flowers). There may be 20 or more kinds of flower seeds in a single mixed packet.

Plant part of the same mixture in a different place or at a different time, and the results will be different. You may not recognize all the plants, so plant seeds in neat, narrow rows rather than broadcast. When they begin to grow, pull out all recognized weeds and anything outside the rows, and let the rest grow. When they bloom, you can easily identify them by looking in illustrated seed catalogs or reference books.

Of course, some plants in the mix will perform better than others and some will appeal to you more. After identifying your favorites, you can concentrate on them the following year. One warning—you will have more elegant results if you buy a superior mix from a high quality supplier. Check our list of resources at the end of the book.

PLANNING

What kind of garden is right for you? What kinds of cut flowers would you like for your home? How many? How much work do they require? How formal should they be? How large? In what shapes and colors? How can they be attractively added to your landscape?

A Cutting Garden For Florida

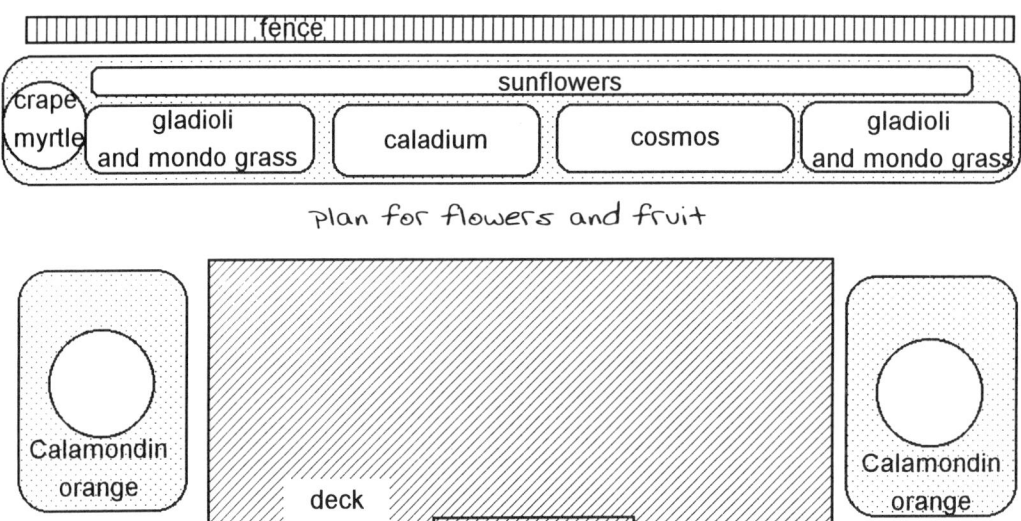

Plan for flowers and fruit

Look at your homesite closely. To what degree does the landscaping already suit your needs? Are you nearly satisfied with your present landscape, but wish to add a patch of flowers for cutting? Are you thinking of a major overhaul? Do you have a new property with plenty of garden space to fill, where you can select all your main shrubs and groundcovers for their dual cutflower/landscape potential? Is space at such a premium that, to fit in plants for bouquets, some other plants will have to be replaced? How much garden work can you take on? Are there views to enhance or eyesores to hide?

How about the soil type and drainage, the amount of sun or shade, your climate, and a source of water? These diverse esthetic and practical considerations are part of good planning. You want to select plants that look attractive outside, appeal to you for indoor use, and are likely to thrive in the growing conditions you provide. Where do you begin?

If you are thinking of undertaking a complete change of a large property, it would be wise to consult a landscape designer, making your wishes for cut flowers very clear. Smaller projects are easier to handle, and there are many approaches.

We usually recommend making a list of your most wanted plants, and then narrowing it down, using practical considerations such as space and each plant's preferred growing conditions. If you pore over a catalog or wander through a garden center, you are likely to add more to your list. It's fun to try some new things along with dependable favorites.

CHOOSING THE PLANTS

Throughout chapters 6 to 10, you'll find alphabetically arranged listings of annual, perennial, and woody plants for cut flower gardens, to help you make your choices. Each listing describes the plant's appearance, frost tolerance, and bloom time as well as its preferred spacing, amount of sunlight, and soil type.

If you garden in a site with difficult growing conditions such as too much shade or poor drainage, it saves frustration to make a list of plants that tolerate that, and then choose among them. If your site is sunny or partially shaded, with good drainage, the choice is wide, so select those that will look the nicest.

Making a Cutting Garden

Keep in mind, too, the indoor area where you plan to use the cut flowers. What colors and types do you prefer? If you will be away part of each year, concentrate on plants that bloom while you are in your Florida home.

Often, the entrance area of a property is well landscaped with evergreen and specimen shrubs, but the sides and back are somewhat neglected. If so, beds for cut flowers can be made along the sides or back of the home, or on the outer edges of the property, perhaps with a fence or line of shrubs for background, or as island gardens in large expanses of lawn.

If there is room only for a small patch for cutting, annual flowers will give you the most production in the smallest space. Even a half whiskey barrel on the patio, filled with rich soil and annuals such as zinnias, will be large enough to give you quite a few bouquets. Container gardens like that can be all of a kind or a bouquetlike mixture of flowers. Another option is growing small, flowery plants in tabletop-sized containers, using them on outdoor furniture or bringing them indoors just to decorate for special events.

If your cutting garden is not to be in a highly visible part of your landscape, you need not worry so much about using colors that clash, or whether it is neat or beautifully arranged. It is mainly for cut flower production, so put in whatever strikes your fancy. Mixtures of colors and flower types are fine. You'll want blooms in all seasons, too. Regardless of which plants you choose, you'll need paths or narrow flowerbeds, so that you can easily reach and cut any flowers in the garden without harming others.

If the garden is visible in the landscape, it will be more pleasant to look at if the colors and shapes blend and contrast harmoniously. Plant large clumps of a single form and color of a plant, and relate the colors to other nearby clumps of flowers and foliage. The colors should suit the indoors where the bouquets will be placed, as well.

In a formal-looking area, or if your cut flowers are to be a prominent feature in the landscaping plan for your yard, their season of bloom and color combinations are much more important. Try to have plenty of bloom in each season and in each section of the yard for continuous color. As you plan, bear in mind which plants in which colors will be blooming at the same time. Keep notes on what blooms when, for future reference.

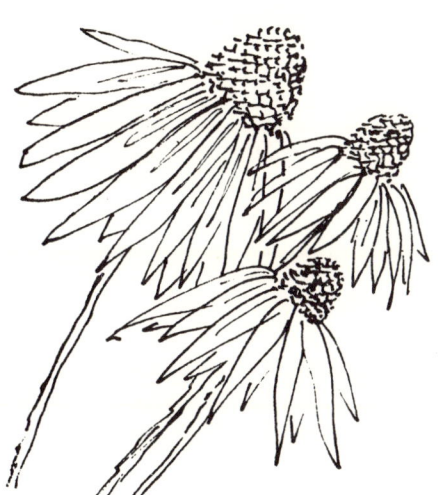

Plan for continuation of bloom. For instance dianthus is both cold and heat hardy, giving a lot of oomph throughout the year. Amaryllis blooms in late winter, more spectacularly but for a much shorter period. Pansies tolerate a little frost but are killed by summer heat. After they have finished providing winter color, remove them and plant something else, such as impatiens, which blooms nonstop during the frost-free times of year, or torenia, which is great for all the warm months.

A Cutting Garden For Florida

In Florida, the growing season is longer than some plants can last. Floridians must make for themselves the decision that winter makes for gardeners up north: when should a row or section of plants be removed for a fresh start. Some annuals such as marigolds will bloom themselves to death. One must be ruthless and remove them as soon as they pass their prime, to make room for something new.

In the beds, have the height of plants increase gradually, the shorter ones to the front and the taller ones to the back. All can get enough sun, and you can readily see what is available for cutting. Grow shade-loving and sun-loving plants in separate beds. Similarly, work with nature and group thirsty plants together, with drought tolerant ones in their own area.

Before you dig, map out the beds, showing the color schemes for each season. You can cut out photos from seed catalogs and rearrange them to test your plan.

Unless you live very close to the Keys, keep frost in mind also. Where a frost-sensitive plant is apt to die back and leave a hole or an eyesore, have other hardy plants nearby to cover the damage and continue the bloom. Pansies bloom right through light frost, so it's nice to have extras for winter emergencies.

CHOOSING A SITE

The spot you select for your cutting garden should be in full sun or light shade. From September to May, full sun is best for most garden flowers. During the hot summer months, most flowers, even those whose seed packets recommend full sun, will grow much better in Florida if grown in bright partial shade. For this reason, nurseries often grow plants below screens or shadecloth.

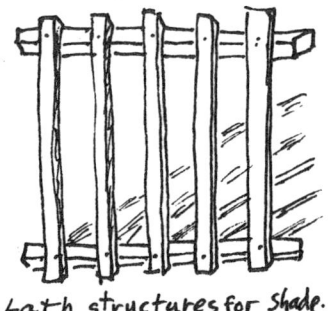

Lath structures for shade.

Choose a flat site to help keep small plants and seeds from washing out. Be sure you have no tree roots, buried telephone or cable TV wires, or other obstacles in the soil. Most utility companies will come and locate underground wires for you, free, if you call and ask.

Easy access to water is vital, especially if you will grow plants from seed. Until the plants are half grown they will need daily or twice-daily watering, soft and gentle. A fan-shaped hose nozzle or a drip watering system will permit you to water freely without dislodging seeds. A lightweight cover made from screen tacked to slender wooden lath strips will shelter them from the blast of a hard rain. Remove or raise it after seedlings have germinated.

The cutting garden can be any size, but it is best to start with a small strip or bed and then enlarge it each year as you gain experience and improve your soil. A space three feet wide and eight feet long will provide many cut flowers. This is narrow enough to permit you to reach in from one side or the other to weed and tend the plants. You'll need pathways in wider beds or those which back up to a fence or wall.

DIGGING IN

To work your soil you will need a spade, a metal garden rake with short tines (not a leaf rake), a sturdy trowel, and garden gloves. Unless you are plowing a vast area, you can do without a rototiller, although it is nice to have one. The soil will have to be turned, fertilized, and, possibly, solarized or treated to prevent nematodes. Be sure to do your spading and any other heavy work in the morning while it is still cool.

Making a Cutting Garden

Most Florida soil is either very sandy or muck. The three main elements of soil are sand (particles of rock or shells), silt (including organic matter), and clay (very small particles of inorganic materials). You are lucky if your garden has muck soil, for it is dark and rich, a grower's dream. Nonetheless, it may need the addition of sand, clay, and compost to give it better texture and prevent erosion.

If your soil is sand, it is pale and gritty, and it is important to keep in mind that it provides no nutrients and does not hold water for long. You are essentially doing soilless (but not bug-free) gardening. You'll have to add soil builders such as compost, peat moss, and manure. Additional humus (organic matter) is needed in all parts of Florida, for it increases the nutrient value and water-holding capacity of the soil. Blooming plants need extra water and fertilizer to make good growth. Soil tests and advice are available from each county's agricultural extension office.

Remove the sod from the area chosen for your cutting garden. If you are in a hurry, dig it out by hand (and plant it or compost it elsewhere), or have a landscaper cut it off and roll it away with machinery. However, if you have more time, you can remove the sod yourself without chemicals or hard labor. Just spread a heavy layer of grass clippings (4 to 5 inches) on it and keep it watered. Without sunlight, the grass plants forming the sod will start to die. In three weeks the sod below the clippings should be easier to turn over. Dig in the clippings and the sod. Don't waste them, for they help build up organic matter in the soil. This can be done at any time throughout the summer to prepare a cutflower bed for autumn planting. This is much better for Florida's underground water supply than using a glyphosphate weed killer such as glyphosphate (Roundup). If weed killer was applied to your grass in the last two months, do not use the clippings over your cutting garden, for the lingering residue will harm your flowers. Instead, cover the cutting garden bed with a layer of black plastic sheeting, which kills sod by blocking the light, and heats and helps sterilize the soil.

Throughout the state, soil should be treated for nematodes. These microscopic worms are present in most soils throughout the country, but in most areas do little damage. In Florida, where there is so much heat and humidity and never enough frost to check the population, they can be a major problem. They infest the soil, then tunnel through roots of plants, stunting their growth. If you pull damaged plants and find knots on the roots that won't rub off (nitrogen nodules will), nematodes are the culprit. There are also kinds that leave less of a signature.

Marigolds, impatiens, and native plants seem relatively resistant to nematodes, and sweet potatoes seem to repel them in some areas. Most other plants are affected to some degree. The damage may be minimal the first year, but will increase in subsequent years if the nematodes are unchecked.

Nematodes are more of a problem in poor soil than soil improved with compost. Organic gardeners fight nematodes by using plastic sheeting, heavy mulch, rotating crops, and improving soil. Even if you add vast amounts of organic matter, you may still have some damage. Although nontoxic methods do not eliminate nematodes completely, we prefer not to use the chemicals that are toxic and go straight down into the underground water supply or into nearby streams and lakes.

Nematodes mainly stay in the top 8 to 10 inches of soil. You can set a plant that is sensitive to nematode damage inside a deep-sided, bottomless pot that has been sunk 8 to 10 inches down. The soil should be nematode-free potting mixture. If the pot extends an inch or two above the ground, it makes for efficient watering. Planting near walls and walks also discourages nematodes because roots can go under the cement and get away from the pests.

SOLARIZING SOIL

During the warm months you can treat soil by solarization. Here's how. Water well, then cover the bed with clear plastic for three or more weeks. The sun will bake and kill many of the nematodes, weed seeds, eggs of insects, grubs, and disease spores, reducing them to an acceptable level.

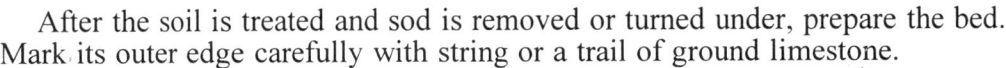
clear plastic over soil

For even deeper treatment, turn the soil after the first solarization and repeat the process. Make use of this deep digging by incorporating soil improvers such as compost and fertilizer at the same time. Most flowering plants prefer fertile, moist conditions.

After the soil is treated and sod is removed or turned under, prepare the bed. Mark its outer edge carefully with string or a trail of ground limestone.

ADDING HUMUS

Spread the bed with a generous layer (at least six inches deep if your soil is poor) of improvers: manure, vegetable matter such as chopped pine needles or leaves, compost, peat moss, and vermiculite, plus several handfuls of ground limestone and slow- or time-release fertilizer (at the rate recommended on the package). Clean kitty litter (for clay), colloidal phosphate, and alfalfa pellets (found at animal feed) stores are also favored by some experienced Florida gardeners.

Then till it all together with a rototiller or by hand. If using muscle power, first scoop out a shovelful of soil at one end of the bed, 10 to 12 inches deep, the depth you'll dig the bed. Dump it into a wheelbarrow or onto the other end of the bed. Then make the next cut, forcing the shovel in only three inches or so behind the edge of the hole. The dirt shifts more easily because the hole gives it air space to move into. Turn the slice (clod) over and dump it into the first hole, including the soil improvers, and work your way around the bed. You'll mix in the soil additives as you go. In Florida sand, this is fairly easy digging. Even so, don't overdo it. Remember, there is no virtue in doing the whole thing in one day, especially if this is a new action for your back.

You cannot get too much humus into the soil (although you must be careful with fresh manures), and will have to replenish it constantly as it decomposes and is used up each season. We like to use our own garden wastes such as chopped leaves and grass clippings as much as possible.

CONSIDERING pH

Another aspect of soil is its pH: alkalinity or acidity. Most soils in Florida have a neutral pH, because the silicon sand is so inert. If, as in some areas such as the Keys, your soil is high in limestone or seashells, it will be alkaline. Acidify it with ground sulfur at the rate of two pounds per 100 square feet (10 x 10-foot area). Adding a generous layer of pine needles and leaves acidifies the soil, too.

Making a Cutting Garden

Areas with a lot of silt may be slightly acidic. Ground limestone makes silty or other acidic soil more alkaline.

Most garden flowers like a neutral soil, neither acidic nor alkaline, with a pH reading close to 7.0. Some, especially wildflowers, have a preference for a high pH (over 7, alkaline) or a low one (under 7, acidic), depending on the soil type in the area from which they come. In our plant listings, we will mention preferred pH only if it is strongly acidic or alkaline. Most compost or loam is slightly acidic (about 6.5), but will bring a strongly acidic soil (say 5.5) closer to neutral, and an alkaline one down to neutral.

FINISHING THE BED

When you finish tilling the garden bed, the soil should be soft and loose and look something like commercial potting soil. In no case should it be white and sandy when you have finished. Add more humus—peat moss and such—if it is. Large, healthy blooms have to be supported by good nutrition and plentiful water.

Trim the edges of the bed with a flat spade or edger, rake it well, and it is ready to plant. Perennial beds and settings for shrubs and trees are prepared similarly. Nutrients will have to be added at intervals as the plants grow; Florida's drenching rains tend to wash them out. This is minimized by good soil preparation and the added humus which, spongelike, holds water and dissolved nutrients near the roots for a longer time.

To keep the soil in improved condition, cover the bed with a layer of mulch. Pine bark chips, chopped leaves, pine needles, and other materials may be used. With routine additions of organic mulch to maintain the amounts of humus, your soil will give better results each year.

AN EASIER METHOD

If you are as lazy as Monica claims to be, you can carry the mulching method one step further and never have to till the soil! Here's her method:

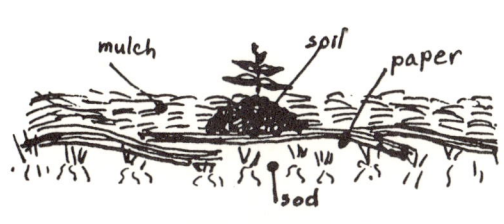

Spread newspaper sections 8 to 12 pages thick over the sod, overlapping them broadly so weeds can't creep in through the cracks. Over this spread a thick layer of grass clippings and/or leaves. After watering well, you can plant immediately. Just pull the mulch back, exposing the newspapers, and place the plants or seeds on the paper. Add soil around the roots of individual plants or over the top of seeds as needed. Dig holes for large plants through the newspapers, removing the bits of sod. Push the the top layer of mulch back up to the trunk after planting.

This method, perfected by ECHO (Educational Concerns for Hunger Organization, in North Fort Myers) for use in third world countries, works very well for Florida gardeners. Monica has used it extensively for many years now and has thereby retired a well-worn tiller. The roots will penetrate the damp newspapers when they need to. Roots can split rocks, so it is not as difficult for them as it may seem.

15

Meanwhile, the newspaper tends to keep the moisture and nutrients at root level and slow down their leaching through the sand. It also keeps the nematodes from coming up and into any roots formed in the mulch, blocks out weeds, and within a few months rots into the soil as humus, since most paper came from trees originally.

WATER-RETAINING GELS

We have also been experimenting with the addition of water-retaining gels such as Soil Moist™ to the soil. They are sold dry and look like crystals. They expand when wet. This is a sound idea, especially for sandy soil, for the gels absorb water and hold it in the root zone where it does the most good.

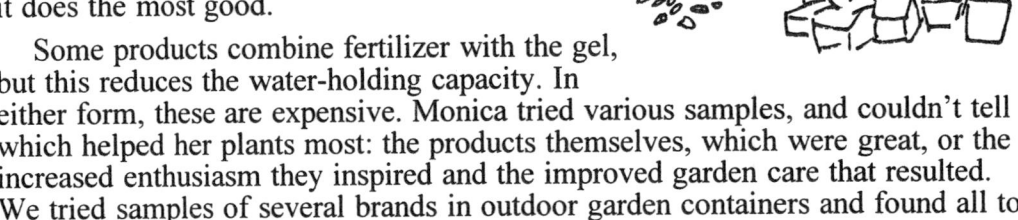

Some products combine fertilizer with the gel, but this reduces the water-holding capacity. In either form, these are expensive. Monica tried various samples, and couldn't tell which helped her plants most: the products themselves, which were great, or the increased enthusiasm they inspired and the improved garden care that resulted. We tried samples of several brands in outdoor garden containers and found all to be helpful in reducing watering needs.

The gel has such astounding water-holding capacity that only a very small amount should be dug in under a planting hole. Add too much and it will expand and push the plant right up and out. If it is not buried deeply enough, the gel expands and rises to the surface of the soil, looking like lumps of clear gelatin. If this happens, dig it right back into the soil, for it quickly becomes useless on the surface. In the soil it is good for several months to over a year, and by that time permanent plants are established well enough not to need it so much.

In containers, especially in hanging pots, the inclusion of gel can make the difference between having to water twice a day or every two days. It is not a necessary additive, but you might find it useful in your own pots and garden, especially as water restrictions remind us of the need to use our resources as wisely as possible.

FROST INSURANCE

Think about starting a small nursery section of replacement plants for your garden, for frost insurance. In an out-of-the-way section of the garden, in the ground or in pots, you can sprout seedlings, take cuttings and root them, and pot up replacement plants. These will be at hand to fill in gaps and help keep your cutting bed in prime condition and production throughout the year. Cover them or bring them into a coldframe or greenhouse, house, or garage on the few frosty nights in the south, up to a few weeks in central regions (sort of a sliding scale with more days in as you go north), and for the whole winter in the north. We found that more days of protection were needed in Orlando than in Tampa, though both areas are in Central Florida.

Also, on the day before a frost is predicted, if not sooner, take cuttings of such plants as coleus, pentas, dracena, hibiscus, copper leaf, croton, allamanda, passion flower, and torenia, and bring them inside.

Making a Cutting Garden

If the frost damage proves to be minor and you don't lose the main plants, you can trade your rooted cuttings, give them away, or grow them as extras. But if frost damage is severe, your replacements are waiting.

See chapter five for more information on making cuttings and divisions. By the way, don't give up too soon on frozen plants, for many, especially shrubs and trees, will reemerge from the roots after the tops have frozen. Sometimes new growth appears on plants that have not shown any signs of life for three months or more.

PEST CONTROL

It is true but overemphasized that Florida has unique and, compared to many regions, greater pest problems. You can have a fine garden here without using poison sprays.

There are several secrets of success. One is the selection of the right kinds of plants for the climate and then of the most pest- and disease-resistant varieties or cultivars of those kinds. Another is to use good cultural practices like soil improvement. Disease and some pests attack weak plants first. Mulch and proper watering and feeding will help to thwart pest problems. Stressed plants invite disease and are easily damaged.

Planting at the right time of year is vital. Petunias will soon be eaten up when summer begins, because they are cool season plants and are weakened by the heat and humidity, so plant them in winter in southern and central Florida, spring in northern Florida.

There are a host of beneficial insects, butterflies, and birds to help keep pests to a minimum. A ladybug can eat 5,000 aphids during her short lifetime. If your children scream when they see their first four-inch long preying mantid, explain that she is a friend. You can buy and import these and other pest-eating aids like green or brown lacewings and trichogramma wasps.

One ladybug vs. 5,000 aphids

mantid

Try to have several flowering shrubs in your garden to offer these helpers shelter and protection. Planning for a succession of bloom will give them a constant food supply. Include open-faced flowers to lure birds and beneficial insects, including alyssum, calendula, coreopsis, dill, gloriosa daisy, purple coneflower, portulaca, sunflower, and zinnia. Some hybridized flowers are so ruffled or tightly shaped that beneficial insects can't get into them.

Also, provide your helpers with drinking water, preferably in a shallow bird bath. Be vigilant about keeping it clean and filled with fresh water.

You will still have a few isolated insect problems. If you take a daily garden walk and watch your plants carefully, you can effectively pick off or kill off the first offenders so they will not become a plague.

When the pests start taking too big a share, get out the *Bacillus thuringiensis*, sold under such trade names as Dipel or Thuricide. This will control unwanted grubs and caterpillars. Insecticidal soap or a solution of hot pepper and garlic, blended with water and strained, will go far to deter other problems such as aphids on your nasturtiums and thrips on your gardenias. Pinesol cleaner diluted with water has been recommended for insect control, mixed at a rate of one tablespoon of the cleaner per gallon of water.

You may want to use a commercial fungicide for roses, especially in seasons when black spot is rampant. Many Florida gardeners are rediscovering antique roses that have survived for decades without fungicide because they have genetic immunity to black spot and other problems. You'll enjoy these without spraying. Try to plant roses in spots with good air circulation. Pick up any fallen leaves afflicted with black spot (they have unsightly yellow patches with black spots inside them) so they won't continue to spread the disease. Pick off yellowed leaves, too. Do not compost diseased rose leaves, just throw them away. Mulch roses to keep disease spores from splashing back up onto the new leaves, and to keep their root zone cool and moist.

GARDEN MAINTENANCE

Maintaining a cutting garden is similar to caring for other kinds of gardens. Any book on Florida gardening will give you the basics. You need to fertilize, water and weed, of course. And you need to prune and deadhead to keep plants to the required size and shape, encourage new bloom, and keep everything neat. But there are several significant differences. It may be that cutting gardens require more fertilizer and water than other gardens, because of the productivity of all the new growth. Mulching your plants will help on both counts (see sidebar) and will prevent weeds as well.

Cutting gardens include plants with lots of flowers. The "job" of a flower is to make seeds. Energy from the plant goes toward ripening those seeds, once they start to form. But as a flower grower, you usually want more flowers or a stronger plant, so it pays to remove the spent flowers right away. Cut them off with sharp little clippers, down near a lower branch or bud. This also makes your garden much more attractive. Have you ever watched professional gardeners at work, waste bucket in hand, snipping deadheads, yellowed leaves, and weeds as they make their way through the beds? Deadheading a cutting garden is not an unpleasant chore because when you cut flowers for bouquets, you are deadheading at the same time.

WHY MULCH

Mulch is a layer of anything that covers the surface of the ground, between the trunks or stems of plants in the bed. Organic mulch such as cedar chips eventually decays back into the ground. Inorganic mulch such as black plastic does not. Water well before applying mulch. Either kind of mulch saves moisture by preventing its evaporation. Mulches prevent weeds from getting the light they need to germinate or grow. Organic mulch helps keep soil temperature steady and eventually turns into soil-improving humus. It helps earthworms and beneficial bacteria flourish.

 Can you get free mulch? Yes indeed. People throw away the makings of good mulch all the time. Grass clippings that are free of herbicides make a tidy mulch, but distribute them right away, while green, to dry to a strawlike mat, in place. This prevents them from getting smelly. Pine needles and chopped leaves are really good. Bark, cedar, and licorice mulches are good but costly.

How much mulch do you need? Well, it depends. Tiny seedlings are smothered by a deep layer, but helped by a thin layer such as half an inch of grass clippings. A mature tree can thrive surrounded by a deep layer of chunky mulch. A 4 to 6 inch layer of organic mulch smothers most kinds of weeds and keeps the bed looking neat.

Chapter Three
A SEASONAL GUIDE

FLORIDA'S PLANT HARDINESS ZONE MAP

According to the USDA Plant Hardiness Zone Map, at right, most of Florida is in Zones 8, 9, or 10, with the Keys in Zone 11. Locate your own garden on the map and use these numbers for ordering plants and seeds by mail. Some of the information for one zone will also apply to bordering areas, especially in microclimate that are unusually exposed or unusually sheltered.

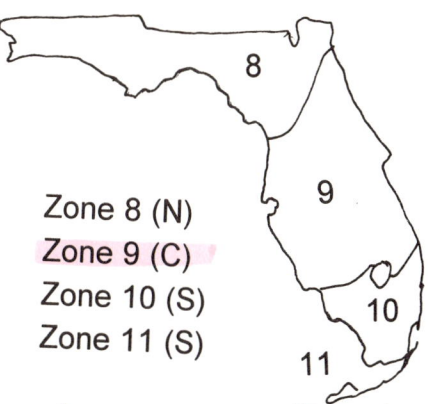

Zone 8 (N)
Zone 9 (C)
Zone 10 (S)
Zone 11 (S)

You may want to see how well warmer or cooler season crops will survive for you. If you live near a border, you might like to use crops recommended mainly for your own as well as some for the neighboring zone. That way, whatever the weather that year, some of your plants are sure to like it. Most of the flowers mentioned in this book, however, will grow in all Florida zones, with more or less frost protection depending on the zone.

More and more catalogs are giving a range of hardiness zones in which a plant will grow, and the southern (higher) number is very helpful. There is a new Heat Zone Map developed by the American Horticultural Society in 1998 to guide gardeners in the warmer zones. In the future, more books will refer to this, but it remains to be seen how useful it will be for Florida. Here it is not so much the heat that kills plants, but the combination of heat with our rainforest humidity.

THE GARDENING YEAR IN FLORIDA

Experienced Florida flower growers think of September as the start of the garden season. It is a good time to prepare soil for cool weather planting of flowers, bulbs, shrubs, and trees. But each month of the year is an appropriate time for starting some plants. If planted at the right time of year, plants from many diverse climates will grow well. Here are our month-by-month suggestions:

JANUARY

Northern Florida. Freezing weather is likely. Prepare soil for spring, but wait before planting.

Central and Southern Florida. Light freezes are possible, so be prepared to cover plants with cloths, newspapers, pine needles, cardboard boxes, insulated (bubbled) plastic sheeting, or whatever you have. Set out frost-tolerant plants of dianthus, calendula, pansies, poppies, stocks, candytuft, petunias, and snapdragons. Buy and start bulbs and tubers of dahlias, crinum lilies, and caladium indoors. Plant and feed freesias and amaryllis outdoors. Try gloriosa lily, a lovely climber in shade. Transplant cold-hardy trees and shrubs like crape myrtle, yucca, and dogwoods.

Prune tea roses, remembering that Florida roses may be pruned to three or four canes three feet high. This is taller than recommended for northern states. It is

> **Microclimates that Stretch the Zone**
>
> Plants that are well watered and fed withstand colder temperatures than others. There are also exposures, or **microclimates,** which decrease frost damage. If it gets cold enough, even these will not help, but many a night they have made the difference between life, death, or long recovery.
>
> **South Side of the House:** The wall of a house absorbs heat during the day and hold the temperatures up a few degrees during the night. One man said, "I can grow anything on the south side of the house. The trouble is I've run out of south side." Put the tougher plants out in the cold, but save the south side for plants of marginal hardiness.
>
> **Sheltered Porch or Patio:** A corner inside a courtyard is a sheltered position. Two walls will hold in heat and keep out wind, giving protection during a light freeze. Cluster your portable plants on a screened porch during the worst of winter, if there is enough light.
>
> **Nearby Body of Water: Swimming Pool, Lake, or Ocean:** When the thermometer dips suddenly at night, plants near water may survive conditions that will nip or kill those further away. Plants thrive in St. Petersburg which freeze in Tampa, farther inland. On a climate zone map, you will see that the warmer zones edge farther north along the coastline. Even the water in an above ground swimming pool can offer some protection.
>
> **Shade:** While shade will cause some plants to bloom and fruit less than they would in the sunshine, it also offers several degrees of protection from frost. In one garden near Gainesville, shrimp plants that were huddled under live oaks, as if under a blanket, were blooming again in early April, while the ones in the open were so badly damaged the gardeners cut them back to the ground. They recovered, but it took many months.
>
> **Portable Planters.** You can move plants in portable planters to a sheltered spot during cold spells. Even plants too large to move can be turned on their side and much more easily be covered with leaves or a blanket on cold nights.

still too early to prune climbing roses; wait until after they bloom. When you prune roses, cut far enough back. It's usually best to cut just above a full leaflet with five segments, not a smaller leaflet with three.

Prune crape myrtle now, but do not prune camellias and azaleas until they finish blooming. Water as needed.

Southern Florida. Refresh beds with new cuttings and plants of perennial tropical flowers.

FEBRUARY

Northern Florida. Set out plants of cold-tolerant flowers like dianthus and pansy, as above. Light frost is still likely.

Central and Southern Florida. It is early spring! Days are getting longer and warmer. Early February for Southern Florida and late February for Central Florida mean time for planting almost anything, including flower seeds. Try a mixed seed packet of annuals in your cutting garden. Space seeds well and save some for another planting a few weeks later. Seeds of babysbreath, sunflowers, strawflowers, shirley poppies, nasturtiums, salvia, and tithonia can go in now, while soil is still cool and insects are at a minimum. Continue to set in the plants that will form the structure of your spring garden. Set in plants of snapdragons, marigolds, petunias, cleome, and zinnias, toward the end of the month. In the north-central Florida, try long-lasting lisianthus (*Eustoma grandiflorum*).

When foliage of paperwhite narcissus and cold-treated bulbs turns yellow, lift bulbs, dry, and store in a cool, dry place.

A Seasonal Guide

MARCH

Northern Florida. Follow central Florida tips for February. Buy and plant shrubs in bloom, to see the exact form and check for fragrance.

Central and Southern Florida. Fertilize lawns and gardens—this is an important growth season. Continue planting flower seeds, including cosmos, marigolds, gaillardia, zinnia, and impatiens. Plant dahlias, gladiolus, and warm-weather bedding plants (see list under May-June). Fertilize and divide chrysanthemums and daylilies. Lift and store bulbs of star-of-Bethlehem. Pinch or shear off tips and old blooms of annuals to encourage branching and continuous bloom.

Keep watching for pests. Look for aphids on the underside of new leaves or on cupped or distorted leaves. Mites thrive in dry weather and suck juices from the underside of leaves. To control them, use a forceful spray of water from the hose, douse with insecticidal soap, or import beneficial insects.

APRIL

Northern Florida. Follow Central and Southern Florida notes for March.

All parts of state. Plant bedding plants of summer flowers. Plant warm-weather bulbs. Put mulches in place to conserve moisture. Remove spent annuals and prune off any branches of shrubs and trees killed by earlier frosts. Weed your cutting garden weekly and check for pests. Plant seeds where necessary. Keep pinching back or harvesting flowers from annuals. April is the beginning of hot weather. From now until the rains begin, usually in June, gardeners have to water often, for our sandy soil dries rapidly.

MAY-JUNE

In all parts of the state, select new daylilies and hibiscus while they are in bloom. Increase watering of all plants unless rainfall is high. Maintain high levels of fertilizer and water it in well. Use an acidic fertilizer for azaleas and camellias. You may still plant summer bulbs like caladium, canna, Aztec lily, butterfly lily, crinum, clivia, African iris, society garlic, spider lily, agapanthus, and gladiolus. Keep weeds under control with weekly maintenance.

Fill in empty spots in the beds with heat-loving flowers such as dianthus, periwinkle, torenia (Florida pansy), ti plant, strobilanthes (shade), gomphrena, portulaca, marigolds, zinnias, cosmos, and celosia. Pinch back tips of chrysanthemums for bushiness. Brighten shade with impatiens, ferns, caladium, and coleus.

JULY-AUGUST

In all zones, maintain watering, weeding, and fertilizing. This season's drenching rains tend to wash out soil, especially that of outdoor potted plants. If you are starting any seedlings, keep them loosely covered with plastic so they won't wash away. Use a "bloomer" fertilizer with high phosphorus and potassium to encourage more blossoms. Prune poinsettias. Compost grass clippings or use them as mulch. Divide daylilies, transplant amaryllis. Prune and fertilize chrysanthemums. Make or clear flowerbeds for fall planting and treat for nematodes.

This is a wonderful time of year to start cuttings. Pentas, coleus, and passion flowers root easily in humid weather. So do other shrubs and vines. Many plants will even root in a vase of water or wet vermiculite. We've both had marigolds, oregano, basil, mint, and coleus root in water while being part of a bouquet. The beginning of the rainy season (its timing and extent are variable) is also one of the best times to plant new trees and shrubs or to transplant perennials.

SEPTEMBER

In all parts of the state, continue clearing and treating beds for fall planting. Scan garden magazines and send for more seed catalogs. Cut flowers for drying. Tie stems together, wrap in cones of paper, and hang upside down indoors. Stake dahlias and chrysanthemums if necessary. Plant seeds of calendula for winter.

Paperwhite narcissus can be planted at intervals from now through October (but not other narcissus and daffodil varieties, which need a cold climate), for bloom from late December through early February. Groom roses.

In Northern Florida, sow seeds of biennials, perennials, and cool-weather annual plants: pansies, violas, alyssum, larkspur, rudbeckia, poppies, stocks, and cornflowers, to name a few.

In Southern Florida, there is still time for quick summer annuals; try a mix.

OCTOBER

In all zones, when the weather has begun to cool and stays below 85 degrees, it is safe again to plant seeds of alyssum, calendula, dianthus, foxglove (only quick-growing types which bloom the following spring, such as 'Foxy'), pansies, petunias, snapdragons, verbena, sweet peas, poppies, phlox, small-flowered sunflowers, Texas bluebonnets, scarlet runner beans, and other relatively hardy flowers in prepared beds. Plant a cut flower mixture. Fine seed may be sown in flats or sixpacks indoors, in strong light. Harden them off by bringing them outside for only a few hours a day at first.

Divide perennials and bulbs that are crowded or which you would like to increase in number. Tulips, daffodils, and hyacinths, bulbs that need winter cold, can now be purchased and held in the refrigerator (not in the freezer) until December or January, then planted out.

In Northern Florida, set out pansy, iceland poppy, viola, and snapdragon.

NOVEMBER-DECEMBER

Northern Florida. Seed planting ends now except in greenhouses and cold frames. There is still time to set out the winter bedding plants listed above.

Central Florida. Much depends on the weather. Why not take a chance with fine seeds of babysbreath and shirley, Iceland, and California poppies, which tolerate light to heavy frost. You may be rewarded with blooms by March. Set out reliable winter bedding plants: statice, geranium, petunias, snapdragons, calendula, pansies, and dianthus. The pansies tolerate more frost than the others.

Southern Florida. At this lovely time of year, many tropical blooms such as hibiscus and bougainvillea are in their prime. This is a good time to seek out and purchase outstanding cultivars. Practically any known annual may be sown or set out this time of year because the weather is cooler and the sunshine less direct. Plant amaryllis and tropicals that grow from bulbs and bulblike structures now.

Now it is planning time for next year. Send for seed catalogs, and check the garden magazines for descriptions of seed and plant introductions. Let the successes and failures of last year's garden guide your plan.

Chapter Four
NURSING YOUR SEEDLINGS

For the most complete choice of cut flowers, grow your own from seed. This is not difficult if you nurse them along with bright light, frequent gentle watering, shelter from pests, and nutritive soil. Usually the larger the seed, the easier it is to grow, for the plant that emerges has more reserves to draw on to maintain its moisture and resist pests. In our charts in the next few chapters, we show the actual seed size.

Before you begin, decide whether to sow seeds in the ground outdoors, or to grow them in pots in a bright, sheltered area such as a window sill, greenhouse, cold frame, or atrium. Small or rare seeds should have indoor protection at first. You will need overhead light bright enough to make a strong shadow or the seedlings will be too weak and spindly. Often, seedlings growing on a windowsill will be leggy for lack of balanced, bright light. Trays of seedlings on shelves just a few inches below fluorescent lights will grow straight and strong, almost as well as greenhouse-grown plants. Remember to change the bulb each year, even if it still works, for more intense light that will strengthen your plants.

If time and space are limited, plant only those special kinds and varieties of flowers indoors that you cannot buy from local outlets.

COLD FRAMES

A cold frame is outstanding for growing seedlings. It is a simple bottomless box covered with glass or plastic. The ideal cold frame for Florida is portable, so you can put it in full sun from October until March, then move it to bright partial shade from April through September. In summer, narrow lath strips, with or without screening or shadecloth, can replace the airtight transparent cover, to prevent overheating. Plants can be grown either in containers or directly in the soil.

Good cold frames are available by mail or from garden centers, or you can make your own. Sides can be made of cedar, cinderblock, or even insulation foam board (very easy to cut and nail). Use window frames or plastic sheeting for the top. The frames can be any size. A useful size is 2 feet deep, 3 feet wide, and 6 feet long. If you plan to utilize an old window or door for the top, measure it and build the rest of the frame to fit. A shade box, which is a cloth or screen topped frame, cuts the force of heavy rain and keeps bugs out, and may be all you need, most of the year, and for hardy plants. An unused corner of a sunny, screened-in patio or swimming pool enclosure is also excellent for trays of seeds!

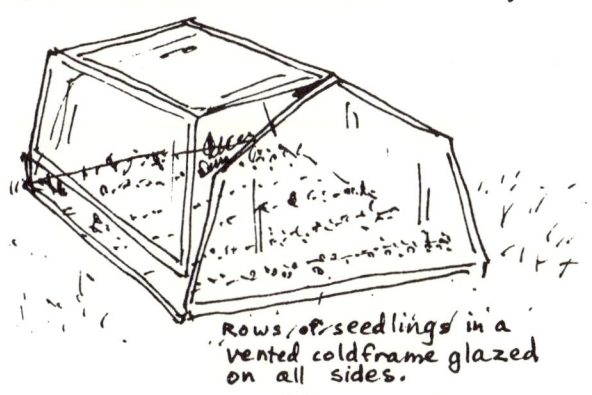

Rows of seedlings in a vented coldframe glazed on all sides.

A Cutting Garden for Florida

Overheating of the tender seedlings can be a severe problem in Florida, especially in a greenhouse or cold frame. Good ventilation prevents the buildup of heat. However, an open cold frame can let in frost, causing great damage to non-hardy seedlings. To prevent excessive heat or cold, a glazed cold frame may need several daily adjustments at critical times, so a frame with automatic venting is the easiest to use. Some systems do not depend on electricity, but instead have a metal, springlike mechanism that coils and uncoils as it contracts or expands with the temperature. Frost is quite rare in southern Florida, but is more frequent the farther north you live.

DIRECT SOWING, OR NOT?

Many excellent plants do better if sown directly in the cutting garden or flower bed where they will grow, without the shock to their systems caused by transplanting them. Some of these are shirley poppy, sunflowers, marigold, zinnia, cosmos, nasturtium, silene, and sweet pea. Correct timing and spacing are needed. They also do well when started indoors and transplanted when young.

Not only does direct seeding prevent transplant shock, it helps prevent crowded roots and develops sturdier plantlets. Outdoor growing also helps prevent damping-off, a fungus that kills emerging seedlings, toppling them over with rot at the soil line. Plants outdoors are more likely to have good light, room for roots and fresh air. When growth is not interrupted by transplanting they come into bloom sooner.

However, summer outdoor conditions are too hot and buggy for most types of seedlings, and winters outdoors are too cold for others. Plant your seeds of cool season crops inside in air conditioning in summer. Start others indoors in warmth in the winter. Especially in northern and central Florida, it can give you a jump on spring or fall seasons. Here are instructions for indoor seeding, followed by corresponding instructions for outdoor seeding.

GROWING SEEDLINGS INDOORS

In addition to seeds, you will need a sterile potting soil. A good mix is made of equal parts of perlite, vermiculite, and milled sphagnum moss. There are many good brands of prepared seed-starting mix. We like to add a tiny pinch of Rootone (a rooting hormone combined with a fungicide) to help prevent damping off. Also, get plastic plant labels for marking your seeds. Wooden ones quickly darken and sometimes rot. Disposable plastic knives are OK for this purpose, as are plastic bread bag tags and strips cut from milk jugs. Use an indelible horticultural pen (available from garden centers or mail order suppliers) or a pencil. Laundry markers can fade in time.

Your seed starting containers can be either bought or recycled. Possibilities include 3-by 12- by 18-inch wooden flats, seed six-packs or four-packs, margarine tubs, flower pots, or foil loaf pans. You will often find the black grass plug trays with their 18 pockets, each three inches square, put out for the trash collector. These are great for seeds because they can be cut apart to fit on window sills, and the size is right for many garden flowers.

Economy tips: Sealed plastic tubs make mini greenhouses for very fine, dustlike seeds. Old plastic plant labels can be scrubbed clean for re-use.

Seedlings

Cutting Garden Flowers That Tend to Reseed or Naturalize

Common Name	Botanical Name	Plant Type	Region
Air Plant	*Kalanchoe* species	perennial	CS
Amaranth	*Amaranthus* species	tender annual	NCS
Blackberry Lily	*Belamcanda chinensis*	perennial	NCS
Blanket Flower	*Gaillardia pulchella*	perennial	NCS
Butterfly Weed	*Asclepias* species	perennial	NCS
Cleome	*Cleome hasslerana*	tender annual	NCS
Emilia	*Emilia flammea*	hardy annual	NCS
Four O'Clock	*Mirabilis jalapa*	perennial	NC
Gaura	*Gaura lindheimeri*	perennial	NCS
Goldenrod	*Solidago* species	perennial	NCS
Hardy ageratum	*Eupatorium coelestinum*	perennial	NCS
Jewels of Opar	*Talinum paniculatum*	perennial	NC
Larkspur	*Consolida ambigua*	hardy annual	NC
Northern Sea Oats	*Chasmanthium latifolium*	perennial	NC
Ox-eye Daisy	*Chrysanthemum leucanthemum*	perennial	NC
Perilla	*Perilla frutescens*	tender annual	NCS
Plume Poppy	*Macleaya microcarpa*	perennial	NC
Purple Coneflower	*Echinacea purpurea*	perennial	NCS
Rudbeckia	*Rudbeckia* species	perennial	NCS
Salvia	*Salvia coccinea*	perennial	NCS
Spiderwort	*Tradescantia ohioensis*	perennial	NCS
Tickseed	*Coreopsis tinctoria*	hardy annual	NCS

> Tip: Plants that are especially easy from seed usually have large seeds that are easy to handle, leading to large, strong sprouts, such as zinnia, balsam, nasturtium, marigold, coreopsis, cornflower, sunflower, gloriosa daisy, ornamental cabbage, globe amaranth, salvia, and rudbeckia.

MONICA'S TOP TEN

The top ten cutting garden plants in Monica's garden near Tampa are:
- Amaryllis, blooming in early spring
- Pentas, blooming all year
- Shrimp Plant, blooming during warm months
- Cordyline, in colorful leaf during warm months
- Silver dollar eucalyptus, in leaf all year
- Pinecone Ginger, in bloom July to December
- Aloe, in bloom and leaf during warm months
- Nasturtium, in bloom from Thanksgiving to May
- Kalanchoe, in bloom from December to May
- Salvia, in bloom all year

These reliable favorite plants are spread throughout the yard and are the basis for lasting color both indoors and out, with a minimum of effort.

A Cutting Garden for Florida

If your seed containers do not have drainage holes, make some with a nail or an ice pick. Heat it to make it go through plastic easily. Wash recycled containers in hot water containing a bit of bleach. Below them, use waterproof liners such as plastic lids to protect tables and windowsills.

For most seeds, containers (with drainage holes) should be about three inches deep. For larger types, use four-inch pots. Mark labels with plant name and date of planting, also plant color and height if you need this information. Make one label per container—this means you may need many duplicates. Moisten the soil (not too wet!) and fill containers to half an inch from the top. Plant at the depth recommended on the pack

For the finest and most difficult seeds, sealed conditions (no drainage holes) that are as close to sterile as possible will give you the highest germination. We have used premoistened seed starting medium, packed into plastic containers with tight fitting, transparent lids (such as yogurt, salad bar, and margarine containers. Dustlike seeds are sprinkled on and gently patted in. The lids are snapped on and the containers left alone under fluorescent lighting until growth begins.

The smaller the seed, the closer to the surface it should be planted. Just tap in dustlike seeds, do not bury them. To spread them more evenly, mix with a spoonful of fine, dry sand or soil. Cover most seeds with 1/8 inch of soil. Plant large seeds such as nasturtium and sweet pea half an inch deep. Put just one or two seeds in each section or pocket, then thin to one plant later on.

For flats, make thinly sown rows three inches apart. Label each row.

For tufted seeds like marigolds, hold by the tuft and slip them into the soil at an angle, leaving the tuft out, just as nature does.

Move containers to the growing area, covering each loosely with plastic (we use transparent grocery bags) and placing a waterproof liner under it. As soon as seedlings emerge, remove the plastic. Water carefully, and never allow the seed containers to dry out.

Fertilize the plants with a safe product, not too strong, beginning when the first true leaves have opened. Use liquid fertilizer at half the recommended strength, increasing the strength when the seedlings are larger.

When plants in flats or crowded containers show four to six leaves, transplant them to individual pots. First fill the pots with damp, fertile soil. Use a pencil to make a hole in the soil!. Then, also with the pencil, pry plants up gently. Hold them by the leaves, not the fragile stems, while firming the soil gently around the roots. Let them grow for several more weeks. When they are a few inches high, give them fresh air and increased sunlight for a few days to harden them off before setting them into the flowerbed.

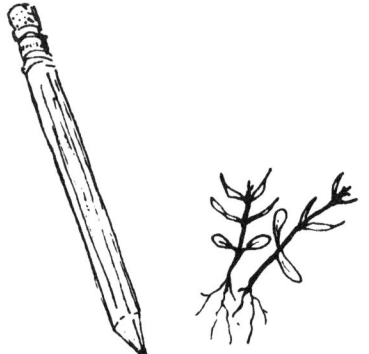

GROWING SEEDLINGS OUTDOORS

Prepare the cutting garden bed (chapter two). Turn the soil again by hand or with a rototiller, adding plenty of soil improvers. The plot should be well worked and fertile. Smooth out any lumps with a garden rake and get set to plant.

Shall it be rows or clumps? Clumps look more artistic, but rows make it easier to tell weeds from flowers, a point that can become very important when sowing something new and unfamiliar.

With either plan, measure out the spots for seeds. Make straight rows by measuring, marking with posts and string, and hoeing a row along the string line. Move posts and string to mark each row. For clumps, rake patches of soil into the right arrangement.

Mark rows or clumps with plastic labels and an indelible pen or a pencil. Place tall varieties toward the back, short ones toward the front, and combine colors for harmony. Leave walkways so you can reach all parts of the bed.

Plant your seeds according to packet directions, or a trace deeper in very sandy soil. As mentioned for indoor seeding, you can also mix very small seeds with fine sand or soil outdoors for more even spread.

If you encounter instructions such as "prefers dry sandy soil" or "prefers poor soil," they do not really mean that we should plant them in soil as dry, sandy, and poor as some of our plainer Florida types. But do select seeds with these preferences, for they are naturally suited to Florida. Also, light shade in Florida is the equivalent of full sun farther north, especially in summer. Full sun here will burn up some tender plants.

Space seeds a little closer together than directions say, for some will probably be lost to pests. When they are three inches tall, thin them. With all that soil preparation, they will be healthy and need lots of room to grow. Water twice a day with a fine spray, unless it is rainy. A hard rain may wash out small seeds. If it does, replant as soon as possible.

Continue watering carefully. Two weeks after the seedlings emerge, broadcast some safe, slow-release, non-burning fertilizer. Four or six weeks later use a bloomer fertilizer with high phosphorus and potassium. Pick off bugs and, if necessary, spray with insecticidal soap or dust with rotenone. Before you know it, the bed will burst into bloom with wonderful homegrown flowers.

SOURCES OF SEED

Some gardeners enjoy saving seed from flowers in their garden, while others disapprove, do not know how, or are afraid to experiment. It's true, there are many pros and cons about seed saving. We both save seeds sometimes, but also use commercially produced seeds and seeds from plant society seed exchanges.

Good reasons for buying commercial seeds are to get special varieties that perform reliably in your garden and to support research done by seed producers. You may want a bed of white snapdragons, and seeds produced under controlled conditions will give you just what you selected. Height, color, and shape will be uniform. You can also buy seeds by mail or on the internet of plants that would otherwise be hard to find. Specialists in flower seeds offer thousands of species and varieties.

SAVING SEED

A good reasons for allowing some of your plants to go to seed, and then collecting and planting that seed, is to develop strains of plants that appeal to you and tend to do well in your soil and climate. If, say, you plant a packet of mixed colors of California poppies, some of the plants will grow better than others, and some of the colors will be prettier. Some seeds from the pack may fail to grow because they prefer drier or cooler conditions. Save the seeds of your most successful poppy plants each year for several years to develop a customized mix.

A Cutting Garden for Florida

Sometimes it's fun to grow some saved seed just to see what will appear in the next generation. Betty saved seeds from a named hybrid pink, dwarf zinnia, knowing that the offspring might not be as special. The result? Most of the plants in the next generation were just the same, but a few were yellow, and a few were taller. The third generation had even more variety, yet all the flowers and plants were attractive.

An obvious reason to save seed is for economy. We're addicted to having masses of flowers around us at all times, and this becomes costly if we don't watch out. We saved seeds of last year's impatiens in envelopes until after frost passed, then liberally sprinkled them in flats and shady beds where needed. They were more reliable than self-sown seeds. At no cost, we got hundreds of plants with an interesting range of color and pattern. Buying that many seeds (not to mention bedding plants) would be pricey.

Add packs of silica gel to jars of stored seeds, to eliminate humidity.

Another reason is to get fresh seed. There are some plants (gerbera daisy is one) whose seeds do not dry and store well. They lose their viability. Fresh seed, freshly planted, from your own plants has a better chance of being successful.

A reader of an earlier edition of this book says she grows a field of snapdragons to sell as cut flowers, from fresh seed which she saves each year, collecting it from the best plants in a range of colors. Her profit margin is not large, and this economy helps make the difference between profit and loss. However, if she were selling bedding plants, she would probably use commercial seeds so customers would know the exact flower color, shape, and size of the plants they buy.

To save seeds, allow desired plants to flower and go to seed. Tie a string around them to mark them. Leave the pods or seedheads alone until they are ripe: usually they turn brown. Each species has its own characteristic form of seed container or capsule. Observation helps you identify them.

In some types, impatiens for one, the pods fatten and explode, scattering the seed. Picked too soon, the seeds are not ripe; wait too long, and they are gone. Get them just before they pop, clasping them so that they pop in your hand. Put them into a cup as you go along, chaff and all. Trial and error is a fine teacher.

Collect the seeds, throw away the petals and chaff, let them dry, and store them in paper envelopes labelled with variety, date saved, color, and height.

Heat and humidity are the worst enemies of saved seed. So it is no wonder we found ours, including leftover commercial seed in packets, losing viability much more quickly in Florida than it did up north, even when stored in the air-conditioned house.

Stored seed should be completely dry. It keeps best in a covered vapor-proof container in the refrigerator or freezer, especially over the summer. Many packets fit into a large jar or coffee can. Freezing does not hurt seeds, even of tender varieties it would kill in the growth stage. Add a packet of silica gel or dry milk powder to absorb moisture. When you remove the container from the cold, let it stand closed until the seeds warm to room temperature, so condensation will not form on the seeds.

For information on dividing plants and rooting cuttings, see chapter five.

Chapter Five
PROPAGATING PLANTS FROM CUTTINGS AND DIVISIONS

We like growing plants from seed because you get such nice surprises: if you plant seeds from a red daylily crossed with a yellow one, you are likely to get flowers in an array of lovely colors. Genetically, each seed-grown plant is distinct. But we like growing plants from cuttings and divisions (vegetative propagation) because we know in advance exactly what we will get. Normally, each plant grown this way is a piece of the parent plant. When it is nurtured separately and grows its own roots, it is a clone of the parent, with the same genetic makeup. If you have a particularly wonderful rosebush cultivar (or allamanda vine, hibiscus, geranium, begonia, coleus, croton, chrysanthemum, amaryllis, impatiens, and so on), you can clone as many more as you wish. Start with first-class parent plants, but observe plant patents where posted. It is illegal to sell patented plants without permission. As we said earlier, it is wise to root backup plants from your favorites, to prevent loss from frost or other problems.

PLANTS FROM CUTTINGS

It is always a wonder to us that so many different plants are so easy to grow from cuttings, either in a cup of water, in a shaded patch of soil outdoors, or in clean potting soil sealed inside propagators made from such ordinary household objects as polystyrene-lidded yogurt containers or plastic sweater boxes. All the cuttings need is a moist, shaded, sheltered spot until the new roots have formed. Stem or tip cuttings of begonia, geranium, scarlet sage, blue salvia, impatiens, fuchsia, rose, passion flower, dianthus, pansy, viola, nasturtium, bougainvillea, hibiscus, viburnum, camellia, barberry, butterfly bush, trumpet creeper, ceanothus, Japanese quince, Mexican orange, marguerite, chrysanthemum, poinsettia, gardenia, heliotrope, hydrangea, petunia, and many others may be rooted without much difficulty.

Usually, the same plant can be propagated in several ways. Butterfly bush (*Buddleia*) may be grown from seed (but flower color and other attributes will vary), started from a division, or started from either a hardwood or a softwood cutting (either in soil or in water). So how do you decide which method of propagation is best? We will give some suggestions, plus further references, but trial and error are of great value. Try the techniques that have most appeal for you first.

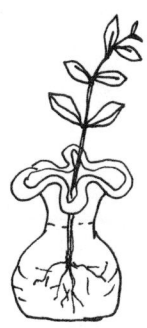

Rooting cuttings in water. Stems of the flowering viny shrub allamanda will root in a glass of plain water on a windowsill. Many other plants do too: impatiens, geranium, salvia, basil, mint, ivy, hydrangea, wandering jew, marigold, croton, and coleus, to name a few. While this is the least professional way to propagate plants, it works well with certain varieties. Betty has also discovered that putting plants that are harder or slower to root, such as impatiens, into the same cup with a plant that roots easily, such as coleus, works very well. Apparently the rooting hormones that make the one easy are shared, and the more difficult one often roots more quickly. Sometimes pieces used in bouquets will have rooted by the time the flowers fade. What could be easier? When the roots are between half an inch and an inch long, set your new plant into the garden, a nursery bed, or a flowerpot filled with moist, rich soil or potting medium. Keep it shaded and moist for another few weeks, then normal treatment will be safe for it.

Rooting cuttings in soil. A more professional approach is to make cuttings and root them in sterile soil or other sterile planting mediums, keeping them shaded, moist, and humid until new roots have developed. This works not only with the easiest plants, but with some perennials, and with most shrubs, vines, subtropical plants, and houseplants. Most plants root from stems, but a few such as begonia and jade plant, will root from leaves. Plants from bulbs seldom grow from cuttings; instead they are divided. The same is true for ferns. Most annuals and perennials do not grow from cuttings, but some do, more than a few.

The depth of soil depends on the type and size of the cuttings, but 3 to 4 inches is good for most purposes. You can use various kinds of containers for this, or do the propagating in a shaded bed outdoors. This is far more risky because of the danger from pests and diseases, but often works with sturdier plants, with Florida's humidity lending aid. Direct sunlight tends to dry and kill cuttings, while shade and fluorescent light are healthier for their development.

Containers. Containers can be flowerpots, planting flats, old dishpans with drainage holes, covered plastic containers like the ones from salad bars, or just about anything that holds several inches of moist potting medium. The big question is whether to use containers with drainage holes or whether to use completely sealed containers, like terrariums. The key to cuttings is keeping the soil moisture steady, not too wet and not too dry. Completely sealed containers are ok indoors. The moisture level must be perfect, and once such containers are planted, they can remain undisturbed for a very long time. If you are rooting in outdoor conditions, it is better to have drainage holes. How many times have we opened a sealed container outdoors just for a little fresh air in there, and then a rain came along and swamped everything! A few drainage holes in the bottom can prevent the excess water from lingering. The same goes for greenhouse conditions, where the watering system can cause similar results.

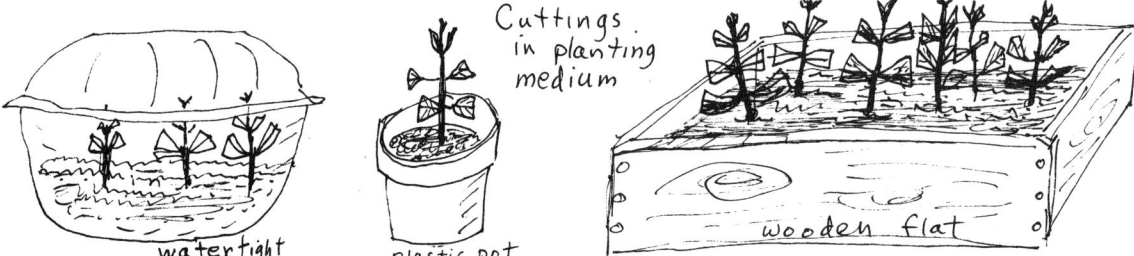

Soil or medium for plant propagation. Good soil for plant propagation is free of pests and holds water without becoming too soggy. It also allows for air to reach the rooting stems. It usually contains organic matter such as peat or humus plus inert minerals such as sand, perlite, or vermiculite, for texture. Some prepackaged brands are already fertile, others need fertilizer. Some mixes contain small bits of charcoal. You can create your own propagating soil using equal amounts of perlite or sand, vermiculite, peat moss, and pasteurized soil or compost. Add some clay, too, if your soil is sandy. Adding a pinch of dried manure makes plants grow faster, but don't add too much or tender new roots may burn. Water-retaining gels can be incorporated, too. The sandier the mix, the faster it dries out. Vary the moisture-holding capacity to suit your plants: more sand for cactus and drought lovers, less for dahlias and moisture lovers.

Garden soil (or garden sand!) harbors harmful, often microscopic pests. However, you can use it in the mix if you pasteurize it. Using an old roasting pan, bake a 3-inch layer of mixed soil in the oven at 275 degrees F for half an hour to kill unwanted pests (when no one else is home—this is smelly). Or, in small amounts in the right kind of container, zap it in the microwave.

TAKING THE CUTTINGS

Cuttings may be made from either branch tips or stems, and may be taken from either **softwood** or **hardwood**. Some plants prefer one or the other, some grow from either. Softwood is younger, with non-woody or easily bendable stems. Stems of softwood cuttings are a fresh green, while hardwood cuttings, which are older and tend to be woody, are darker green, brown, or gray.

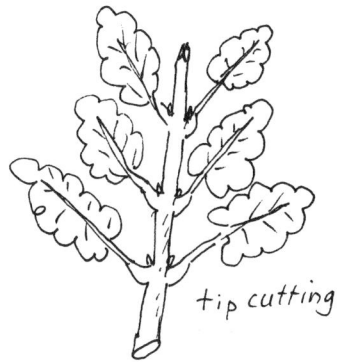

Usually, softwood cuttings are taken in spring or summer, preferably spring, during moist, mild weather. Cut them with a sharp knife or clippers from the ends of healthy stems. Clip just above a stem bud so the parent plant can make new growth without deadwood. Each piece should be 4 to 7 inches of mature new growth, which bends without snapping. Some kinds of plants, especially vines and tropical plants, will root from pieces of stems even without the tip. If in doubt, use stems with tips only.

Hardwood cuttings (usually from trees, shrubs, and vines) are often taken in fall or, in southern Florida, in winter. Cut 6- to 8-inch long, pencil-width sturdy stems. Each should have three leaf buds, and you will cut just below the lowest one, but taking care not to nick it.

INSERTING THE CUTTINGS

Remove leaves from the lower third of the cutting so that they do not rot beneath or at the ground level. With some plants that have very large leaves, such as angel wing begonias, hydrangeas, or ti plant, you may want to cut off more of the leaves or parts of them to reduce transpiration of moisture. Remove flowers and buds to send the strength of the cutting into the making of roots. Dunk the cut ends in rooting hormone if you wish. Sometimes this is very helpful; with easier cuttings at favorable seasons it may not be necessary. Then make a hole in your potting soil with pencil or screwdriver and insert your cuttings (top side up—most won't grow upside down) 1 to 2 inches and firm the medium or soil around the base. Keep them in a lighted place that does not get too hot. Make certain soil stays damp but not soggy. Some cuttings will wilt at first until they begin to perk up as new roots develop enough to take in moisture. Misting to increase humidity is crucial during these first days. In 1 to 4 weeks, your softwood cutting should develop a good new system of roots. Hardwoods may take several months. The time varies greatly by species. Let the roots develop well before you transplant.

> Tip: Let geranium cuttings dry out for two days, inside or in the shade, before sticking them into the propagating medium.

Softwood cuttings and plants with tropical origins root well indoors in temperatures between 50 to 80 degrees and bright but soft lighting. You may want to cover the containers with glass or plastic to trap humidity. Use a propagating box or put them into plastic bags in which you have made a few inch-long slits for ventilation. An empty aquarium makes a great propagating box. Do not put the covered cuttings into direct sunlight or they will overheat and rot. Indirect or fluorescent light is best. As roots begin to form, loosen covers and increase light in gradual stages.

Outdoor cuttings need protection from intense sun, but still need light. You can shade them by setting them in a coldframe that is under a leafy tree, or by making a cover of heavy screening (shadecloth) or lath strips. Unless the cuttings are in a sealed container that traps moisture, mist them daily and water them as needed.

Outdoors, climate and season make quite a difference in your rate of success. Root most hardwood cuttings outdoors in the fall or after hot weather begins to moderate. Other cuttings, especially softwoods, root outdoors in weather that is not too cold or hot. Tropical plants, vines and shrubs root any time of year you can provide warm, moist weather. Sometimes you can get plants to take root just by sticking pieces into damp garden soil at the right time of year.

The practical, usual size of cuttings ranges from about 3 to 8 inches long. Size varies, however, depending on the species and conditions. Some subtropical plants root so readily that large branches or whole trees can be used. A friend of Betty's in Longwood moved some tall crape myrtles two inches in diameter (from a place about to be bulldozed) by sawing them down near the base and resetting the trunks in the garden about three feet deep. It was rainy, and new roots formed!! (By the way, we do not recommend this!) On the other hand, in tissue culture, tiny pieces of a growing tip are rooted.

Cuttings can be unpredictable. It is not unusual for the pieces to root with varying rates of success. You may prepare 10 identical-seeming cuttings and treat them equally, and eventually find that 6 take root and 4 die. Forget the losses and be pleased with the successes. Sometimes trying again at another time will improve the results considerably, so never give up.

MOUND LAYERING

Woody plants are sometimes hard to root with cuttings, but mound layering is an alternative. This works for some plants that have a single stem and cannot be divided, like rosemary and lavender. It works on azaleas and rhododendrons, vines, evergreens, roses, and many other shrubs and plants. The new plant forms roots before it is cut away from the parent plant.

Scratch the skin on several of the lowest branches on the undersides to expose the cambium layer that is just beneath. Then bend these branches to the ground. Or just do this with one branch. Pin them down with wire or pipe cleaner if necessary. Or hold it down with a rock. Mound up good soil over the scratched points, water, and cover with mulch. Keep it

expose the cambium layer where the branch touches the soil.

moist all during the rooting period, which will vary depending on the plant and the conditions.

Rooting this way can take one to several months. Pull gently or dig down carefully to check, once a month or so. Don't be too eager! When the roots below the scratched points seem to have anchored firmly into the soil, lift the entire new plant without detaching it and have a look. If it does not seem that enough roots have formed, re-cover the stems and roots and wait longer. If roots seem sufficient, cut the rooted branches from the main plant. If multiple root clumps have formed, you can separate them into pieces appropriately, being sure each has enough roots. Plant them in the ground or in individual pots at once. Give them extra care for several weeks while they take hold, even more care than cuttings or divisions.

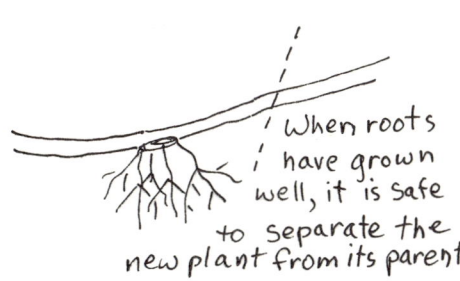
When roots have grown well, it is safe to separate the new plant from its parent.

DIVIDING PERENNIALS

There are two reasons to divide your plants, to keep them from getting overcrowded and to get more of them. Usually it is easier to divide perennials than to root cuttings, because the pieces already have roots and can begin to grow right away. You'll have best results if you do your divisions when conditions are favorable. For most plants, this is in early spring (or late winter in frost-free zones) when new growth begins. Another good period for making divisions is in fall after the weather begins to cool. Incidental weed control is another important benefit of digging and dividing your plants.

Operate on your plants during cool, or at least moist weather, not when it is hot and dry. Some, but not most, perennials have strong preferences about the time of year to be divided. The more tropical the plant, the warmer the weather should be when you divide it. If you have to divide plants during unfavorable weather conditions, protect the replanted pieces the same way you would protect cuttings, using loose, moist soil plus covers and shading to keep humidity up and temperatures moderate.

Which plants grow well from divisions? Daylily, chrysanthemum, iris, fern, rudbeckia, African daisy, bird-of-paradise, liriope, ginger, plume poppy, canna lily, and calla lily are just a few.

When you divide plants, you are either separating individual plants that are growing too close to each other or cutting a mature plant into pieces, depending on the species. As you learn what kind of hidden underground growth your plants make, you will be able to divide them better. You will find that some plants, like daylilies, eventually grow into a tight bushy clump of crowded plantlets with a big ball of tangled roots. Others, like chrysanthemums, reappear the next year on many different stems in a somewhat spreading circle around the original plant. Each plantlet is at the end of a stolon, or runner. Some plants, African iris, for instance, have tough woody or fibrous roots that must be divided with a sharp knife.

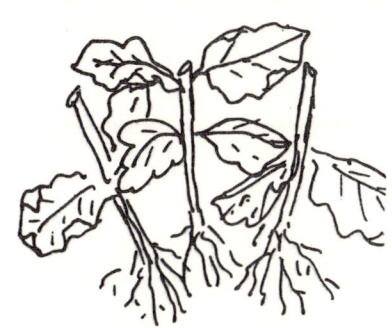
Pull apart chrysanthemum divisions carefully and reset at proper spacing.

A Cutting Garden for Florida

Other plants, like zephyranthes, gladiolus, and amaryllis, come from individual bulbs or corms. When they multiply, more and more bulbs or corms become crowded together. With these, it is important not to cut the individuals, but to pull the intertwined mass apart and move some of the bulbs or corms elsewhere.

With large or loose clumps such as aloes or sweet potatoes you can cut rooted pieces away from the edge without disturbing the main plant at all. But dividing plants with compact roots is often called "lifting" because you begin by digging up the plant you will work on. Before you set in a spade or trowel, try to figure out where roots are and how deep and far they spread. Dig carefully to limit root damage. Put the clump on the ground (on newspaper if you like to be neat) and look at it. If you are not familiar with the kind of roots the clump has, shake off enough soil for a look. Otherwise leave the soil in place.

How many plants are there? One big one surrounded by many small ones? A mass of small plants? Thin roots? Fleshy roots? Woody roots? Bulbs or corms?

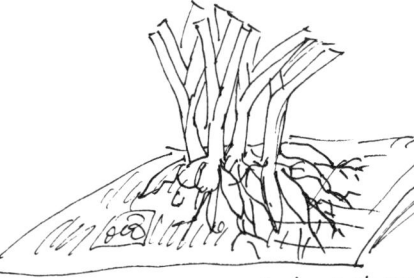
Four daylily plants in a clump, ready to be divided and replanted at better spacing.

Decide how to separate or divide with the least damage to individual plants. If you can see individual plantlets clearly, as with individual bulbs or with rooted stems of chrysanthemums, set each one into the garden at the appropriate spacing. Carefully break or cut apart the plant or plants and replant at the same depth in good soil. If in doubt about how fine to split the pieces, just cut or tease the clump into two halves and replant them at improved spacing. Replant the divisions immediately, and water well after replanting. Discard any diseased portions, and any bulbs or corms that are sliced or damaged. If you divide plants early in the growing season, when new growth has barely begun, do not cut back the leaves.

If you divide in the middle or end of the growing season, trim back the leaves and stems by half or a third to let more plant energy go into new root formation. Whenever you dig up the root or bulb clumps for division and replanting, plan on accomplishing the job in one fell swoop. Choose an overcast or even rainy day for the operation. After replanting, if the weather is hot or dry, cover the divisions with lightweight cloths or floating row covers for a week or so. Sprinkle them with a hose to raise humidity for the first few days afterward, then gradually let the plants adjust to normal conditions.

After you garden in the same place for awhile, you'll probably run out of room for all these new plants. We like to replant some in the garden and pot up others to keep around until the next plant swap or friendly visitor comes along. This chapter has been just a short summary of techniques for plant propagation. We list several of the many excellent books on the topic in the bibliography.

Chapter Six
CUT FLOWER CHOICES: TENDER ANNUALS

Here and in the next few chapters are some of the many kinds of flowers and foliage that may be grown in Florida. Of those we have grown or have seen thriving somewhere in a Florida garden, the following are the best for cutting and arranging. They will perform best if conditioned—soaked for several hours in deep water containing floral preservative, in a cool place indoors or in shade. For those flowers and foliage types with special conditioning needs, tips are included in the entries. Conditioning and harvesting are discussed in detail in chapter twelve.

Almost any annual, tender or hardy, will grow in Florida if planted at the right time of year for its type. Annuals are excellent for cutting because each plant produces flowers abundantly for several months, rather than blooming once per year.

You can grow annuals from seed, starting indoors or out, or purchase them as bedding plants at garden shops and centers everywhere. Shop early in the season for the best selection of plants. If your need large quantities (several dozen flats), you may be able to order at a discount from growers in your area.

CHOOSING GOOD BEDDING PLANTS

The best bedding plants are not necessarily those with the most flowers. Instead, look for young, healthy, dark green plants which have not been overstressed in cramped conditions. Some plants never recover from the dwarfing effect of being grown in too little soil. A cell-pack filled with bushy or branched plants in bud, or with just one or two blooms, is usually better in the long run than one with leggy plants in full bloom. See if you can learn when your favorite garden center receives fresh stock. It is often delivered on Thursdays or Fridays in preparation for the weekend.

CUT FLOWER CHOICES

It is hard to choose from so many varieties of flowers. Try to grow those which thrive in the conditions your yard offers, requiring the least special preparation such as wind or frost protection, or a drastic change of soil type. Of those that are most likely to thrive, choose what will look best in your vases indoors as well as in your flowerbed. Choose long-stemmed cultivars over short-stemmed ones. Think like an interior decorator and select flowers for their color, size, shape, and degree of formality. Choose some with a linear shape, others that are round and bold, and others with a sprinkling of small flowers, for filler. For surprises and to experiment with many types of cut flowers, try a mixed packet from a good seed supplier.

ANNUALS, TENDER AND HARDY

Annuals are plants that produce roots, stems, leaves, flowers, and seeds within a single year, then die. The terms tender and hardy, as we use them here, refer to cold tolerance, which varies greatly among annuals. **Tender annuals** are sensitive to or killed by light frost. Plant seed or set out bedding plants of these in spring when daytime temperatures remain at about 70 degrees F. Or sow seed earlier indoors or in a coldframe. **Hardy annuals** survive light to heavy frost. In Florida, plant them in

A Cutting Garden for Florida

SEED STARTER'S GUIDE TO TENDER ANNUALS

Start these seeds outdoors after the danger of frost ends, or earlier indoors.

Name	Seed Size	Germination	Sun/Shade	Spacing	Height
Ageratum		5 days	○ ◐	10-12"	6-30"
Amaranthus		10 days	○	12-18"	2-3'
Callistephus (China aster)		8 days	○	10-14"	1-2'
Capsicum (pepper)		10-14 days	○	12-24"	1-3'
Catharanthus (vinca)		15 days	○	10-15"	8-24"
Celosia		10 days	○	10-12"	6-24"
Cleome		10 days	○ ◐	15-18"	3-5'
Cosmos		5 days	○	12-20"	1-4'
Dahlia		6 days	○ ◐	12-24"	8-36"
Gomphrena		15 days	○	10-12"	6-24"
Helianthus (sunflower)		5 days	○	16-36"	1-8'
Heliotropium		25 days	○ ○	12"	12-18"
Impatiens		10-14 days	○ ◐	10-12"	8-24"
Nicotiana (tobacco flower)		12 days	◐	12-18"	15-30"
Perilla		12 days	◐ ●	8-12"	24-36"
Salvia splendens		15 days	○ ◐	12"	12-30"
Solenostemon (coleus)		10 days	◐ ●	10-20"	8-30"
Tagetes (marigold)		5 days	○ ◐	8-12"	8-36"
Tithonia		10 days	○	24"	3-6"
Torenia		15 days	◐ ●	8"	8-12"
Tropaeolum (nasturtium)		8 days	○ ◐	10-12"	8-48"
Verbena		20 days	○	18"	6-12"
Zinnia		5 days	○	12-14"	6-36"

Notes: Seed size is drawn actual size and shape. Germination shows the approximate number of days. ○ shows full sun, ◐ shows partial shade, and ● shows deep shade. Spacing and height refer to mature plants and are approximate. Nearly every type of annual has short and tall named forms. Dwarf and tall sunflowers range from 1 to 8 feet tall.

winter, spring, or fall, preferably in fall or winter, like biennials. Biennials and hardy annuals are covered together in the next chapter.

Tender annuals grow throughout the year in frost-free parts of Florida. There are some mixups in plant classification, for some of these, though grown as annuals in cold-winter areas, have a tendency to become perennial if climate permits. But where frost does not end their growing season, in some cases heat will do the job, especially in full sun and sandy soil. Yet other tender perennials are so heat tolerant that they can be set out as bedding plants even in the hottest part of the summer.

Conditioning Tender Annuals

Tender annuals for Florida are warm season plants, so, usually, icy cold conditioning water does not suit them. Cut them early in the day, immediately placing them in a bucket of deep, tepid to cool water, 60 to 80 degrees F. In your work area, recut stems, remove lower leaves, and return them to buckets of deep, fresh water. Let the flowers continue to soak in a cool place for several hours before arranging them

Most annuals for cutting are easy to grow but need ample fertilizer and water. In full sun, they may need water every day. Frequent picking and deadheading of flowers will keep the plants from going to seed and dying young. When plants become too old and unattractive, remove and replace them. Here are some of the best tender annuals for growing during frost-free times of year:

TENDER ANNUALS

***Ageratum houstonianum* (floss flower).** These small fluffy bunched flowers, blue, violet, pink, or white, are used for edging, bedding, and cutting. Varieties are available in uniform heights from 6 to 30 inches, but the tall ones are hard to find except as seeds. 'Blue Horizon', 'White Bouquet', and 'Red Top' are 30-inches tall and are great for cutting and bedding too. The blooms last 4 or 5 days in bouquets. Start seeds or plants in early spring in any soil and in full sun or light shade. The small seeds need shelter but are not hard to grow. Bedding plants of short-stemmed types are widely available in 4-inch pots and 4- or 6-packs. Ageratums need lots of water but little else once started. They are easily increased from cuttings and often spread almost like a ground cover in Florida gardens. They last from frost to frost and seldom look shaggy. If they do, shear off the old flowers.

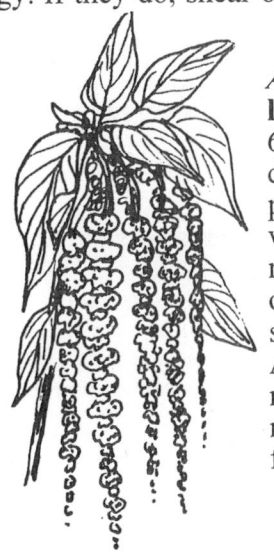

***Amaranthus caudatus* (tassel flowers or love-lies-bleeding).** Bright, gaudy leaves embellish 2- to 6-foot, heat-loving plants. Some varieties have drooping swags of chenille-like flowers, some are more plumelike. Plant in full sun. It is best to sow directly in warm average soil, anytime but winter, keeping in mind that they need several months to mature. Water often until germination, but when established this species will survive with only occasional watering. Avoid root disturbance or dampness that could lead to root rot. Heat resistant and easy to grow, this tends to reseed a lot. Harvest the chenille types only when the flowers are mature; they are used fresh or dry.

A Cutting Garden for Florida

The "Joseph's Coat" type, **Amaranthus tricolor,** also known as summer poinsettia, is grown for its colorful red and yellow leaves. With a bright golden swirl of leaves atop tall green plants, 'Aurora' is spectacular. We also like *Amaranthus cruentas* 'Hot Biscuits' with coppery plumes on 5-foot plants.

Callistephus chinensis **(China aster).** Seed catalogs show pink, rose, burgundy, blue, yellow, and white varieties with fluffy blossoms ranging from daisy form to pom-pon to ostrich plume. Cut when in full bloom for they do not continue to open as well as other flowers. To keep them fresh in bouquets, remove foliage and recut stems. Blooms range from 2 to 6 inches wide. Tall varieties are best for cutting but may need staking. Plant seeds indoors six weeks before last expected frost or outdoors after danger of frost is past. China asters like full sun to partial shade and rich soil. Water regularly but do not place mulch against the stems or rot may occur. Transplant with care and protect from nematodes and baking sun. Choose wilt-resistant varieties and plant in new ground each year because asters are prone to soil-borne diseases.

Capsicum annuum **(ornamental pepper).** Small white flowers are followed by shiny little round or pointed peppers. Often there are several colors on the same plant, for the peppers change hue as they ripen. The range includes green, red, yellow, orange, and purple. Some types are edible, hot or sweet. 'Thai Hot' and 'Super Chili' are covered with fiery, narrow, pointed red peppers. There's a sweet (not hot) cultivar called 'Cherry Pick' with loads of small round red fruits. Several types, including 'Pretty in Purple' have purple leaves and lavender fruits that ripen to red. Peppers like full sun, regular water, and well-drained, fertile, loamy soil. Plants often become short-lived subshrubs in frost-free areas. They grow well in pots, so it's easy to provide frost protection in winter. For bouquets, harvest branches filled with peppers; condition by slitting the bottom of the branch stem and immersing for several hours in cool water before arranging. Branches of peppers are nice for accent in holiday arrangements, and individual peppers can be made into wreaths and ristras. Caution! Wash hands well and don't touch your eyes if you've been handling hot peppers.

Catharanthus rosea **(periwinkle, vinca).** So well suited to all parts of Florida that it is often found growing wild, periwinkle, with its bright pink, lavender, purple, or white flowers, blooms amid green leaves and always looks neat. Vinca grows in sunny, sandy soil and often reseeds. Easily grown, its flowers last 3 to 5 days when cut, and buds continue to open for a week. The glossy foliage alone is useful. Short types (a foot tall or so) are best for bedding but

Tender Annuals

taller ones work better for cutting. Cut when 2 or 3 flowers on each stem are fully open. Buds showing color will open. Split stems, condition overnight in cold water. Remove some foliage to show flowers better and make them last longer. Remove spent flowers as they fade. Plant from March to July in northern Florida, all year in southern regions. Some newer varieties have had disease problems that are still absent in the older types. Protect from slugs and snails.

Celosia cristata (**cockscomb**). Bright plumes or ripples of velvety flowers in a wide range of warm colors are excellent and long-lasting in fresh or dried bouquets. There is another type, *C. a. spicata*, known as wheat celosia, which makes a spiky backdrop in the garden and is superior in dried bouquets.

Cultivar names are 'Flamingo Feather' and 'Pink Candle'. It has the same silky shine and grows like the others. In full sun, sow seed in rich soil from March to September for central and southern areas, March to July in northern parts of Florida. For seedlings, temperatures should be above 70 degrees F, and water should be steady so that growth will not be checked. All the celosias need only occasional water when mature, love hot weather and sandy soil, and are easy to grow and dry. For more on drying, see page 105.

Cleome hasslerana (**spider flower**). These gigantic background plants quickly grow three to six feet tall. The rangy spikes are densely studded with tubular, spidery, strongly scented flowers. In bouquets, cut off the seedpods and lower foliage. Try combining the pink and purple flowers with purple foliage such as

opal basil or perilla. Cleome is an old-fashioned southern favorite that does well in warm weather, but also tolerates chilly weather. If cut for a bouquet or deadheaded, it will branch and reflower. Leave some flowers to ripen into long, tan seedpods if you want it to self sow. Only a few are needed. The self-sown seedlings withstand a touch of frost. Flowers can be pink, violet, rose-purple, cherry, or white. Plant seeds or plants outdoors in March or April. When plants are eight inches tall, thin to ten inches apart, later to twenty. Cleome grows in any soil in full sun to light shade, and prefers warm, dry weather once established. There is a similar form, *Cleome serrulata*, which is thornless.

Cosmos bipinnatus **and** *C. sulphureus.* Cosmos is a graceful, old fashioned flower for cutting that is fast and easy from seed. Plants bloom for months with many long-stemmed flowers 2 to 5 inches in diameter. Their gold centers are

framed by ray-like petals. Many new cultivars have recently been introduced but there's nothing wrong with the old ones. *C. bipinnatus*, 2 to 5 feet tall, is the main type for bouquets and comes in soft tones of violet, rose, or white, and also magenta. Separate or mixed colors are available. These are long lasting when cut. Shorter types need no staking. 'Gazebo' has huge and abundant flowers on 4-foot plants. 'Versailles' is similar at 3 feet. 'Early Wonder' with 4.5 foot plants replaces the old 'Sensation' series. For something different, try chocolate colored *C. atrosanguineus*.

C. sulphureus, including the 'Klondyke' series, is shorter, usually 1 to 3 feet tall, and comes in gold, orange, and fiery red. Recent award winners 'Cosmic Orange' and 'Cosmic Yellow' look strong and promising. The blossoms of *C. sulfureus* are much smaller than *C. bipinnatus* and do not last more than a day or two in bouquets. Plant seeds of either species in full sun to light shade from November to February in Zones 10 and 11, after danger of frost in other regions. Both types can be grown from seed in the flowerbed or field. Cosmos prefers rich, moist soil but will tolerate less ideal conditions.

Replant all species of cosmos several times a year for continuous bloom. Thin seedlings to 10 or more inches apart and pinch back once for bushiness when they are about 8 inches tall. Plants can get seedy rather quickly, but often self sow. We have had good results from seed saved from our best plants. Constant harvesting of fresh flowers and deadheading will prolong bloom. Remove and discard plants if they become unattractive.

Dahlia **hybrids.** These famous cut flowers are tricky to grow in Florida because of high heat and damp weather. They are easy enough to start from seed planted indoors (difficulties with hot weather are apparent later on). Some hybrids come into bloom as fast as zinnias, and in Florida, speed is a help. 'Piccolo' is small and speedy. 'Double Pompon' is long-stemmed and nice for cuts. Larger dahlias are just as easily started from seed, but take a few weeks longer to start blooming. If you don't want to bother with seed, set out bedding plants when they appear in the market, or buy tubers and plant in mid- to late winter, after the danger of frost passes. Many sizes, colors, and forms are available. Categories are single, anemone-flowered, collarette, water lily, decorative, ball, pompon, cactus-flowered, and miscellaneous. Seed catalogs often say that dahlias like full sun, but we find that they cannot tolerate the strength of Florida summer sun. They do well in cooler weather here, especially in southern Florida winters, or under shelter, screen, or lath. Pamper them with rich soil and frequent gentle watering. After blooms are spent, dig and store tubers in a cool, dry place, rest for a few months, and plant again. In bouquets, remove lower foliage on stems and condition them in cool water. Even so, they may droop in hot weather.

Gomphrena globosa **(globe amaranth).** Here's a tidy plant that likes hot sun and sandy soil. The 1-inch everlasting flowers of gomphrena resemble strawlike cloverheads. The color range includes white, purple, red, orange, and pink. The whites and pale pinks often look dull and gray, so the darker reds, purples, and hot pinks are more satisfactory. 'Bicolor Rose' has deep rose colored flowers whose centers fade to white. Gomphrena is easy to grow from seed and tolerant of drought. Its compact growth helps make it a good bedding plant. It is found in most mixtures of seeds for dried flowers. It thrives in hot, sunny places, even in poor, sandy soil if it is well drained. Plant in spring for summer bloom and hang to dry. Dwarf types are a foot tall, others up to three feet tall.

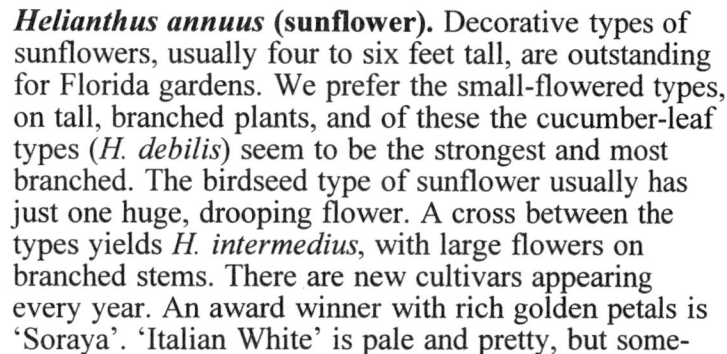

Helianthus annuus **(sunflower).** Decorative types of sunflowers, usually four to six feet tall, are outstanding for Florida gardens. We prefer the small-flowered types, on tall, branched plants, and of these the cucumber-leaf types (*H. debilis*) seem to be the strongest and most branched. The birdseed type of sunflower usually has just one huge, drooping flower. A cross between the types yields *H. intermedius*, with large flowers on branched stems. There are new cultivars appearing every year. An award winner with rich golden petals is 'Soraya'. 'Italian White' is pale and pretty, but sometimes can be hard to germinate. 'Go Bananas' has very little pollen, which makes it easier to handle, for with others the pollen can stain your hands as well as tablecloths and furniture. 'Giant Sungold' is a fluffy double yellow. Tall, bushy sunflowers are the most productive for cut flowers, but there are many dwarf types ('Solar Babies' for one) that grow quickly and are excellent for living arrangements in container gardens. There's no limit to sunflower forms, whose cultivar names often hint at the color range: cream, yellow, red, rust, purplish brown, and bronze. Conditioning is critical to keep sunflowers from wilting. Slit stem bases and condition for several hours in a bucket of deep, cool water.

Although sunflowers are usually classed as tender annuals, in our experience the newly sprouted seeds withstand a touch of frost, although they do not need it. Plant them early in the year, ahead of bugs and pests: January in southern Florida, February or March in central Florida, and in March or April in northern sections. Though they are known for loving sunshine, in our climate they do well if very lightly shaded. Give them rich, sweet soil and room to grow. Plant seeds one foot apart. Thin seedlings to two feet apart when plants are a foot tall, and for the tall types, later thin to four feet apart and pinch out the central tip when they are two feet tall, for bushier plants with more flowers. Sunflowers are easy to grow and a favorite for children. But they can frustrate you if you have rabbits, squirrels, or deer eating the plants.

Heliotropium arborescens **(heliotrope).** A small, bushy shrub in zones 10 and 11, where it is hardy, this is more often grown as a tender perennial. The small purple or lavender flowers form lovely fruit-scented clusters. It will reach 1 1/2 to 2 ft tall and wide by the end of its first year. It grows best in full sun with well-drained, fertile soil, and plentiful water. It does well in large pots and may be trained as a topiary standard. Pinch back tips to promote bushiness. Prune plants if they become leggy. Take cuttings in fall. Sow seed, barely covered, at temperatures between 70 and 85 degrees F.

Impatiens walleriana. Except in winter, you can always find impatiens in bloom, so it is handy for quick bouquets. It grows indoors or out, and blooms whether plants are small or large. It is particular about conditioning and should be cut early in the day and retrimmed with a sharp knife. Although perennial in

A Cutting Garden for Florida

frost-free areas, it is usually used as an annual, in gardens and indoor and outdoor containers. Single flat or roselike double two-inch flowers are available in colors ranging from white through all shades of pink, peach, orange, and red, with a few lavenders. Foliage may be green, bronze, or variegated. Dwarf to tall types grow six inches to over three feet tall and wide. Pinch back for new flowers and to shape plants. New Guinea impatiens withstands more sun than other types do and has larger flowers. Shade, rich soil, and plentiful moisture keep this favorite plant happy. Their only faults are that they need a great deal of water and if they are in too much sun, they will wilt in summer heat, no matter how much water they have. Cuttings root readily at any time of year, and plants also self sow. If colors clash, transplant the volunteers to other parts of the landscape. Conditioning tip: cut early in the day, slit stem bases slightly, and condition in deep, cool water. Very dwarf forms are easy to use in living container-garden bouquets.

Nicotiana alata **(flowering tobacco).** Although this is a short-lived tender perennial in the warmer parts of Florida, it is usually grown as an annual. Garden types are one to three feet tall. Long, scented, tubular flowers with star-shaped faces bloom in soft shades of green, white, pink, red, and purple. Check out 'Havana Appleblossom Hybrid' with pink-blushed white flowers on one-foot plants. *N. sylvestris* is a tall, bold background plant, 4 feet tall, with pendent white flowers in generous clusters. If you pinch the central growing tip when the plants are half grown, they will branch more.

In Florida, plant nicotiana in loamy, rich soil in bright partial shade. Buy bedding plants or start seeds in small containers, on surface of soil, in light, under warm, moist conditions. Space them one foot apart in the garden, more for tall types. Plants may become dusty if set too near the road, for the leaves have a sticky texture.

Harvest nicotiana early in the day. If stems are split and conditioned in deep water, flowers last a week in the vase, but may droop a bit nonetheless.

Perilla frutescens **(beefsteak plant).** This foliage plant with metallic purple, crimped leaves is a striking filler in bouquets, especially with pink flowers. A herb, it is also used to give color and flavor to herbal vinegar, and as a garnish for food. It grows 1.5 to 3 feet tall with broad leaves up to 5 inches long. The color may not be as dark in Florida as it is in the North. It tends to fade to green as the hot summer goes along. 'Purple Hedge' has good form and a metallic sheen. After spires of small lavender flowers appear, perilla self sows rather weedily, and can be a pest. However, it is easy to control if you deadhead to prevent seeds from forming, if they are not desired. Grow it in average soil, average moisture, and partial shade for best results. Seeds prefer warm moist conditions, barely covered with soil. Start new plants two or three times a year, for they are most

Tender Annuals

attractive while they are young. Slit stem ends and condition in deep water before arranging. You may find that stems sprout roots in the vase water, after a week or so, and can be planted in the garden.

***Salvia splendens* (scarlet sage).** Familiar red spires of tubular flowers bloom on bushy plants. Also available are rose, peach, lavender, a fine deep purple, and white. Perennial salvias are hardier, but this annual bedder is killed by frost. Scarlet sage does not last long in bouquets but is striking for a day or two. Monica's best results came with salvia plants placed where they received morning shade and afternoon sun. One big, bushy plant bloomed all winter long, protected by the house from light frosts. The white, pink, peach, and purple strains of *S. splendens* need more shade than the red ones. Salvia tolerates mildly acid soil but likes lots of water. Most gardeners purchase bedding plants, but it is easy to grow salvia from seed or cuttings.

***Solenostemon scutellarioides* (coleus, formerly *Coleus* hybrids.** Familiar old coleus has been developed into fabulously fashionable new styles and colors, and has a new botanical name besides. The bright or dark foliage of this houseplant and bedder makes good, long-lasting filler in bouquets. Its color range includes variants of white, yellow, pink, red, purple, green chartreuse, violet, and near black. Leaf sizes range from smaller than a penny to longer than a dollar bill. Leaves may be smooth or frilly, with either barely serrated or deeply cut edges. 'Jade Wizard' is lovely with mottled, lobed leaves of ivory, green and chartreuse. 'Carefree Mix' grows quickly and easily in a broad array of colors. The small seed of coleus is not too hard to start indoors (barely cover with sterile soil and do not let the medium dry out), but it is much easier to take cuttings. They root in a week in the rainy summer. Sometimes coleus branches root in water while still in the vase.

Coleus is killed by frost and drought, but is easy to grow. Old varieties prefer shade, but some new varieties are great in either sun or shade. The amount of light affects the color tones in the leaves. They do best with rich soil and ample water, in the garden or in pots. In landscaped beds, coleus has more impact if only one of the many color combinations is used, but mixtures are fine in the cutting garden. When shopping for coleus, check for special individuals in the mixed packs, for you may find a gem that you want to propagate into a colony. Since frost kills the plants, protect your favorites by bringing cuttings indoors, and always keep a few backups on hand.

***Tagetes* species (marigold).** This heat-tolerant favorite shows up in catalogs in an unbelievable array of forms on plants from six inches to three feet tall, all with warm, vibrant colors of yellow to orange to bronze or bicolors. There are

A Cutting Garden for Florida

forms such as 'Mr. Majestic' with yellow and mahogony striped petals, revivals of Victorian types. There are petite signet marigolds, short, bushy, French marigolds with bicolored petals, and tall, somewhat rigid, large-flowered African marigolds in a single color, solid yellow, orange, or off-white. 'Snowball' is close to pure white. All marigolds trace back to Mexico and other parts of the New World. They are easy to grow from seed, and some types flower in only six weeks. Plants are readily available, even in summer. Make successive sowings from February until December in the south, to July in the north, in sun and moist soil. Remove faded blooms. Remove plants after a few months if they look seedy or weedy.

Marigolds are herbs with a flavor similar to tarragon. The small-flowered signet types have a better flavor than others and are most often used this way. The flowers are edible, and the petals are an edible accent in salad, while whole flowers can be used to garnish platters of food. Golden-yellow 'Tessy' is an attractive cross between a signet and a French marigold. Marigolds are somewhat effective as pest and nematode repellants, but need protection from mites, slugs, and snails. 'Golden Guardian' from Park Seed is recommended for nematode control.

Marigolds look nice in bouquets when they are massed in low bowls. Cut marigolds for bouquets while the centers are tight and remove all foliage below the water, for less odor. Some people object to the fragrance of the leaves. Cultivars vary, so check the listings to find so-called odorless kinds.

Tithonia rotundifolia (**Mexican sunflower.**) Red-orange or golden yellow flowers look like single dahlias or sunflowers. Most types are 6 feet tall and these are used commercially as cut flowers. 'Fiesta del Sol' is a recent all-American Award winner, with red-orange flowers on wind-tolerant, 3-foot plants. Other 3-foot and under types are 'Goldfinger' (yellow) and 'Aztec Sun'. Leaves sometimes look rather coarse or weather-beaten, and are best seen from a distance. Tithonia takes a lot of space but is well worth it, for it stands up to summer weather and produces long-lasting, bright flowers that the butterflies love. Plant seeds six inches apart or set out plants two to three feet apart in early spring, after frost, in sun in average soil. Thin seedlings. Pinch plants back for bushiness when two feet tall. Spray with insecticidal soap for unmarred blooms. Water rarely once established; tithonia may be used in xeriscape gardens.

Torenia fournieri (**Florida pansy, wishbone flower, blue wings**). Versatile and rugged, these violet blue tubular flowers touched with white and yellow appear from late spring until frost. Torenia tolerates high heat if given extra water. The tallest types grow about a foot high. Though small, it is cute in arrangements. Easy to grow from seed or plants and to root from cuttings, it does best in enriched soil with ample water, in partial shade. Plant from February to May. Pink and white varieties are available, but the blue ones are the charmers. 'Clown Mix' is still available but the newer 8-inch 'Happy Faces' is quick and easy. Petite 'Duchess Mix' is free blooming and gives a lot of color in pots. There is a similar species, *T. baillonii* 'Suzie Wong' which is bright in shade with its gold flowers with black eyes.

Tender Annuals

***Tropaeolum majus* (nasturtium).** Nasturtium flowers are charming in small vases, and the flowering vines of the tall types can be used in larger arrangements. They offer bright colors, unique spurred form, succulent texture, and tangy fragrance. The circular leaves look very nice as well. All parts of nasturtiums are edible. Leaves and petals add zest and color to salads, if they are pesticide-free (and pest-free, too). Refrigerate the flowers for two hours in a bowl of water, drain, and use to garnish serving platters. Stand long-stemmed flowers in cold water for several hours to condition them for bouquets.

nasturtium

There are many choices of color and size, either viny or bushy. 'Whirlybird' is an old standby with low, bushy form and lots of flowers, held above the foliage. It is early blooming and a good choice for hanging baskets. Monica likes the climbing mixes and grows them next to her screened porch. 'Alaska' has leaves variegated with white but is less vigorous than some of the other climbers. 'Moonlight' is a vigorous, climbing type with butter-yellow flowers. 'Copper Sunset' has great color in the flowers and the leaves.

Canary creeper (*T. peregrinum*) is another nasturtium climber with lobed leaves and bright yellow, deeply fringed flowers. *T. azureum*, another climber, has blue flowers but is said to need a cool, stable indoor climate. If you try it in a climate-controlled sunroom or greenhouse, let us know how it does!

In Florida, nasturtiums are easy because of their large seeds. Soak seed overnight in lukewarm water before planting for much faster germination. The branches (6 or more inches long, with multiple leaves and buds), will easily root in water or moist potting medium. Plant nasturtiums in full sun or partial shade while the soil is cooler, from fall to spring. They need protection from frost but have no trouble in temperatures in the mid-thirties. They are great winter plants in southern Florida. Seed packets say nasturtiums thrive in bad soil, but they need better soil than the average unimproved sandy type here. Add manure and peat moss to the bed, and mulch to keep roots cool. Protect them from aphids with sprays of water or of insecticidal soap. In winter, nasturtiums like full sun, but when temperatures climb, shade will give them longer life before they burn out in summer weather.

***Verbena* hybrids (vervain).** Although this flower is perennial in ideal conditions, neither too warm nor too cold, that does not describe Florida, so we have included it here with tender annuals. Discs composed of many flaring, tubular florets bloom constantly in shades of rose, red, white, blue, and purple. They always look cool and refreshing, especially the pastel shades. Some are scented.

A Cutting Garden for Florida

Most types are under two feet tall. Their form may be upright or trailing. Set out bedding plants after danger of frost passes, 18 inches apart, in deep, rich, moist soil. Or start seeds indoors in December. Pick when heads begin to open, slit stem ends, and start their conditioning in warm water containing a pinch of sugar.

verbena

Zinnia* species.** ***Zinnia elegans. This popular type of zinnia has been hybridized into so many colors and forms that choice is unlimited. This species is one of the few flowers that can be planted during Florida summers, for it does unusually well in heat. Or plant any time after frost, from February to June in northern and central Florida, until September in southern Florida, directly in the garden in full sun and average soil. Zinnias need only occasional water during the dry months. Mildew can be a major problem during hot humid weather, such as summer anywhere in Florida. Some zinnia types are resistant to mildew.

When plants are a few inches tall, pinch the central stem once for bushiness. Or for really big blooms, pinch off side buds and develop just one superior flower. After plants begin to bloom, cut them on long stems while centers are still tight. Put them into water immediately, carrying a bucket with you as you cut, or they will wilt and have trouble recuperating. Indoors, remove most of the leaves (otherwise they'll stink up the vase water), run hot water over the stem ends, and stand the flowers in deep water to condition. Handle them carefully, for the big types have hollow stems that can easily break or crack. In arrangements, the flower heads may change position as they bend or turn toward the light You can dry the flowerheads of zinnias in silicon gel, or hang long-stemmed flowers upside down to air dry.

We like cactus flowered types and 'Ruffles' hybrids because the colorful petals have a twist of texture, and 'Chippendale' which has single bronze flowers tipped with gold. We plan to try 'Oklahoma' for it is said to have long life in bouquets.

Zinnia angustifolia (once called *linearis*) has narrow leaves and small, daisylike flowers in great abundance. They come only in white, golden yellow, primrose yellow, and orange. They only get 10 to 12 inches tall, so they are more filler than focal points in bouquets. But they are much easier to grow in Florida than *Z. elegans* because they like the hot, humid weather and do not get mildew. They even survive light frost. Monica has had some last into their second year. Start them from seed or buy them as bedding plants. 'Profusion White', an award-winning hybrid of this type, grows up to 20 inches tall.

zinnia

Zinnia haageana (Mexican zinnia) withstands heat and stormy weather. It has bright, double, mostly bicolored flowers in rich shades of gold, maroon, copper, cream, yellow, orange, and deep red. Butterflies love it. 'Persian Carpet Mix' is an All-America winner of this type which grows 15 inches tall. Flowers can be two inches across, and last well in the vase.

Chapter Seven
CUT FLOWER CHOICES: HARDY ANNUALS AND BIENNIALS

Biennials are plants which grow leaves their first year, live through the winter, and bloom profusely the next spring, for instance hollyhocks and pansies. Then they make seeds and die. They often self sow in the garden. Hardy annuals, which tolerate light to heavy frost, complete the same cycle in similar manner but in a shorter time.

In most regions of the United States, biennials are planted in summer, hardy annuals in early spring. In Florida, both groups do best if planted in fall. They both provide lots of short-lived bloom in late winter or early spring, but the annuals are easier to grow. Winters are so mild that shirley poppies, larkspur, stocks, annual phlox, and many other favorite hardy annuals for cutting survive them with no trouble. As the days get warmer and longer, they respond with fantastic bursts of bloom—in a hurry to set seeds during favorable weather. Apply extra fertilizer and water before and during bloom. If weather is hot, an extra shower at midday helps revive your flowers.

By the time the annuals and biennials finish blooming, they are branched and ragged looking. Remove plants and put them on the compost pile. Probably seedpods have formed. Collect any seeds you are interested in, save them in paper envelopes, label them carefully, and plant them the next fall. If we could say only one thing about growing cut flowers in Florida, it would be this advice: make good use of the coolness of winter to grow lots of these beautiful biennials and hardy annuals. Less heat-tolerant perennials which bloom the first year from seed can be grown this way, too.

NORTHERN FLORIDA

Biennials do very well here in the cooler parts of the state. There is a definite winter, but it is short and mild. Biennials survive it easily and have an early start for spring. Pansies, lunaria, campanula, sweet william, foxglove, Iceland poppies, silene, and viola are good choices here. Hardy annuals such as stock, bachelor's button, shirley poppy, pansy, and larkspur will be equally successful. Start seeds in October for best results.

CENTRAL FLORIDA

Here, hardy annuals thrive in winter because it is so mild. We have had best results with verbena, dianthus, nasturtiums (only in low-frost winters), pansies, poppies, blanket flower, daisies, scabiosa, snapdragons, and sunflowers. Hardy annuals may be grown like biennials here, and so can some perennials such as the gloriosa daisies, which tend to die in summer. The secret is to plant biennials, short-lived hardy perennials, and hardy annuals late in the fall, after nights have cooled, instead of in summer. December is not too late, but November is ideal. Mixed cut flower beds of biennials are highly recommended for early spring flowers. Often, mixed wildflower seeds are mostly biennials and hardy annuals, well-suited for planting in fall, and cutting the next spring. A few of the many good choices to plant in fall for spring bloom are shirley poppies,

A Cutting Garden for Florida

SEED STARTER'S GUIDE TO HARDY ANNUALS AND BIENNIALS

Start these relatively easy cold-hardy seeds outdoors in cool weather, late fall in Central Florida, winter in Southern Florida, and late winter (February) or earlier in a cold frame in Northern Florida.

Name	Seed Size	Germination	Sun/Shade	Spacing	Height
Alcea rosea (hollyhock)		10 days	O ◑	24"	24-60"
Ammi majus		15 days	O ◑	12"	24-36"
Antirrhinum majus (snapdragon)		10 days	O	12"	6-36"
Brassica (ornamental cabbage)		10 days	O ◑	12"	12"
Calendula species		10 days	O ◑	12-24"	12-24"
Centaurea spp. (bachelor's button)		10 days	O ◑	12"	12-24"
Consolida ambigua (larkspur)		20 days	O ◑	10"	15-36"
Coreopsis tinctoria (tickseed)		5 days (L)	O ◑	10"	8-30"
Dianthus species and hybrids		5 days	O ◑	12"	6-28"
Digitalis species (foxglove)		20 days	◑ ●	15"	18-30"
Dimorpotheca species (African daisy)		10 days	O	10"	12"
Emilia flammea (tassel flower)		8 days (D)	O ◑	8"	12-18"
Eschscholzia species (California poppy)		20 days	O ◑	10"	10-24"
Gaillardia pulchella (blanket flower)		20 days	O ◑	12"	12-18"
Gypsophila elegans (babysbreath)		10 days	O ◑	12"	24"
Helichrysum bracteatum (strawflower)		10 days (L)	O	12"	12-30"
Iberis umbellata (candytuft)		20 days	O ◑	12"	10-20"
Lathyrus odorata (sweet pea)		15 days	◑	10"	8-48"
Lavatera trimestris (mallow)		20 days	O ◑	24"	24"
Limonium sinuatum (statice)		8 days	O ◑	15"	24-30"
Linaria marrocana (toadflax)		8 days	O ◑	10"	10-28"
Matthiola incana (stock)		12 days	O ◑	12"	18-24"
Nicandra physalodes (shoo-fly plant)		10 days	O ◑	15"	15-24"
Nigella damascena (love-in-a-mist)		10 days	O ◑	12"	15-24"
Papaver rhoeas (shirley poppy)		20 days	O ◑	10"	15-24"
Petunia hybrids (petunias)		10 days	O	15"	12-24"
Phlox drummondii (phlox)		15 days	O	12"	12-24"
Rudbeckia species (black-eyed susan)		10 days	O ◑	15"	18-36"
Scabiosa atropurpurea (scabiosa)		20 days	O	12"	12-24"
Silene species (silene)		10 days	O ◑	10"	10-24"
Viola species (pansies and violas)		10 days	O ◑	8-12"	6-12"

Notes: Seed is drawn actual size and shape. Germination shows the approximate number of days but this varies greatly. O shows full sun, ◑ shows partial shade, and ● shows deep shade. Spacing and height refer to mature plants and are approximate. There are short and tall forms of most types of annuals. For instance snapdragons range from several inches to several feet tall. The letter "L" indicates that this type of seed needs light (no soil covering it) to germinate, and the letter "D" indicates that it needs darkness.
Thanks go to Park Seed for some of the germination information.

Iceland poppies, California poppies, carnations, dianthus, scarlet sage, larkspur, delphinium (difficult, choose fast-growing dwarf types), statice, snapdragon, gloriosa daisy, pansy, phlox, and viola. Their sturdiness as outdoor-grown winter seedlings may surprise you. In addition, take a chance with other annuals in winter; if the weather happens to be warmer than usual you will have early cut flowers of many kinds. Some our best sunflowers were ones that were planted in fall and lived through a winter that happened to be mild enough to allow them to survive. Make a fall planting of a seed mixture, for some of the types are likely to succeed, even in an unusually warm or cold winter.

SOUTHERN FLORIDA

Except for certain northern perennials that need cold and dormancy, most flowers will grow here at some time of the year. Cold-tender annuals like vinca, salvia, coleus, impatiens, and verbena are perennial in this climate. Most biennials grow in southern Florida if planted in November or December, and so do annuals like nasturtium and shirley poppies that like cool weather.

FLOWERS FOR FALL AND WINTER SOWING

Here, briefly described, are some of the many hardy annual and biennial flowers for Florida, plus a few short-lived, heat-sensitive perennials to treat as biennials. For best selection, grow most of these from seed in fall, but you may find that some will also be available at garden centers as blooming bedding plants in the spring, ready for the garden.

Alcea rosea **(hollyhock).** Here's the ultimate in cottage garden flowers. But, be warned, it is very tricky in the subtropics. This short-lived perennial is grown like a biennial, sown in fall, the year before it should bloom. Cultivars vary in growth time needed, so select smaller types, which come into bloom in the shortest time. Height ranges from 2 to 6 feet, depending on cultivar, in all colors but blue. Double or single flowers a few inches wide bloom in progression on tall spires, from bottom to top. 'Summer Carnival', a fluffy double-flowered type that comes in all the hollyhock colors, is your best bet, for it goes from seed to bloom in as little as four months. That would be early December to early April. Provide ample fertilizer, compost, and water to keep up the speed of growth. You are in a race with Florida's steamy summer heat. Hollyhocks went out of fashion years ago because of problems with rust disease. Now, with new rust-resistant varieties, it's fun to grow them again. But not in southern Florida.

Ammi majus **(Bishop's flower, false Queen Anne's lace).** Hardy annual. From March until hot weather these are clouds of feathery bloom, over 50 flowers per plant. They are glorious for over two months a year in Monica's garden. Similar and slightly larger is *A. visagna* 'Green Mist' (Park Seed). Sow in fall in sun, in any soil. Their shiny compound leaves grow slowly, like carrots. Thin and transplant with care, while plants are small. In early spring the plants shoot up to five feet tall and may need staking. Before this growth spurt occurs you can transplant the small plants. The blooms last well as cut flowers and may also be dried if picked as they just begin to open.

A Cutting Garden for Florida

Antirrhinum majus (snapdragon). Hardy annual. Showy spikes of tubular florets bloom in bright or soft colors of white, red, orange, pink, or yellow. Varying heights are available. 'Rocket' hybrid is the classic, colorful tall type. Choose any of the taller types for bouquets. Snapdragon is one of the best annuals for a spire form, and one of the most frostproof. Sometimes the plants live for a year or more, although they usually burn out in hot summers. It takes several months for seed-grown plants to reach blooming size, so most people buy bedding plants. Though small, the seed is not all that hard to handle if started indoors under lights and later set out. Snapdragons need sweet, fertile soil and a sunny spot. Add lime in most parts of the state. Cut when the bottom half of the spike is open. Continue to pick flowers, or cut plants back to six inches to renew bloom. If plants form a mat of foliage with no flowers in winter, just mulch them and be patient, for they will explode with bloom when warm weather returns.

Bellis perennis **(English daisy, double daisy).** This is a very short-lived perennial, usually sown in fall for early spring bloom. Neat, low plants bear daisies one to three inches wide, single or double, on strong stems. Pink, white, or rose are the usual colors. Bellis prefers moist, fertile soil and partial shade; it is not at all suited to hot weather. It combines well with pansies in winter gardens and bouquets. Mulch it to prevent the soil from becoming dry and hot.

Brassica oleracea **(ornamental cabbage or kale).** As easy to grow as regular cabbage, these ornamental cabbages and kales come in various leaf colors, and in both rippled and fern leaf forms. They are biennials, used for winter bedding. The main color combinations are of green with pink, red, cream, yellow, or purple—or all of these together. The contrasting leaf colors may not show up until 3 months from sowing. If you sow seeds, start them inside in August or outside in September, for an early enough start. Otherwise, buy plants in the fall. Either way, they will thrive all winter and look good as foliage plants until the weather gets warm the next spring. Some gardeners carry them over, for in spring, the yellow flowers, like blooming broccoli, grow in a fountain of bloom from each stalk. This can look decent in a mass planting but will look weird with just a few plants.

Flowering cabbages and kale are handsome plants in the garden, and you can add the leaves to bouquets and salads alike. Plain red cabbage leaves look great in bouquets, too. To use any of these brassicas in arrangements, bend the leaves to the shape you want, then submerge them in icy water for one to two hours. They are quite striking. If you can't get the whole leaf base into the oasis, shave off the sides and make the midrib into a point. After arranging, do not keep them around too long or they will develop a characteristic cabbagey odor.

Calendula officinalis **(English or pot marigold).** This hardy annual with elegant cream-colored, gold, or orange blooms resembles chrysanthemums. Heights and sizes vary. So does heat tolerance, but calendulas are partial to cool weather. These are excellent winter plants for all of Florida. Start them in fall to

Hardy Annuals and Biennials

earliest spring from seeds, which are large and easy to handle, or get plants. Calendulas like full sun and moderate amounts of water. They are susceptible to nematodes, but otherwise easy to grow. They last really well as cut flowers.

***Campanula medium.* Canterbury Bells.** Pretty bellflowers bloom in many in soft shades of blue, pink, and white. They symbolize constancy, but they are short-lived as cut flowers. Most Florida gardeners can grow these lovely biennials. Though they tend to self-sow in northern states, we have not noticed this here. In fact, they are quite difficult in the southern half of the state. Replant each fall in full sun in rich, moist soil. Perennial campanulas (there are many species, short and tall) can sometimes be grown in Florida as biennials, but normally are not reliably hardy here because of a lack of chilling in winter or too much heat for too long a time in summer. Go for the annuals when you find them. *C. isophylla* 'Stella' is an annual, 8 inches tall and covered with white or blue bells. It would be very pretty in tabletop flowerpots.

Centaurea cyanus **(bachelor's-button, cornflower)** Hardy annual. These old-fashioned favorites come in a lovely blue, also pink, white, burgundy, purple, and bicolors of round, tufted blossoms on long stems. For the largest, strongest spring plants, sow seed outdoors in fall. Seed may still be planted in early spring; plants will be less robust but still very pretty. Plants respond to day length, and fall and spring sowings bloom at about the same time. Plant in any improved, well-drained soil in full sun or bright partial shade. Keep picking to prolong bloom. When flower quality deteriorates too much, discard the plants. Avoid the frosted types with petals tipped with white, for they look prematurely aged in bouquets. Thompson & Morgan has 'Cut Flower Mixed', 36 inches tall. Tall types make better cut flowers. Also good is 'Blue Diadem,' intensely blue, 30 inches tall, and large-flowered. There's a similar and related flower, Sweet Sultan (*Amberboa moschata*) with white, pink, or yellow flowers, and a chocolatey scent.

larkspur

Consolida ambigua **(Larkspur, annual delphinium).** This is a good choice for spires of violet, white, pink, and blue early in the year. Plant in winter, where you want them to bloom, for fast growth in spring. These can really be gorgeous flowers! Everybody loves the rich blues such as 'Earlibird Blue' and 'Blue Bell'. Plants need full sun (maybe a tiny bit of shade) and average soil, and like mulch to keep roots moist and cool. Where they are happy they will self sow, improving every year. For fresh or dried bouquets, harvest stems when the bottom third of blossoms are open, and the other buds will continue to open. With fresh flowers, remove foliage for longer vase life. Sometimes if stems are hollow, moist cotton is tucked inside to keep flowers fresher, longer. To dry, hang upside down in small bunches.

A Cutting Garden for Florida

***Coreopsis tinctoria* (tickseed).** This hardy annual grows best if planted in fall (also early spring in northern Florida). It copes with Florida's interseasonal temperature fluctuations quite well. In fact, coreopsis is Florida's official State Wildflower, and is widely planted along roadsides and in highway median strips. It can be planted near the sea if sheltered by buildings or fences. Daisylike flowers on wiry stems bloom in gold, orange, and rusty red, and often are bicolored. Short and tall types are available; the tall ones are more productive but need staking. Plant in any soil with average moisture, in full sun or partial shade. Harvest while the centers are still tight.

***Dianthus armeria* (pinks), other *Dianthus* species and hybrids.** You see this neat, pretty, clove-scented relative of the carnation, usually only eight inches tall, as a bedding plant all over Florida, in white, pink, red, and red-purple. Though classed as an annual, it behaves like a perennial here because it tolerates both of the big killers: light frost and summer heat. It takes full or near full sun and regular watering. Use bloomer fertilizer. Plant seed or bedding plants in fall, winter, or spring. Monica loves its relative, sweet william (*D. barbatus*), and has gotten plants to live, but never bloom in her Tampa garden, where other forms of dianthus thrive and sometimes live for more than a year. Sweet william grows more reliably in northern Florida than warmer areas. Local garden centers have good types of dianthus for your area.

***Digitalis* hybrids (foxglove).** Except in the northwestern sections of the state, you can't really grow this typically English perennial well in Florida, even as a biennial, but sometimes you can get blooms (once per plant) from a fast hybrid such as 'Foxy' before plants burn out in spring heat. Keep plants cool and moist, and provide loamy soil in shade.

***Dimorpotheca* species (African daisy).** This hardy annual daisy is easy to grow from large, flat seeds sown in late fall through late winter. Plants are about a foot tall with loads of daisies from 2 to 2.5 inches across. The color range of *D. sinuata* is a pleasing range of pastel yellow, cream, white, orange, and peach shades. *D. pluvalis* 'Glistening White' is aptly named, with shiny white petals enhanced by dark eyes. At the moment, both are available from Park Seeds.

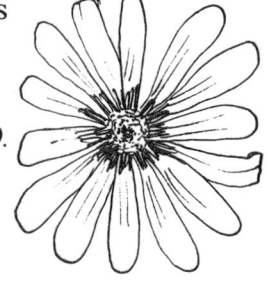

***Emilia flammea* (tassel flower, cacalia).** Sow this annual in fall, in a sunny spot with average, well-drained soil, where you want plants to grow. Plants self seed unless kept picked, and may seem weedy when they come up in the wrong place. To get emilia established, make successive sowings. 'Scarlet Magic' is a red strain; there are also golden and orange types. This grows wild in southern Florida. Stems are 1 1/2 feet long, and bear loose clusters of petite daisylike flowers. Thin seedlings to about eight inches apart. In the vase, the red blooms makes a nice accent when combined with larger flowers, especially lacelike white *Ammi majus*.

Hardy Annuals and Biennials

***Eschscholzia californica* (California poppy).** Bright, sunny golden chalice-like blooms on blue-green, ferny foliage make this an outstanding choice for bedding or cutting, though it is short-lived in bouquets. It also comes in tones of red, rose, cream, and peach, including some bicolored on the reverse side of the petals. Plant outdoors from October to February in full sun or partial shade in nearly any well-drained soil. Too much fertilizer will limit blooms. It tolerates drought and often reseeds, but dies out in hot weather. Pick in morning, just as caps begin to pop off, while blooms are still tightly furled. Very easy; recommended.

***Eustoma grandiflora* (lisianthus, prairie gentian).** Beautiful, silky, cup-shaped blooms open from long, tapered buds and last very well. They come in shades of pink, purple, and white and in single and double forms. Some are bicolored. Heights vary from short bedding plants to tall border types. Taller ones with their long stems are better for bouquets. Seaside gentian (*E. exaltatum*), a close relative, grows wild in central and southern Florida, so it is not surprising that lisianthus tolerates salt and may reseed. Plants seeded in fall bloom in spring, which is fairly slow. Fortunately lisianthus does well as bedding transplants, which are widely available from nurseries in spring or fall. Plants may survive through summer heat, but they definitely prefer cooler weather in semishade, ideally in morning sun with some afternoon shade, in moist, enriched soil. Pinch plants back once or twice for the maximum number of flowers. Harvest in the morning and condition in cool water. Cut flowers often last for more than two weeks.

Gaillardia 'Red Plume'

***Gaillardia pulchella* (blanket flower).** Sow this annual form of blanket flower in late fall or early spring. Choose from double (globe-shaped) or single (daisy-shaped) types. Stems are nice and firm and flowers last well in bouquets. The plants are about two feet tall, with flowers about two inches wide. Colors are mostly cream, gold, red, orange, and plum. Blanket flowers bloom prolifically and tolerate heat very well, which is unusual in a hardy annual. They thrive in average, well-drained soil in full sun, and there's a related blanketflower that can be seen growing wild on dunes near the ocean.

***Gypsophila elegans* (baby'sbreath).** This hardy annual blooms with two-foot clouds of tiny white or pink flowers that are a florist's standby. They grow from seed easily, but are hard to find ready-started. Plant them outside while the soil is quite cool; frost won't hurt them. Make successive sowings from fall to early spring. They prefer poor to average soil with some lime added, and do fine in full sun or with afternoon shade. When hot weather arrives, they say farewell. 'Covent Garden' is the classic type and blooms in only about eight weeks from seed. There's a perennial gypsophila but usually it is not successful in Florida.

A Cutting Garden for Florida

***Helichrysum bracteatum* (strawflower).** Hardy annual. Looking like double daisies fashioned of colored straw, in glossy orange, yellow, pink, magenta, rust, peach, or white, these seem almost unreal, especially before the flowers have been dried. Plants are 1 to 4 feet tall and blooms are 1/2 to 3 inches wide, depending on variety. Flower seed specialists offer them in separate or mixed colors, in several sizes. Strawflowers are under-appreciated in Florida: few gardeners know that, due to their Australian heritage, they tolerate hot and cold weather and adapt to sudden changes of temperature. They are showy in the border, too. Plant them in sun any time of year in central and southern Florida, in early spring in northern Florida. They grow in well-drained, average soil. They like sandy soil and are drought tolerant once established. For fresh or dried bouquets, cut while centers are still covered by inner petals. See page 105 for information on drying them.

***Iberis umbellata* (candytuft).** The annual type of candytuft is free-blooming in pink, purple, rose, white, or crimson. Hyacinth-flowered types are tall columns of florets, while other types form round heads. Some varieties are fragrant. Plants are very cold hardy and salt tolerant, but do poorly in hot weather. Plant in late fall in most of Florida, or very early in spring (six weeks before the last frost) in northern sections of the state. Seeds are large and easy to handle. Bedding plants are not hard to find. Plant in full sun or partial shade and provide water regularly. Harvest blooms when the outer petals open.

***Lathyrus odoratus* (sweet pea).** Hardy annual. With our mild winters we can grow lovely sweet peas, if it doesn't get unseasonably hot. Soak their large seeds overnight for easy sprouting and plant from November through January. Protect them from hard freezes, but a light frost is no problem. These are fragrant, unusual cut flowers for the home. Some are climbers, some bedders. In seed catalogs you'll find a wide selection of frilled sweet peas in white, mauve, yellow, blue, pink, or violet. However they are meant for a cooler climate or a greenhouse. Grow them only in cooler weather in sun or bright partial shade, in rich soil with regular, plentiful watering. It helps to plant them in a shallow trench, then gradually add soil and compost around the stems as the seedlings grow, in order to make them deep rooted and protect the roots from heat and drought.

***Lavatera trimestris* (mallow).** This hibiscus relative has four-inch flowers in early summer. The pale to deep rose pink color is lovely. It needs space, for it grows quickly to almost shrub size. Plant in a sunny spot in spring and water generously. It likes rich soil and cool weather and is easy to grow. If this is new to you, try it!

Hardy Annuals and Biennials

***Limonium sinuatum* (statice, sea lavender).** Bright sprays of papery flowers in white, yellow, purple, blue, rose, or lavender bloom on 18-inch stems above neat rosettes of leaves. These sturdy plants tolerate sea air and wind. Plant seeds in February in northern Florida (or earlier in a coldframe), from September to January in central and southern parts of the state. The plants need time to make a basal rosette of leaves before they start to form flowers on stalks. Timing is critical to success. The flowers are long-lasting fresh and very easily dried. Plants bloom periodically from late spring through fall. Grow in sun in any well-drained soil for bedding and cutting. Cut when flowers are half open for fresh bouquets, half to three quarters open for drying (page 107). Harvest or deadhead often to keep plants productive.

***Linaria maroccana* (toadflax).** This hardy annual is easy in sandy soil, if planted during cool weather. Betty found this charming miniature snapdragon after growing a packet of mixed seeds, then identified it, and has grown it ever since. Sow seeds in fall, then enjoy clouds of jewel-bright, spurred flowers on stems up to two feet tall in late winter or spring. 'Northern Lights' is good for cutting because of its long stems. Leaves are threadlike and delicate, stems wiry. Colors are white, yellow, rose, red, and every shade of purple. It likes full sun and well-drained, average soil, and can tolerate drought once established. The flowers, though small and delicate, last over a week in bouquets. Delight a child with the tiniest bouquet, just right for her dollhouse.

***Matthiola incana* (stock).** This cabbage relative has columns of deliciously fragrant single or double florets. In the garden they are never as tightly arranged on the stem as are the greenhouse spires, but are lovely nonetheless. The taller types are best for bouquets. Plant in the fall in central Florida, early spring in the north, for they like cool weather but freeze out at about 25 degrees. Give them full sun to partial shade, average to rich soil, and plenty of water. Cut when a quarter or half of the florets are open, but BEFORE the ones at the base begin to fade. Remove the lower leaves to prevent the cabbagey odor. Split the woody stem bases and condition overnight in very cold, deep water. Mist the double types of flowers and their foliage daily to prolong bloom. Use rather acid sugar water (3 teaspoons sugar and 2 tablespoons vinegar per quart) to help make flowers last from five to 12 days in the vase.

***Molucella laevis* (bells of Ireland).** Interesting and fragrant apple-green bells grow on two to three foot spikes. Seedlings of this hardy annual tolerate cold weather, but germination occurs during warmer weather. Soaking seeds overnight in warm water softens the coats and speeds germination. Plant in fall or spring in any well-drained soil. Cover very shallowly for they need light to germinate. Grow the plants in full sun or light shade. Mulch helps. Effective and increasingly popular, use bells of Ireland either cut fresh or dried in arrangements. After drying, the green eventually fades to tan, as do grasses.

A Cutting Garden for Florida

***Nicandra physalodes* (shoo-fly plant).** A cousin to tomatoes, this plant has large leaves and a unique spreading habit. The flowers are delicate lavender-blue cups with white centers that only stay open part of the day, but stems make a good filler in arrangements. The five-sided seedpods are decorative when green or dried. Once it starts blooming, while still quite small, the plant is effective in reducing flies, though these are seldom a problem in Florida. It has followed Monica into every garden since it saved her sanity on an Iowa farm years ago. Plant seeds indoors or outdoors in early spring, in full sun and average soil. The first ones may germinate sporadically, but once you have them, plants will self seed but never invade. Treat them like tomatoes. They are even easier to grow. Give them room toward the back of the garden and enjoy their novelty.

***Nigella damascena* (love-in-a-mist).** With multi-petalled, pastel flowers nestled in frothy, threadlike leaves, nigella gives an airy look to bouquets. The color and texture are lovely, but the flowers last only a few days. Tall varieties are best for cutting. Balloonlike seedpods are useful and everlasting in dried arrangements. Plant seeds in December in southern Florida, and at about the time of the last winter frost in central and northern sections, or earlier with protection. Nigella prefers good, loamy soil, full sun or partial shade, and average moisture. Plants are likely to die during prolonged high heat, but are otherwise very easy, and often self sow.

***Papaver rhoeas* (shirley poppy, Flanders Field poppy).** Hardy annual. This delicate, papery looking flower comes in scarlet, white, and shades of pink and salmon, in single and double forms. Start seeds outdoors in late fall or early spring while the weather is cool. Sowing them in late fall yields larger plants. Shirley poppies like sun but will tolerate very light shade, too. Give average soil but not too much fertilizer, and water plants only occasionally. Cut as buds begin to open. Flowers last only a day. Singe stem ends for all-day vase life and add sugar to the water, or yours will wilt in an hour. This excellent cutting garden choice is guaranteed to be a favorite once you succeed with it. Try! Also try *P. nudicaule*, Iceland poppy, a heat sensitive perennial that makes a good one-season show in Florida when treated like shirley poppies.

***Petunia* hybrids.** With a dazzling array of colors and bicolors, petunias are as reliable in Florida as elsewhere, but at different seasons. The singles are more weatherproof than the doubles. Petunias are slow to grow from seed, but widely available as bedding plants. They grow all year, with enough water, yet in summer, drenching rains and high humidity drown the plants. In northern Florida, they may die in winter in colder years; mulch deeply to prevent this, or get new plants. Petunias are very cold tolerant, and the plants survive light frost even though buds and blossoms freeze. Give them sun or partial shade and moist, fertile soil. They grow well near the sea. Pick off spent blooms. Pinch back leggy stems. Cuttings are easily rooted for new plants, during cool, moist weather—this was more commonly done many years ago. Try petunias as cutflowers in a large bowl, intermixed with ivy or other foliage.

Hardy Annuals and Biennials

Phlox drummondii. This very hardy annual grows wild in many parts of the state, blooming by the field and ditchful in March and April. It can be grown near the sea with only a little shelter from salt spray. The bloom of wild phlox is quite wonderful, with masses of flat-faced or starlike tubular flowers in shades of rose, peach, burgundy, white, yellow, red, and purple, on plants about 1 foot tall. Many have a contrasting eye. They grow just as well in the garden if planted in fall, and bloom from spring into summer. To harvest, cut above a stem joint before half the flowers in the cluster open. Many forms are available but the classics are best.

***Rudbeckia* species (black-eyed susan, gloriosa daisy).** These tall, sturdy plants usually have golden orange blooms with dark centers. Some are bronze and bicolors. Breeders give us dwarf, medium, and tall forms. The dwarf forms such as 'Becky' and 'Toto' are under a foot tall and can be planted in baskets to show off on picnic tables. 'Indian Summer' provides large, golden daisies on strong plants, 3 feet tall. Heat and sun loving, the rudbeckias are good perennials that bloom the first year from seed. However, they are normally short-lived, and especially so in Florida, so they are treated in our book and in Florida gardens as biennials. Double types are not as graceful as singles. Cuttings and divisions root easily. To save seeds, let the flower mature fully and tap the little black seeds into an envelope to save them for the next planting. While plants are blooming, use soap spray often for perfect blossoms, keeping aphids away. If you cut the stems while the flower centers are tight, split stem bases slightly, condition flowers in cool water, add a pinch of sugar to the vase water and change it often, the flowers last up to two weeks in the vase.

***Salvia* species.** Salvias, even short-lived types, tend to live more than a season in Florida. See the salvia section under perennials.

***Scabiosa atropurpurea* (mourning bride, pincushion flower).** In spite of the unappealing names, this easily-grown hardy annual will provide you with lovely, disclike, composite cutflowers in desirable shades of blue, violet, white, rose, wine, and purple. Some types need staking more than others. Get seeds from a well-known supplier for types with stronger stems. 'QIS Scarlet' is a strong grower with wonderfully rich cranberry red flowers. Plant scabiosas during cool weather in good soil, in full sun or light shade. Keep soil evenly moist. Buds must be well developed to open after cutting. Split stems. Seedpods are also effective, fresh or dry. Flowers last 4 to 8 days. Perennial scabiosas grow only in the cooler parts of Florida.

***Silene compacta* (catchfly), *Silene coeli-rosa* (syn. *Viscaria elegans*).** These dainty members of the pink family grow just under to just over a foot tall, blooming on slender, wiry stems. Catchfly is usually electric pink with tiny flowers in vivid clusters, above neat mats of grayish green foliage. Leaves and stems are sometimes sticky, hence the name. Viscaria has masses of pink, deep rose, blue, or violet flowers about half an inch wide, with silky petals. Both are best grown as biennials, planted in fall or winter for spring bloom. Catchfly is very hardy, even in Pennsylvania. Both types like a limy, well-drained, average to rich soil in full sun or bright partial shade. Seed is very small, but try growing it because plants are rarely available from garden centers. For best results, sow on soil surface where plants are to grow or in individual pots, and keep very moist until plants are about an inch tall. Thin or transplant carefully. After plants mature, average to dry soil is satisfactory.

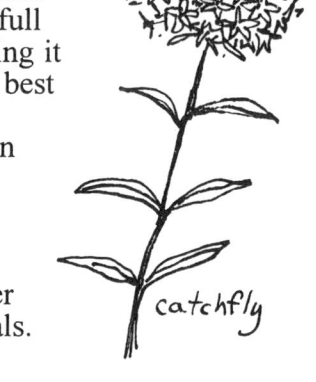

Tropaeolum species (nasturtium). Although classed as tender annuals, nasturtiums share many attributes with hardy annuals. See the plant entry on page 45.

***Viola* species (pansies and violas).** Most of these popular species are biennials and hardy annuals. Set out plants from the cool part of fall through early spring. Or grow your own from seed if you are patient. Start them indoors in late summer. Seeds dry out at their peril, so you can grow them in covered containers, or else presoak seeds for two days in a moistened paper towel enclosed in a plastic bag, and then plant with tweezers in small pots or cells. Grow the small plants indoors for another month or two, under lights or in a bright window. Pansies tolerate frost and may be grown under deciduous trees where they receive full sun in winter, light shade in spring. They like rich, moist soil. Pick often or shear back plants to prevent legginess. Shearing will stimulate new growth which can be used to make stem cuttings for new plants, or longer stems for bouquets. The new shoots root easily but the old, hollow stems do not. To save seed from your own plants, collect ripe pods when they turn tan, before they shatter.

Though small, pansies and violas are lovely in informal bouquets. To condition them, submerge them completely for several hours in cool water. Do not try to force the tender stems into floral foam, just use them in water-filled vases. Sprinkle the bouquets with cool water for longer vase life.

Chapter Eight
CUT FLOWER CHOICES: PERENNIALS

Perennials are non-woody plants which live for years, growing fresh foliage and flowers each year. **Hardy perennials** tolerate freezing weather, and many require a period of chilling in winter. Most freeze or die back to the ground each winter, then grow back from the roots. They tend to flower once a year for several weeks, but there are exceptions. They take up a lot of space in the garden, but earn it by blooming year after year without replanting. Some popular types for northern gardens can be grown here through winter, but die during a long Florida summer that is much too hot for them.

Tender perennials live for years, but only if protected from frost. Some, like impatiens, are usually grown only as annuals in places with cold winters. They can become much larger and shrubbier in frost-free areas. Since tender perennials are accustomed to a warm climate, they usually bloom more frequently or for a longer time than the hardy ones. A few are sensitive to high heat, but most thrive in it.

In this chapter, we have tried to include the more reliable, longer-lived perennials for Florida. Plant your perennials in well-prepared, fertile soil, for they will grow in the same site for many years. Keep perennials attractive by harvesting or deadheading frequently, removing yellowed or spoiled foliage, dividing them when crowded (see chapter eleven), and refreshing soil with fertilizer and mulch several times a year.

NORTHERN FLORIDA

Somewhere between northern and central Florida is the dividing line between temperate and subtropic gardening. North Florida gardeners interested in perennial borders which reflower each year can follow standard gardening guides for the southern and central East Coast. Many classic perennials will grow in northern Florida but will not grow reliably in central or southern parts of the state. Peonies, hostas, bleeding hearts, coral bells, perennial asters, bearded iris, oriental poppies and perennial babysbreath are examples.

CENTRAL FLORIDA

This part of the state is the most difficult for which to recommend perennials, because some years it has hard freezes and other years it does not. Many perennial flowers are unpredictable or impossible here, so we have listed only the ones that usually do well. The others tend either to burn out in summer sun or fail from irregular winter weather patterns.

SOUTHERN FLORIDA

Here you will definitely have to get along without astilbe, peony, hosta, and other northern perennials, but for every plant that won't grow, you'll find ten to take its place. Exotic tropical plants like split-leaf philodendron, bird-of-paradise, anthurium, New Guinea impatiens, Australian tree fern, datura, and orchids make up outstanding beds of perennials.

PERENNIAL POSSIBILITIES

Abelmoschus **hybrids.** These plants with dogwoodlike flowers (but with five petals, not four) are sometimes grown as annuals, yet can last for years. They are close relatives of hibiscus and okra. *A. manihot* blooms in shades of coral pink to cherry red, and will bloom from seed in about 100 days. Seed prefers warm conditions for germination. The leaves are dark, almost green, but reddish in winter, and are deeply, palmately lobed. The flowers are about two inches across and only last for a day, but they are striking enough to be worth the work of replacing them in bouquets, or you can let new ones open up along the stems. The dried seedpods are decorative.

Plant any time from seed in central or southern Florida, spring in north in full sun or light shade. Abelmoschus thrives in sandy soil and would do even better in muck since the mallows love damp soil. Yet it blooms well with only occasional watering. Prune as you pick to shape the plants. They grow to 2 1/2 feet. Monica's plant bloomed continually for several years, until struck by a very hard frost. It then came back strongly from the thick roots.

Acanthus species (alligator cactus, mountain thistle, bear's breeches). This plant has dramatic thistle-like leaves and long lasting pink, purple, or mauve flower spikes that bloom in winter and early spring. The seed pods are also interesting for dried bouquets. Plants grow 3 to 5 feet tall and prefer light shade, though they withstand full sun. The flowers especially and the leaves to some extent are frost tender, but so far have always come back in Monica's yard. These leaves were the inspiration for the decoration atop Greek Corinthian columns. They will be imortalized in your mind if you try to handle them without gloves, for they are definitely prickly. These are good barrier plants. *A. spinosus* is hardier and more spiny thant *A. mollis*, and author Allan Armitage says *A. spinosissimus* "should only be grown by masochists."

Achillea **species (yarrow, milfoil).** Reliable only in northwestern Florida, these natives with their flat-topped clusters are trim and stylish in bouquets. They come in yellow, gold, peach, brick red, and white, and are tolerant of sandy soil. They are popular in fresh and dried bouquets. In zones 8 and 9, they grow in any soil and in sun or partial shade, self seeding and spreading where they are happy, but they tend to burn out in high heat. Some types bloom in spring from seed planted in fall. See also page 102. Achillea is difficult in central Florida, and as for South Florida, don't bother.

In Tampa, with its south/central climate, Monica has had luck at last with *A. millefolium.* It is doing well in a spot with morning sun and afternoon shade. Other gardeners tell her that the pink and white species are best in this climate. In warmer parts of the state, you may have best results with a fast-growing type such as *A. m.* 'Debutante', which can flower the next spring from a fall planting.

Perennials

Harvest achillea when slightly over half the tiny flowers in the cluster are open. For fresh bouquets, condition in deep, cold water with two tablespoons of salt added to each quart of water. To air dry, hang upside down in small bunches, for several weeks.

Aloe **species (burn plant).** Aloes are easy-to-grow succulents in the lily family. The name, burn plant, refers to the healing gel inside the thick, succulent leaves. They need winter protection in northern Florida but are hardy in southern and central parts of the state. *Aloe barbadensis* has branching spikes of tubular red or orange and gray flowers that are striking in arrangements, especially when combined with foliage of silver dollar eucalyptus. Flowers last 4 or 5 days in the vase. Plants prefer full sun to light shade and can be easily started from divisions of the offshoots. In fact, you'll need to dig from the edges to restrict the spread every few years. Monica puts the extras out by the mailbox with a sign "free aloe plants" and they always disappear.

Angelonia grandiflora **(angelonia)** is an increasingly popular tender perennial from South America that looks like lobelia at first glance, but is more airy and delicate. The green leaves are long and thin with toothed edges and the flowers are either dark purple or purple mixed with white. They are found loosely arranged along the vertical stem. They average two feet in height and do best in full sun. They root fairly well from cuttings and have survived several years of light frosts in central Florida for us. Few catalogs offer this, but plants are available at nurseries. It is a fine cut flower accent in mixed bouquets, and plays the same role in mixed container gardens.

Anthemis tinctoria **(golden marguerite).** These petite fern-leaved daisies are popular pot plants and grow well through the cooler part of the year. They constantly sport one-inch flowers of a bright sulfur yellow. Provide light shade and average soil. Divide if crowded, or increase by cuttings. They are more reliably perennial in northern and central Florida than they are farther south. Cut them while the centers are still tight.

anthurium

Anthurium andraeanum. When cut and arranged, the firm, waxy flowers of anthurium, related to calla lilies, last three to four weeks, making a Florida statement of exotic style all the while. Strangely shaped, glossy flowers (the heart-shaped spathe sports a linear spadix in a contrasting color) may be red, pink, peachy, greenish, or white. The redder they are, the more unreal they look. The heart shaped green leaves are large and handsome, useful as foliage in bouquets as well as in the garden and in pots. A true tropical plant, it is easy to grow indoors or in a greenhouse, but outdoors it needs protection from frost and cold weather. Plants vary in size as well as color. The larger the leaves, the larger the flowers will be.

A Cutting Garden for Florida

***Aquilegia* species (columbine).** Though perennial in northern states, this flower is best as a biennial in Florida, if grown at all, in Zones 8 and northern parts of 9 only. If you are lucky, some may bloom again another year; they are temperamental as well as poetic. They are most likely to be perennial in a few northwestern counties. Start seeds indoors in summer or outdoors in fall. Set out plants in cool, moist weather and water twice a day until they are established. They prefer a shady, moist, loamy bed with good drainage. The pretty, spurred, bicolored flowers bloom above ferny leaves. The wildflower *Aquilegia canadensis* and faster hybrids such as 'Music' are best bets for the northern third of Florida. Condition blooms in deep, cold water. Cut flowers last 5 to 7 days.

***Asclepias* species (butterfly weed, milkweed).** These native plants of several species are heat-tolerant enough for all parts of Florida. They will grow from divisions, cuttings, or seeds.

A. tuberosa has been hybridized and now comes in red, rose, and gold shades in addition to the usual fiery orange. Plants are rugged and handsome with sprays of bright, long-lasting, heat-loving small flowers. Hybrids are shorter than wild forms; both are excellent garden and cut flowers.

A. canadensis is also easy to grow and attractive with its pink flowers.

A curassavica grows 3 feet tall with sprays of yellow or red flowers. It can be grown as an annual, too, for it flowers in 20 weeks from seed.

The milkweeds are easy to grow in full sun in average soil, and adapt well to wet or dry conditions. They attract a variety of insects without suffering much from their presence. Even when larvae of the swallowtail butterfly deleaf some of the plants, they come back well. Singe the stem ends and condition in deep water. Flowers lasts 5 to 8 days when cut. Pods can be dried.

***Asparagus densiflorus* (asparagus fern).** A houseplant in northern states, asparagus fern is used as a groundcover in most of Florida, Zones 9 to 11. Often three or more feet long, its trailing, feathery green fronds are excellent as filler in bouquets, although the narrow leaflets will start to drop in a few days.

The tuberous roots make this plant very drought tolerant, but it also can become tangled and invasive. For good color, grow it in fertile soil in partial shade, otherwise leaves may be too yellow. At times, small pink or white flowers appear amidst the foliage, followed by a sprinkling of red berries. Transplant volunteer seedlings if they are wanted. Cut tops of mature plants back before dividing. Plants freeze to the ground but come back with new sprouts in early spring. To rejuvenate an old bed, cut it back to the ground, preferably in February or March, and then divide and reset plants in improved soil. Water and mulch. New growth will appear very quickly.

***Belamcanda chinensis* (blackberry lily).** This very hardy member of the iris family is a native of China and Japan. It blooms mostly in the summer, in northern, central, and even the upper part of southern Florida. It has many flowering stems that can reach four feet tall and each one branches with many flat, star-shaped yellow or orange flowers dotted with red and up to two inches across. Later the rather typical iris seed pods turn tan and burst open to show tenacious, shining, jet-black seeds resembling blackberries. Both flowers and seedpods are showy in the garden and good in cut flower arrangement.

Perennials

Set the plants in full sun to light shade. The sword-shaped foliage is fairly attractive. Propagate by carefully dividing the rhizomes (thickened roots), or start from seeds, which take 2 to 3 weeks to germinate. Plants usually bloom the second year from seeds, and fall-sown seeds sometimes bloom the next spring. Though somewhat drought tolerant, plants prefer fertile, moist conditions.

Individual florets last only a day or two in bouquets, but the cluster continues to open for up to seven days. Cut them when the first one or two florets open. Condition for several hours in deep, cold water. Hang the mature seedpods upside down to dry and they will keep indefinitely. You can use the seedpods fresh or dry, and in the green or the tan stage.

BROMELIAD	**REGION**	**LIGHT NEEDED**
Aechmea species (vase bromeliads)	S	medium
Ananas comosus (pineapple bromeliads)	CS	high
Billbergia species (vase plant	CS	medium, high
Cryptanthus species (earth star)	S	high
Dyckia brevifolia (dyckia) terrestrial	CS	medium, high
Guzmania lingulata (orange star)	S	medium
Tillandsia species (air plants)	NCS	medium, high
Vriesia splendens (flaming sword)	CS	low

Bromeliads

Several bromeliads are fine for bouquets, and others for ornamental arrangements of living plants. Many types, from tiny to spectacular, do well in gardens throughout central and southern Florida with very little care. They come in many colors and shapes; there are types for soil and others that grow up the trunks or on the branches of trees. Both edible and ornamental pineapples fall into this class and are very rewarding to grow. The ornamental ones have brightly variegated leaves and when one blooms, you can cut the fruit and some foliage for a dramatic centerpiece that will last for several weeks.

Using bromeliads as cut flowers often means that the blooms will last a few weeks in the vase, compared to a few months on the plant, so you may not want to cut them all. But many such as *Billbergia* and *Tillandsia* bloom with enough abundance to bring some indoors to the spotlight. For others like the earth star with its many-colored leaves, you can use small offshoots as accents in your arrangements, then root and replant them later.

A Cutting Garden for Florida

***Centratherum intermedium* (Manaos beauty).** This plant grows wild in Florida. It has blue-green foliage and soft, thistlelike purple blooms 1 inch across. It grows 2 feet tall in either sun or shade, is tolerant of varied soil types and moisture, withstands difficult conditions, comes easily from seeds or cuttings, and blooms throughout the year.

***Chrysanthemum* (*Dendranthema*) species and hybrids.** Northern and Central Florida gardeners have a wide choice of chrysanthemums. They have been in a nomenclatural tug-of-war, but by any name are great garden plants. All the late-blooming ones have time to flower here, and the early ones do well also. Most kinds bloom both in spring and fall in this climate. Mums will grow in almost any soil in full sun to light shade. Low-growing types can be used as groundcover in shade; they'll bloom on and off.

Chrysanthemums can be grown from seed for bloom the first year, though most gardeners buy plants. Set out plants at any time. Cuttings are easily rooted, even ones with flower buds.

In Florida, chrysanthemums need more pest control and more pinching back for bushiness (until early August) than in the North, and must have at least occasional water during the winter to do well. In zones 10 and 11, there is not enough chilling for most types, so buy frost-tender types only, from reliable or local sources.

Chrysanthemum frutescens (Marguerite or Boston daisy). These bright daisies are often found at nurseries or can be started from cuttings. They grow up to 3 feet tall in full sun and bloom constantly, yellow or white. The ferny foliage is perky and green. Cut the flowers when completely open but with centers still tight. Recut the stems under cold water and condition in same, overnight or longer, up to 24 hours. When arranging, allow for lengthening of stems. Flowers will last 6 to 12 days

With other types of chrysanthemums, pick flowers while they are young and just beginning to open. After harvesting, slit the stem bases slightly and place the flowers in deep, cold water. As cut flowers, if conditioned well, they will last one to three weeks. All chrysanthemum species are highly recommended.

Coreopsis grandiflora, C. verticillata. Daisylike golden flowers on straight stems can be easily grown and do not take long to come into bloom. Sow seed or buy plants. *C. verticillata* has threadlike leaves and is long-lived. 'Moonbeam' has pale yellow flowers; 'Zagreb' is golden. *C. grandiflora* has swordlike leaves. Though easier to grow from seed, it is not long-lived. Some types are short, other two or more feet high. Shorter types do not need staking. 'Early Sunrise' is an award winner with 2-inch semi-double flowers, Plant in fall through early spring in sun, in any well-drained soil. They need little water once started, but shower them on hot days to keep them cool. Thin or divide plants each year, if crowded. They may self sow if they get ample water at the right time. Cut the flowers while their centers are still tight. They need long conditioning in cool water, and even then last only for a few days.

Crossandra infundibuliformis (**crossandra**). This shrub-like perennial grows to 3 feet and has glossy dark green, opposite, tender leaves and showy stems topped with funnel-shaped flowers in orange-red or soft apricot yellow. It grows easily in partial to light shade and blooms mostly in the summer, but it will continue as long as the weather is warm. Frost will nip it back, but it recovers quickly. It is sensitive to nematodes, so mulch it well. Start new ones from cuttings, but don't be surprised to find some seedlings, though it is never rampant. It is reliable in spite of low salt and drought tolerance. Cut the flowers when they are colorful. Split stems ends and condition in cool water. A few flowers will drop after a few days, but the others stay bright and new buds continue to open for a week or more. Use crossandra mostly for filler. Even the rich green foliage is useful in arrangements.

Delphinium **hybrids.** The many types vary greatly in heat tolerance, but the tall, classic types are virtually impossible here, even in the northwestern region of Florida. Thompson & Morgan and some other seed suppliers list the zone range for each different species and cultivar. Delphiniums will bloom once in late spring after a November planting, if you are lucky, but may not survive long after blooming. In Florida heat these are all difficult, for they prefer cool, moist weather. *D. cardinale*, a red delphinium, is said to be quick to bloom from a fall sowing. Delphinium flowers, if you manage to get them to grow, require a long conditioning in cool water. If you have no luck with perennial delphiniums, instead try larkspur (*Consolida ambigua*), an annual or biennial delphinium which grows everywhere with ease, from a late fall planting after the weather has cooled. See page 51 for more information.

Dianthus caryophyllus (**Florist's carnation**). Long-stemmed carnations are classic cut flowers, but are usually bred for and grown in a greenhouse. They are quite a challenge, and not only in Florida, for they do poorly in high heat though they withstand a lot of chilling. Select shorter, fast-growing carnations such as the 'Knight' series, which grows well in late winter and early spring. 'First Love' with white flowers fading to pink also grows in Florida. Carnations prefer full sun to light shade. 'Knight' takes about five months from seed to bloom, so start it in a cold frame or greenhouse, or buy bedding plants. One potful can sometimes be divided when setting out. Cut and conditioned, carnations last up to 10 days in the vase. Some of the annual dianthus species last many seasons in Florida. In northern Florida, you may have good results with Dianthus plumarius and other perennial dianthus species for the garden.

Dietes vegeta (**African iris**). These plants are wonderfully graceful and delicate looking, even though they are among the sturdiest, most heat- and insect-proof plants in the garden. The white blooms touched with lilac speckles appear in spring and sporadically at other times. The two-and-a-half-foot swordlike foliage never droops or straggles. Soil should be average and

A Cutting Garden for Florida

well drained. Partial shade is the best exposure, but full sun is tolerated. Buy plants at garden centers. This landscape plant rarely needs division, but in time forms huge fibrous clumps.

Digitalis. See Hardy Annuals and Biennials, page 52.

Echinacea purpurea (purple coneflower). Here is a tough plant that grows from Maine to Florida. Large, rose-pink daisies with dark, prickly, cone-shaped centers bloom on long, sturdy stems up to three feet high. 'Magnus' is a strong, pink hybrid. There are white forms, too, such as 'White Lustre'. Give coneflowers plenty of space, full sun, average soil, and moderate watering. They are not difficult from seed, and their heat tolerance is superior. This is a good butterfly plant. However, insects sometimes eat whole young plants the night after they are set out, so protect them with insecticidal soap, pepper spray, or a mayonnaise-jar shield until they become established. Abundant flowers can be up to eight inches across and will last over a week in arrangements if stems are recut and water is changed. The spiky centers can also be used with the petals removed, in fresh or dried bouquets and wreaths. We recommended this highly.

purple coneflower

Erigeron hybrids (fleabane). Clusters of small, daisylike wildflowers bloom in shades of pink, rose, and lilac, with gold centers and soft petals. Two-foot types such as 'Jewel Mixed' are best for cutting. They grow well in central and northern Florida, but may not be long-lived. Sow seeds in fall or set out plants in spring, in well-drained, average soil in sun.

Gaillardia grandiflora (blanket flower). This rugged perennial does so well in Florida that it has naturalized as a wildflower. Big, bright two-toned yellow and red daisy-form flowers with fringed petals look fine in vase or flowerbed. It loves heat, sandy soil, and full sun, and will survive with only minimal watering, even on sandy dunes. Choose tall types for cutting and plant in winter or spring, spacing well. Bedding plants are widely available at garden centers. 'Goblin' is red with yellow tips, while 'Burgundy' has solid, wine-red petals. This is a good seaside plant. Cut while centers are tight and petals are open. Split the bottom of the stem slightly. Highly recommended.

Gaura lindheimeri (gaura, whirling butterfly). This pretty perennial is an American native, found wild in Texas, Louisiana, and central Mexico. It is hardy from Zones 6 to 9, so Monica tried some seeds, which were easy. She grew several clumps with narrow-leaved stalks.

Perennials

They bloomed the first year with delicate spikes of 3/4-inch star-shaped flowers, pink or white aging to rose. Cultivars vary in depth of color. Gauras bloom, a few flowers at a time, for a long time in warm weather and last well in the vase. They are used in France for summer bedding and are considered half hardy annuals. However, Monica's plants have lasted over two years so far. Plants range from 2 to over 3 feet and thrive in sandy, well-drained soil. They resist drought but look better with enough water

***Gazania* species (treasure flower).** This low-growing bedding plant's 5-inch bloom looks like a multicolored sunflower on a short, compact plant. If you are patient it is not hard from seed. Gazanias are popular and can be found at garden centers. Hot weather and sunny, well-drained, rich soil will usually give good results, but set in the plants during cooler weather in early March so they can become well rooted before the heat begins. Although attractive, gazania is unstable as a cut flower because the flowers open and close during the day according to the level of light in the room and other factors.

***Gerbera jamesonii* (Transvaal daisy, African daisy.)** From South Africa, these long-lived single or double daisies will bloom all year in southern Florida, and for most of it in the rest of the state. They come in many heights and sizes, with flowers up to four inches across in rich, vibrant gold, red, rose, and peach, on unbranched stems up to about 2 feet tall. Cultivars under a foot tall are also available. Flowers attract butterflies and are excellent for cutting gardens and flower beds. They need a sweet soil and full sun; add lime. It is best to start with plants, for the seed is short-lived and difficult to germinate. For color and style, select them while in bloom.

Set the plants into the ground at the same depth as in the pot, taking care to keep the leaves above the soil. They respond well to bloomer fertilizers, rich soil, and ample water, and like it alternately wet, then dry. Protect them during heavy frosts and they will live for years, with a large basal rosette of leaves from which the straight stems of flowers grow. Divide when crowded, but only if several plants are clumped together. Take care not to harm each plant's deep taproot. Protect foliage from slugs and snails.

Harvest with long stems. For best vase life, cut off the bottom half inch of stem and split the stem base slightly. Condition overnight in cool water up to the flowerhead, but keep petals dry. Flowers last five to seven days in bouquets, if conditioned well.

***Hedychium* species (ginger lily, shell flower), and other gingers.** Hedychium, or butterfly ginger, grows 3 to 6 feet tall and bears very fragrant pastel flowers during the warmer months. The flowers flare widely from long tubes, emerging in clusters near the tips of lush, deep green, long-leaved stalks. The butterfly-shaped flowers in white, yellow, or pink are generally about two inches across, in clusters up to a foot long. The gingers like a hot, frost-free, moist environment, but will survive moderate dryness and light, infrequent frosts. They usually come back from the spreading rhizomes (running roots) with rapid

A Cutting Garden for Florida

growth even in northern Florida, and grow 3 to 6 feet tall. Plants are available at nurseries. Plant the roots shallowly in early spring, in rich soil. In later years, divide them at this time if they have become clumped and crowded. Keep them fertilized.

True ginger (*Zingiber* species) is similar in form and size, it prefers shade and rich, moist soil, but will grow well in any good soil with ample water, and will tolerate full sun and some salt air. In subtropic conditions, with plenty of water, you might also try shell ginger with its long, pink flower, or pinecone ginger with its green, pinecone-like bloom atop a long, straight stalk. Pinecone ginger cones turn red at maturity, and can show color from the Fourth of July until New Year's day. The red cones don't show up much under those big green leaves, so you might as well cut some of them for bouquets, where they can serve as dramatic focal points. Interestingly, the flowerheads produce lanolin, a lotion-like juice that is nice as a hand or face wash. You can continue to squeeze the flowerhead softly to release the juice, even while it is in the vase. Edible ginger has inconspicuous flowers in cones similar to those of pinecone ginger, but only a fourth the size. The cones can be used in arrangements, and the leaves and roots are used in Asian cooking.

Dichorisandra thyrsiflora (blue ginger) blooms in the fall with lovely, deep blue spikes. It is a relative of wandering jew and has similar leafstalks with striped or mottled markings. Blue ginger grows in the shade, and looks very well with purple-leaved ti plant. It is not edible. If it gets nipped by frost, it comes back. It is the only ginger that can be started from cuttings. Plant in humusy soil in light shade. It lasts very well in the vase.

All gingers spread rapidly where conditions suit them. With mulch, they grow with ease in central and southern Florida. Some go dormant in the winter. In all zones, gingers grow well in large containers.

Helianthus maximilianii **(prairie sunflower).** This dramatic perennial sunflower is easy to grow from seeds, or you can buy plants. Sow the seeds in early spring for bloom the first year. In late summer and fall, they will be six feet tall with dozens of 3-inch, yellow, single flowers. These die down in winter but come up in greater abundance every spring. At this point, you can divide them just as new growth begins. Give them full sun and pinch them back a few times, or you'll have to stake them. Cut the branches when half of the flowers are open, split the stem bases, and condition overnight in deep warm water, 80 to 100 degrees F, and they should last a week or longer. Other perennial sunflowers for Florida are beach sunflower (*Helianthus debilis*), wild sunflower (*H. angustifolius*) and, for moist areas, swamp sunflower (*H. simulans*).

Perennials

***Heliconia caribaea* (Wild plantain, flowering banana, lobster-claw).** These close relatives of the banana and bird-of-paradise are among the most exotic and tropical looking you can find for the garden. The waxy, brilliantly colored inflorescence is outstanding for bouquets. The flowers reside in stylized, showy chains of beautiful scarlet and yellow bracts, 6 to 8 inches long, sometimes more. Varieties and species vary in appearance. Most grow more than six feet tall. Leaves are leathery and large on clump-forming plants. There is a Heliconia Society for devotees. Grow heliconias in full sun or partial shade, in moist, fertile soil. Do not let the soil dry out, and fertilize every year during growth. The bracts can be preserved for longer use in bouquets by spraying with Pam or a waxy antidesiccant to hold in the moisture. We recommend this for frostless gardens or as an exotic plant for ultra large pots. Heliconia is fairly salt tolerant.

***Hemerocallis* species (daylily).** This carefree plant has only one drawback as a cut flower: the lilylike blooms close at night. If you use daylilies in a bouquet on the dinner table, be sure to dine early. Some of the newer and more expensive tetraploid hybrids have more substance and stay open longer hours, but nevertheless remain open only for a single day. However, unopened buds on branched stems continue to open for several days in the vase. Some people have luck refrigerating the blooms during the day, tricking them into staying open at night. This keeps flowers fresh for use as edible garnishes on party platters.

Daylilies are highly recommended anyway because they are truly perennial and pest-free landscape plants. They do not flower as abundantly in Florida as in the North, but the bloom season lasts most of the year. Plants from a first rate local supplier are worth the investment, but those from northern suppliers may not be as hardy here as those bred for Florida. In South Florida, buy evergreen types and plant very shallowly.

Plant or transplant daylilies anytime to improved soil in full sun or partial shade. They will survive with only occasional water, but flowers and leaves will look more luscious with lots of water and fertilizer, especially during bud and bloom time. In central and southern Florida, cut the foliage of established plants back to the ground in September, simulating a dormant period (winter), to induce them to bloom again. This is the time to divide them, too, if they are crowded, and reset the divisions in fresh, rich soil. In northern Florida, divide in late winter.

A Cutting Garden for Florida

Hibiscus moscheutos (rose mallow). This dramatic perennial hibiscus is showy and easy to grow. Mallow flowers are large, even dinner-plate size, in shades of white, pink, rose, cranberry, and red. 'Anne Arundel' is a deep pink and 'Lord Baltimore' is cranberry red, both with 10-inch flowers on 5-foot stalks. 'Southern Belle' has flowers about the same size, on four-foot plants, and comes in an array of colors, from seed. The plants closely resemble hibiscus shrubs, but the foliage dies to the ground each winter. Plants prefer a bit of shade in Florida, and lots of moisture. Mulch is very helpful. They are short-lived as cut flowers, so before you use them for party decorations, test their longevity. A single blossom floating in a bowl is a bouquet in itself.

flowers of perennial hibiscus moscheutos can be as large as a dinner plate!

***Hosta* species.** Hostas, dwarf or large, are great foliage plants, but are not a prime choice for much of Florida. They can turn to mush on a hot, muggy Florida day. The green ones are hardier than the blue, yellow, or variegated types. If you live in or near the Panhandle you may have success, and if you do, you'll find the leaves ideal for background material in bouquets. Condition them by totally submerging them in cool water for several hours. Check for heat tolerant cultivars. Hosta breeders, are you listening?

Ipomoea batatas **(Sweet potato vines).** These perennial vines are excellent in hanging baskets, cascading over the edge of containers, or as groundcovers in sun to light shade. 'Blackie' has deeply cut, dark purple leaves and 'Margarita' has large, slightly textured, chartreuse leaves. They are not nearly as rampant as the regular sweet potato. My purple one was well into its second year before starting to spread much. 'Tricolor' is a bit more difficult to grow because variegated plants are, as a rule, less vigorous. All the ornamental sweet potatoes are relatives of the morning glory, hardy here except a hard frost. In that case, take cuttings; they root easily and may root even in the vase. They require very little water and thrive in sandy soil. I have, on rare occasions, seen inch-long light pink to lavender flowers, but these are grown mostly for their ornamental foliage. They do produce tubers that are edible. Most of these are hybrids. Cut single leaves or stems ends and condition in cool water. They will last about a week.

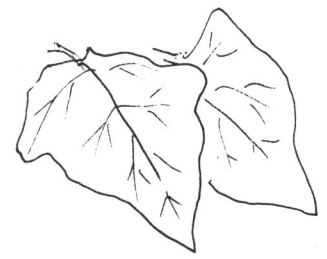

***Iris* species (Louisiana and Japanese iris, blue flag, walking iris).** While the spectacular bearded iris are rarely seen and never thrive in Florida because the wet summers rot their rhizomes, we have some substitutes that are almost as good. There are some excellent Louisiana iris hybrids that bloom with large flowers of red, yellow, blue, white, or purple. These need so much water that they are best grown in ponds or wet areas or in pots set constantly in pans of water. They bloom briefly in spring or summer. Several species of native iris, including *I. hexagona* and *I. virginica*, both called blue flag, like acid soil and wet areas and grace many a pond in the spring with lavender and white flowers. Japanese iris, *I. kaempferi*, have flat reddish-purple blooms in the spring.

Perennials

African iris (*Dietes vegata*, page 65) grows with wiry grace, impervious to most pests and problems. The swordlike, waxy leaves can spike up a boring bouquet.

All of the above do best in full sun. In the shade and in central and southern Florida try walking iris, *Neomaria* species. They are very easy to grow, spread quickly, and come with smaller but charming and fragrant blooms of yellow, white, and blue. Cut when the fist bud is just about to open. Flowers of all will last 1 or 2 days in the vase, with buds continuing to open on the stem. Better plant a lot, so you'll have enough to cut.

***Justicia* species. *Justicia brandegeana* (shrimp plant).** The flowers are actually showy, layered bracts which look like shrimp and come in yellow, rusty orange, or red. They bloom almost year round, with few pests. They like high shade to full sun and are not fussy about soil, but do not tolerate salt. Water often until established; mulch. Plants tend to die back in hard frost but often come back from the roots. Extension agent Sylvester Rose had some that lasted for twenty years. Shrimp plants root easily from cuttings and make good container plants. Cut flowers last 5 to 7 days.

***Justicia carnea* (jacobinia).** This is a good choice for frostless locations, and grows several feet tall with rather large leaves. The exotic clusters of curved flowers in red, yellow-apricot, pink, or orange bloom from April to August, and will last up to five days in bouquets. The waxy foliage is evergreen. The plants do best in shade but will tolerate some sun, but dislike salt. They like moderately fertile soil with abundant moisture. Where damaged by frost, they often grow back from the roots.

***Justicia betonia* (white or silver shrimp plant).** This perennial should become better known. It grows to 4 feet and has glossy small leaves and almost succulent stems that break off easily. Flowers are small and pink but bracts are silvery white in spires 3 to 5 inches long and very showy, especially when used or grown in combination with blue flowers. They are easy to grow, spread extensively, are nipped back by frost but come back from the roots. Cuttings root easily. Plants bloom continuously except in cold weather and last well in the vase. They dry well hung upside down in bunches and are good for wreaths or dried bouquets.

Cut all justicia species for bouquets when the bud tips are showing color. Split bases of woody stems and condition in warm water overnight or until far enough open to be colorful.

***Kalanchoe* species.** There are several species of Kalanchoe that thrive in central and southern Florida. The most common, *K. blossfeldiana,* has flat clusters of tiny four petaled flowers that continue to open and fade neatly over a period of several weeks. They can be pink, yellow or white, but most often are a reddish orange that blends well with nasturtiums. There is also a *K. tomentosa* called pussy ears for its fuzzy leaves, and *K. gastonis-bonnieri* that is called life plant.

A Cutting Garden for Florida

All are so easy to start from cuttings that you can just stick them in the ground. They like full sun but will grow in partial shade, just not as robustly. In the north they are valued as long blooming houseplants.

Kalanchoe pinnata is called miracle leaf, live-forever, or curtain plant because if you pin the leaf to a curtain, it will still send up tiny little plantlets from every notch in the scalloped, succulent leaves. The flowers are nodding, pale pinkish-green inflated bells in great number on a branched stem. They come in late winter and can be nipped by the frost. Otherwise, and depending on how much sun they get, they can turn purple as they mature. The plant is supposedly hardy in Zone 10, but Monica's has lived in Tampa since she moved there in 1987, though the flowers have been lost during cold spells. A stem or two makes a bouquet. Flowers last for weeks and tend to dry in the vase.

***Leucanthemum* x *superbum* (shasta daisy)**. Shasta daisies grow well in Florida, for some gardeners, but may be short-lived, especially in the southern half of the state. Plants bloom in spring from a fall sowing. Thin clumps and reset plantlets in fall to keep plants strong. Try several different strains, for they vary in uprightness and strength of stems, as well as height and bloom size. Pick while centers are bright and tight. Strip lower leaves and condition in cool water for blooms that last about 5 days in the vase.

***Liriope muscari* (lily turf)**. Grasslike mats of glossy lily turf can be used as a groundcover that doubles as a generous source of lavender flowers on spikes. The plants with dark green, linear leaves are about a foot tall, somewhat taller while in bloom. Some forms have variegated leaves. The shorter but similar species, *Ophiopogon*, will not provide cut flowers. *Liriope* grows throughout Florida in shade, and is easy to find at local garden centers. For best appearance, separate and reset the clumps in rich soil when they become crowded, and fertilize every spring. If foliage freezes, trim off browned sections. The flowers will grow much more attractively in good conditions. Plants are propagated from divisions of roots and from the shiny, round black seeds. Cut flowers with long stems and condition in cool water for a few hours. They last several days before they shatter.

***Lobelia cardinalis* (cardinal flower)**. Spires of intensely red flowers attract hummingbirds. This plant grows over four feet tall in lightly shaded areas with plentiful moisture, particularly near streams, in northern and central Florida. However, this plant is of borderline hardiness in cental Florida, absolutely requiring a cool, moist, shady setting. Set out plants or sow seed in early spring. Seed may perform better if prechilled in the refrigerator for several weeks. Blooming plants may need staking. Dip stem ends in boiling water and use warm water for conditioning, we are told.

Perennials

Lupinus species (lupine, bluebonnet) Bluebonnet and other lupines, which have spires of pea-like flowers in a wide range of clear, bright colors, often do well in northern and central Florida. *Lupinus diffusus* and sundial lupine, *L. perennis,* grow wild in Florida. Avoid Russell types, which are easily grown from seed, but, to grow well, need cooler weather than can be found in Florida. *L. arboreus* and *L. argenteus* (silver lupine) are shrublike and better suited to our climate. Plant lupine seed in fall in full sun, in any well-drained soil; seedlings burn out when planted in summer.

Macleaya microcarpa **(plume poppy).** This huge perennial is easy to grow from seed, and self sows so readily that it could become a pest if it did not pull out so easily. It has fascinating, irregularly shaped silvery leaves, somewhat hand-shaped, but squarish. They are small at the top of the plant but much larger than a hand at the bottom. The plants can grow from 5 to 8 feet tall, and have plumes of pinkish beige flowers with a subtle fragrance.

Plume poppies are good background plants in the garden, and also handsome in a narrow garden against a wall. The leaves and plumes of flowers last well in arrangements. Rarely seen in Florida, they are still a good choice for part shade, and you only have to plant them once. Seeds are available from Thompson & Morgan and others, and plants from suppliers of perennials. Set out plants during cool weather and keep them moist until they are well established.

Ocimum kilimanscharium x *basilicum purpureum* **(African Blue Basil).** This is one of the easiest, hardiest, and by far the most reliable of the many basils or Ocimum species and hybrids sold by herb growers. The entire plant, foliage and flowers, have a purplish-blue cast from the purple stems and leaf veins. The spires of pink and purple flowers make it quite decorative enough to be grown

for its blooms alone. The sweet camphor scent is strong and pleasant. Some find it inferior to other basils and do not use it at all as a seasoning, but others of us do use it, especially when the other basils have died out. All basils are members of the mint family and have the square stems. Leaves and stems are dotted with tiny oil glands that release fragrance if touched or even moved by a breeze. African Blue gets three feet tall and a bit more in width. Since it is a hybrid cross between the dark opal and camphor basils, you will have to start it from a cutting rather than seed. Plant it in full sun for the best bloom. Cuttings root easily in water or soil, and they last well in a vase as well. None of the basils mind the summer heat at all, but they are sensitive to cold. Basils are also annuals and so have a limited life span, but we have known the African Blue to last as long as three years with mild winters or protection from frost.

Orchids. Details about this varied group of plants are beyond the scope of this book, but here are a few basic notes. *Cattleya* orchids are considered easy to grow in Florida. They are epiphytic, clinging to trees or supports with fibrous roots, but are not

parasitic. They can be purchased from orchid specialists, better garden centers, and giftshops of many of our botanical gardens. Hang their pots on tree branches, where they will receive partial shade so they will not overheat. The light should be bright enough to keep the straplike leaves a deep green. Water frequently, but be sure the pots have good drainage. Use warm water, for cool water on sun-warmed leaves will spot them. Feed them often, for the soilless medium they are planted in (usually fibrous bark chunks) is quickly depleted of nutrients. Use a 10-20-20 or similar blossom booster fertilizer formula from late summer until bloom, which usually occurs in winter. Bring plants inside to a sunny window before frost. As cut flowers, stems of orchids may last up to two weeks, but they will last longer on the plants. Orchids may be dried in silica gel, with or without a microwave (see page 111).

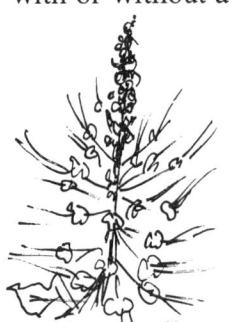

Orthosiphon stamenis **(cat whiskers)** is a plant we had not seen until a few years ago. Monica bought a white one and finds it multiplies easily from cuttings. It dies down in severe frost but usually comes back, and blooms with charming feathery spires in continuous flushes throughout the warm weather. Monica's have lasted for years but stopped blooming when they became woody. If this happens, take cuttings and start over. There is also a "blue" variety that is actually pale lavender. Each plant grows about three feet tall and spreads at least that wide. It thrives both in full sun and partial shade, but survives frost better in the latter. Take cuttings in northern and central Florida when a frost is expected, or to keep it over the winter. The blooms last well in arrangements. We know no source of seed, but plants are often seen at nurseries.

Pardancanda norrisii **(candy lily).** Originally from Park Seed, this is a cross between *Pardanthopsis* and blackberry lily. Star-shaped flowers resemble those of blackberry lily. Candy lilies are very easy to grow from seed and come in a wide range of colors and multicolors on three-foot plants. They tolerate heat and drought and are well suited to light shade under trees in Florida. They flower frequently, but blooms do not stay open long indoors, only a day or two.

Passiflora **species (passion flower).** This vine bears waterlily-like flowers three inches wide that can be floated in low bowls or used with their trailing stems in grand bouquets. But keep your eye on the flowers, for they can close unexpectedly and spoil your arrangement. We like the red form, *P. coccinea*, especially. The blue and purple forms are lovely, too. Plants can be propagated easily from seed or cuttings, but can become quite invasive, eventually. Vines can be trained to a support of any size; a ten-foot trellis is ideal. Plants are killed by frost but mature plants are likely to come back from the roots, especially if mulched. Provide full sun to partial shade, ample moisture, and good soil. The edible fruits of *P. edulis* flavor Hawaiian punch. They may need hand pollination in order to set fruit.

Perennials

***Pelargonium* species and hybrids (geranium).** The name *Pelargonium* is derived from the Greek, *pelargos*, a stork, for the seed pods are shaped like the beak of a stork. There are other plants that are *Geranium* by botanical name, but we have not seen them in Florida. Pelargoniums may be perennials or shrubs in central and south Florida, but are best grown as hardy annuals in the colder parts of the state. They will survive light frost but need protection from a freeze. All have fragrant foliage, some with variegation and color. Trailing, ivy-leaved types are excellent for hanging baskets. The upright garden geraniums bloom with familiar globes of white, red, pink, rose, peach violet, or magenta flowers, single or double, and can grow 2 to 3 feet tall. The scented ones are grown mostly for their foliage, with many variations of leaf shape, and a range of fragrance that includes lemon, rose, peppermint, apple, pine, apricot, coconut, and nutmeg.

Geraniums do best in Florida from early fall through June, but tend to suffer in the summer rains. Though they grow easily from seeds or cuttings, most people start with bedding plants to get the colors and scents they want. Take cuttings in late spring and put them into containers in some shade and they should survive the summer and be ready to start blooming again when the weather cools. Cut back if leggy and deadhead frequently. Remove yellow leaves. For bouquets, cut flowers when the buds start to open and some color shows. Scented types can be used for their foliage. Remove lower leaves (dry and save them for potpourri) and split the base of the stem. Condition in warm water. Buds will continue to open for 5 to 7 days.

***Pentas lanceolata*.** These shrublike flowering plants are among the easiest and most colorful for central and south Florida. They grow quickly from cuttings to plants four feet high and wide. The abundant, starlike blooms are in terminal clusters in red, white, and shades of lavender and pink. They are not fussy about soil and will survive with only occasional watering once established. Monica once planted a rooted cutting that bloomed constantly for three years, until a hard freeze killed it. Now she takes new cuttings and brings them inside before a freeze is predicted, just in case, and they root with ease in about two weeks. For bouquets, cut pieces with stems, leaves, and one or more bunches of flowers. Remove the lower leaves and condition in cool water. In arrangements, it will be about a week before the first little stars begin to drop. Parks offers pentas from seed; most nurseries have plants.

***Physostegia virginiana* (false dragonhead, obedient plant).** Spikes of foxglove-like pink, white, or lilac flowers can grow three feet tall in north or central Florida. There is a type with green and white variegated leaves. They bloom from late summer through autumn. Frost kills the tops, but plants come back vigorously in spring. Plant in full sun or light shade. They prefer rich, moist soil but are adaptable. Start from seed or division. These excellent cut flowers will hold any curve, thus the name obedient. Harvest before the first flowers on the spike begin to fade.

Rudbeckia **species (black-eyed susan).** See listing in biennials, page 57.

Rumohra adiantiformis **(leatherleaf fern).** Central Florida gardeners with partial shade under trees can easily grow this useful bouquet filler as a groundcover. It prefers rich, loamy soil and average moisture. Mulch is helpful. Harvest mature fronds, which last over a week in bouquets. Condition by immersing whole fronds in cool water for several hours. This is the glossy, green fern used by florists.

Salvia **species (salvia, sage).** There are hundreds of attractive salvias, and most of them thrive in Florida with minimal care and a maximum of color. Almost all attract butterflies. Some are neater in the garden than others and some are neater in the vase. Some, like sky blue bog salvia (*S. uliginosa*) bloom only in the morning. Some, like yellow-flowered *S. forsythia*, need frequent pruning but are worth the trouble. All root easily from cuttings and many send up additional seedlings once established. A few are short lived, but many last longer than two years, including the following two species, which are both excellent for cutting. Pineapple sage (*S. elegans*) is several feet tall and has deep red, edible flowers and fragrant, edible foliage that is good in tea or fruit drinks. Mexican sage, *S. leucantha*, grows like a shrub, but it is not woody. It loves full sun and is easy to grow, and easily reaches eight feet in all directions. Its many white stems bear long, narrow, gray-green leaves and showy eight-inch spikes of purple flowers. These last well, fresh, and will dry in the vase or even on the plant, keeping the purple color remarkably well in dried arrangements.

Salvia farinacea **(blue sage, mealycup sage)** is a choice salvia which can be perennial or nearly so in Florida. It produces multitudes of slim blue or white spires on wiry stems. It's a good cut flower to be used fresh, or dried by hanging upside down. This plant tolerates light shade. 'Victoria' is a prizewinning cultivar, a deep rich blue which combines well with other flowers, especially in rose and red shades.

The many other species and cultivars come in lovely shades of blue, red, pink, silver, white, and yellow. *Salvia riparia* and *Salvia azurea* are natives with good cutting qualities. Check with local nurseries and look for special sales to expand and refine your own collection. Cut the flowers for bouquets when half to three quarters of the florets on the spire are open. Split the stem bases and condition in deep warm water overnight. Many will last five to ten days in the vase. Cut spires from several types at once to see which ones last best. Those with papery texture can be hung upside down to dry or be allowed to dry in the vase.

Salvia leucantha **(Mexican sage).** This excellent small shrublike perennial forms a clump of few to many white stems which bear long, narrow, textured gray-green leaves. The plants can grow as tall as four feet. Soon each stem starts opening many showy long spires of white flowers surrounded by fuzzy lavender

Perennials

calyces. These last indefinitely and can be hung to dry. Tall stems tend to fall over, but before you finish cutting them a new bunch is coming up from the crown. New plants may be started from softwood cuttings. Mexican sage does best in full sun and enriched soil, and looks good in combination with pentas. It is carefree, but needs water occasionally.

Solidago species (goldenrod, blue mountain tea). There are many species and hybrids of this native plant that vary in height from 2 to 5 feet. You will seed golden masses of them growing wild by the roadside or in open fields. They are easy to grow in full sun from seeds, cuttings, or divisions. Once established, they need little water. They bloom with spires of mustard yellow blooms in summer and fall of the first year. Thereafter they both return from the roots and spread from seeds. Contrary to rumor, goldenrod does not cause hay fever. Other plants that bloom at the same time are the real culprits. Cut them at any stage for fresh bouquets, even with just a few flowers open. Condition in cold water for 4 hours or overnight. Flowers will last for 1 to 3 weeks in the vase and then dry to a rich, mellow golden shade and last for years. The goldenrods can be a bit invasive, but we have never found that to be a problem.

Stokesia laevis (stokes aster). This Florida native is one of the best perennials for the whole state. Branched, bushy plants grow two feet tall and produce an abundance of 2- to 4-inch wide, shaggy, blue, white, or lavender flowers flowers from May to September. 'Blue Danube' is popular for deep blue flowers. Plant *Stokesia* in full sun to light shade. It likes fertile soil but will live with less. Cut flowers last six to ten days. Split stems. Recondition in warm water if wilting occurs. Add sugar to water, one teaspoon per quart.

Strelitzia species (bird-of-paradise). Long-lasting, spectacular, crane-shaped flowers are usually multicolored in parrot colors: orange, blue, and white. There is also an all-white flower form, and both are truly fantastic in arrangements. *Strelitizia* is an evergreen banana relative that is killed by heavy frost, so this exotic plant is ideal for southern Florida plantings, and elsewhere if in protected spots or containers. It blooms best in full sun, but leaves stay nicer in light shade. Give it good soil, good drainage, and average water. Cultivars range from 1 to 7 feet tall at maturity. Flowers last 1 to 2 weeks when cut. Condition them in water brought to pH 4 by adding three heaping teaspoons of sugar and up to two tablespoons of vinegar per quart of water, depending on the acidity of your water. The blooms dry well even after use in fresh bouquets.

A Cutting Garden for Florida

***Talinum paniculatum* (jewels of opar).** The blooms of this plant shoot up about two feet, providing large, airy decorative panicles which are masses of buds, little pink or lavender flowers, and small, shiny, round, red seedpods, all about a quarter of an inch wide. Stems are slender and succulent, rising above dark green leaves about three inches long. Similar forms have variegated or chartreuse leaves. The leafy part of the plant is only a foot tall, so it can be placed in front of other plants, the better to see the dainty plumes of bloom, which appear the first year.

Monica started hers from seeds Betty sent and has had them for years. They appear here and there in the garden and in almost any watered container, but are not rampant enough to be a nuisance. They are too dainty to be more than a filler in bouquets, but they are interesting and maintenance free. Put them in sun or partial shade and don't worry about frost, for they come back from what soon becomes a tuberous root. They also grow easily from cuttings. The stems last well in bouquets, and actually dry in the vase. In dried arrangements the beadlike seedpods keep their red color for weeks, eventually turning brown but holding their form. Seeds are available from J. L. Hudson and other sources.

***Tradescantia ohioensis* (spiderwort, trinity flower).** The lovely blue flowers of this plant color Florida roadsides in spring and attest to their ease of growth. Catalogs offer cultivars in shades of white, pink, lavender, and blue. Some are bicolored and some are semidouble instead of having only three petals per flower. Sizes vary, too. This easy plant likes moist but well-drained soil and either sun or partial shade. Use foliage or flowers in bouquets. Each flower lasts a day but the clusters open a few flowers at a time and look fresh for several days. However, they are open only in the morning. Slugs can be a problem.

Chapter Nine
CUT FLOWER CHOICES: FLOWERS FROM BULBS

Bulbs are easy to grow. In a bulb, such as that of a paperwhite narcissus, the flower is stored in there, in miniature, ready to unfold quickly when conditions are right. The food supply stored inside bulbs makes them very reliable for Florida gardeners. They do not need as much nurturing as do small seeds and plants. Some bulbs, like amaryllis, are so well primed to grow that when they begin, change is visible from day to day.

In gardening, the word bulb is sometimes used more loosely than it is in botany, and serves as shorthand to include storable tubers, rhizomes, and corms, like those of canna lilies, anemones, and gladiolus. These are also easy to grow, but are not as quick to grow as true bulbs, which technically speaking are underground leaf buds modified for storage of energy.

The handling which bulbs and bulblike structures receive before you purchase them is crucial to their performance. Check before you buy. They should be firm, not flaky or soft. If they have been overheated in storage, they may have been damaged. Buy bulbs from the best growers. Avoid any which have grown long sprouts in storage, for they may not grow straight in your garden. Flowering stems from bulbs should not be pinched back. If a friend offers bulbs straight from the garden, say yes. Just dig them up even if they are in leaf, and treat them like any other transplants, planting them right away.

Though bulbs are well prepared for bloom the first year, they need rich soil and careful watering to build up their reserves for the next, so prepare the soil well. Follow the grower's planting depth instructions, but in Florida sand, it is advisable to plant about 20 percent deeper, at least in the northern part of the state. In southern Florida, bulbs resist rot better if planted shallowly. After blooms fade, deadhead the plants. Allow the green foliage to turn yellow or tan before you remove it. If soil is well drained, bulbs can stay in the ground; otherwise dig, dry, and store in labelled paper bags filled with dry sand and set in a cool, dry place until time to replant. A closet or bureau drawer is fine, but a garage may be too hot.

In general, bulbs and bulblike structures do best in full sun or very light shade. Standard commercial potting soil mixes, compost, clean kitty litter, and slow-release fertilizers are good additions to sandy beds of bulbs. Bulbs also do well in potting soil in terra cotta pots on patios, especially screened patios in full sun. The only drawback is that, blooming in pots, they look too pretty to cut.

In this chapter you'll find many good choices for cutting gardens, and the chart on page 80 has recommended planting times for Florida's climate zones.

Achimenes **species.** Graceful plants produce an abundance of waxy, long-keeping flowers 1 to 2 inches wide. Their pinks, white, blues, and purples are elegant when mixed in a pot or hanging basket. They are also good for shady beds in average soil, but are not salt or nematode tolerant. After a long season of bloom through summer, dig and store the roots (rhizomes) or simply dry off pots for a rest period in fall and winter. For more plants, gently separate crowded clumps of rhizomes and replant.

A Cutting Garden for Florida

 # BULB PLANTING GUIDE FOR FLORIDA

NAME OF PLANT	PL. DEPTH	SPACING	** BEST PLANTING TIMES		
			N. FLORIDA	C. FLORIDA	S. FLORIDA
Achimenes	.5 in	2 in	Mar-Apr	Mar	Jan
Agapanthus	Cover	18 in	Mar	Feb	Jan
Allium	Varies	Varies	Nov-Jan	Nov	Nov
Alstroemeria	6 in	24 in	Mar	Feb	Jan
Anemone	2 in	12 in	Nov-Dec	Nov	Nov
Caladium	2 in	24-36 in	Mar-May	Feb-Apr	Dec
Canna	3 in	Varies	Mar-Apr	Feb-Apr	Nov-Apr
Crinum	Varies	Varies	Nov-Dec	Feb-Apr	Nov-Mar
Crocosmia	5 in	12 in	Mar-Apr	Feb-Apr	Nov-Mar
Dahlia	Cover	12 in	Mar	Feb-Mar	Nov-Jan
Eucharis	Cover	12-24 in	Apr	Mar	Jan-Feb
Freesia	4 in	4 in	Oct	Nov	Nov
Gladiolus	5 in	6 in	Mar-May	Feb-Jun	all
Glad (mini)	4 in	4 in	Mar-Jun	Feb-Jun	all
Gloriosa lily	Cover	18 in	Mar-Apr	Feb-Mar	Dec-Feb
Hippeastrum	Cover	12 in	Feb-Mar	Nov-Feb	Nov-Feb
Hyacinthus	4 in	6 in	Nov	Nov	Nov
Iris (Dutch)	4 in	6 in	Nov	Nov	Nov
Ixia	3 in	3 in	Mar	Feb	Jan
Leucojum	3 in	6 in	Nov	Nov	do not plant
Lilium	Varies	Varies	Nov	Nov	Nov
Lycoris	3 in	4-6 in	Nov-Mar	Nov-Jan	Nov
Narcissus	6 in	6 in	Nov	Nov	Nov
Oxalis	2 in	4 in	Feb-Mar	Feb	Nov-Feb
Polianthes	2 in	8 in	May	Feb	Nov
Sparaxis	3 in	4 in	Nov	Nov	Nov
Tritonia	3 in	3 in	Mar-May	Feb-Jun	all
Zantedeschia	Cover	12-24 in	Feb-Mar	Nov-Feb	Nov
Zephyranthes	1 in	3 in	Nov	Nov	Nov

* PL. DEPTH: Cover with this much soil. ** See Chapter Three for hardiness zones. Also check plant entries for more information.

Bulbs

Agapanthus africanus **(lily-of-the-Nile, African lily).**
Agapanthus grows from fleshy, bulblike root divisions and has blue or white globes of starlike flowers on 2 foot stems. Plants are perennial where winters are nearly frost-free and should stay in the gound where they are hardy. Available cultivars vary in their cold hardiness, some being hardy as far north as Washington, D.C. The straplike leaves are evergreen if they do not freeze. In northern Florida, protect plants from light frosts by mulching roots, or grow in tubs. In all regions, plant in autumn or winter for bloom during late spring, summer, or early fall. Give them average to rich soil and full sun to partial shade. Divide when crowded. Cut when a fourth of the flowers on a stem are open, and condition in deep, cool water. They should last 5 to 7 days.

Allium **species (ornamental onions).** Some alliums will grow in Florida, but the many species vary in their climate preferences. Note recommended zones in catalogs. Plant in full sun or light shade in average soil. Heights, colors, fragrance, and vase life vary with kinds, but some last up to 3 weeks in bouquets, and seedheads can be dried for arrangements. Pick when buds begin to open. Change water often. Check for oniony odor before using them for a party.

Alstroemeria **species (Lily of Peru).** These trumpet-shaped, summer-blooming flowers are beautifully spotted and marked. With care, they can be grown in northern or central Florida in shaded, northern exposures and good soil. Plant 10 to 12 inches deep, 12 inches apart, and fertilize with manure before flowers form. Some plants will live outdoors for years, but some may need to have their fleshy roots lifted and stored in dry sand for a dormant period after blooms fade and foliage ages, for in damp conditions they might rot. In the right conditions they become very deeply rooted and somewhat invasive. They can be grown in deep tubs, which can be placed in the garage for a winter rest period. Pick when clusters start to bloom and condition in deep water.

Anemone **species (windflower, anemone).** The florist's (poppy-flowered) anemone is best for cutting. Hardiness varies with species. Anemones from tubers prefer slightly dry soil. Try to plant the tubers with the central stem scar upward after soaking them overnight in water. Plant in full sun to light shade in a humusy soil. Dig up and store indoors in paper bags of dry sand, for if damp in summer they will not come back. Anemones can be grown from seed, but this is a challenge. Cut stems for bouquets before flowers fully open and recut stems under water.

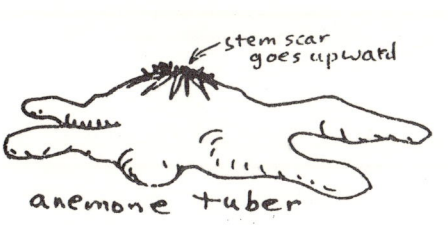

***Caladium* x *hortulanum* (caladium).** With their lovely large spade-shaped leaves, caladiums are easily grown from tubers. The color range includes white, pink, green, and red, with distinctive edgings and veinings in multiple shades. Green and white veined types look cool in the shade. They can be left in the ground except in the north, where they should be dug and stored indoors over winter to protect them from frost. They die down in late fall in central and southern Florida and come back and multiply in the spring. Give them full sun or high, light shade and rich, organic soil, away from salt air. After cutting, split stems and condition overnight in deep, cool water or submerge them completely for half an hour. Leaves last five to ten days in bouquets. Monica sprays undersides of leaves with Wiltpruf (a clear plastic) to prevent their curling.

***Canna* x *generalis* (canna lily).** Some cannas are native, and all grow easily throughout Florida and can be left in the ground. They need plenty of light, water, and fertilizer and will bloom from April to August. They grow well in marshy ground and anywhere near water, but also in average garden conditions. Flower colors include yellow, pink, peach, deep red, and orange. The tropical looking large leaves may be purplish bronze, green, or variegated green and yellow. Cut the flowering stems back after they bloom unless you want some seedpods for arrangements. Divide clumps each year and fertilize throughout the growing season, several times a year. Treat for leaf roller caterpillars if necessary. Without proper care, these can get rather weedy looking. The shorter forms stay neater. For arranging, cut the flowers when 2 or more florets in the bunch are open, split stems, and submerge all parts until crisp, then continue to condition in cold water overnight. Florets last 2 to 3 days and buds continue to open, extending the blooming period. Foliage lasts 10 days. Flowers grow better in sun, but foliage looks fresher in shade.

***Crinum* species (milk-and-wine lilies).** These natives are among the best bulbous flowers for the entire state. Most bloom in spring and summer with majestic clusters of fragrant white, pink, rose, or striped flowers, with as many as 25 large flowers per umbel on some types. With great variation, they grow 2 to over 4 feet tall and wide and can be left in the ground until crowded. Winter is the best time to divide them. Give them plenty of room, partial shade, rich soil, and plenty of water. Mulch them deeply in the north, where they may die back to the roots each winter. Bulbs of larger crinums are quite heavy and expensive. If flowers are left on, flowerheads sometimes form small onionlike bulbils. These are easily collected, planted, and grown on to full size, although it takes several years for plants to mature. Betty grew some from an untended ornamental planting near a bank's parking lot! Cut flowers when the first row of florets open and a single stem will continue to have flowers opening for up to 2 weeks. Just cut or pull off the spent ones as they fade.

Crocosmia **species (montbretia).** 'Lucifer' is a wonde[rful] cultivar, devilishly red. Others range from yellow thro[ugh] red-orange. Swordlike foliage is 3 feet tall, and plants ... robust. Tubular flowers are borne profusely in late spring on gracefully branched spikes. Plant corms in winter or, in northern Florida, early spring, in rich, well-drained soil in full sun to partial shade, but blooms are best in sun. Mulch where frosts occur. Plant corms a foot apart and let them spread into big clumps. Cut flowers before any on the stalk have faded and condition in deep water.

Dahlia **hybrids.** See under annuals (page 40). Buy tubers in late winter. Set them out immediately in central and southern Florida, but start them indoors in northern Florida, for earliest flowers. Dig and store the tubers in sand, after they finish blooming.

Eucharis grandiflora **(Amazon lily).** This is a popular pot plant that can also be grown in the garden in the central to southern part of Florida. Both the dark green foliage and the clusters of waxy white fragrant flowers are good for bouquets. Like stephanotis, this is often used in wedding bouquets, but Amazon lily has long stems. Plants like rich soil, moderate to deep shade, and crowded conditions. Monica's stay in the ground and always return after a frost. Farther north than Tampa, you may want to bring them indoors before frost.

Freesia **hybrids.** Easily grown outdoors from corms, fragrant freesias are excellent cut flowers and will naturalize very well. Delicate, trumpet-shaped, fragrant flowers open along slim arched stems in single or blended tones of white, yellow, orange, purple, pink, and cream. In central Florida, they bloom in February. Plant bulbs in well-drained soil in fall for late winter for spring bloom in full sun or partial shade. If you can only get them in winter or spring, plant them anyway. If you receive them as potted plants, set them in the garden after they bloom. First-year results may be poor but survivors will improve and multiply in subsequent years. Mark the spots where they are planted, for foliage disappears during the hot weather. Bulbs will flower once each year if they are not damaged. Divide them after foliage yellows if they become too crowded. Wrap flowers loosely in plastic to preserve the fragrance during the conditioning period, several hours or overnight in deep water. Highly recommended.

freesia

Gladiolus **hybrids.** Ranging from under 2 to over 4 feet tall, showy glads may be red, lilac, salmon, yellow, green, violet, rose, or white with varied marking and ruffling. Look for disease resistant types. Gladioli are easy to grow in sun with average soil and water. For a succession of bloom, plant a few bulbs each week for bloom three months later. Plant in fall or winter in southern Florida, after frost in late winter in northern or central Florida. Although year-round bloom is possible in southern Florida, summer and fall blooms may have poor quality.

A Cutting Garden for Florida

New corms can be planted every year, or corms can be left in the ground. The old corm dries up and new ones form in its place. Usually that is two main ones and some smaller ones. However, if soil is not well drained or summer weather is too wet, you'll have to lift the corms after the foliage yellows, and dry and store them until planting time. In well-drained soil, they will be reliably perennial. Any over an inch in diameter should bloom; smaller bulblets can be grown on until they are large enough.

G. acidanthera is a graceful glad, 2 to 3 feet tall, that loves hot weather. Its white, star-shaped blossoms have purplish black centers and an elusive but delightful fragrance. Easily grown from corms in average soil, the plants bloom briefly several months later and each following year. The spearlike foliage is neat and attractive.

Gloriosa rothschildiana **(Glory lily).** The name is no exaggeration of these showy, recurving, lily-like flowers in bright red and yellow. With tendrils, plants climb as high as six feet. Plant 4 to 5 inches deep at any time, usually spring, in full sun to light shade in well-drained soil, and give plenty of moisture during growth. Tubers are usually left in the ground. If you feed heavily when new growth starts, a vigorous vine can bear many flowers, up to 20 or 30. Flowers last 4 to 5 days. Cut when petals have turned back. Split stems and condition overnight in cold water.

Hippeastrum **species (amaryllis).** Clustered, lilylike flowers of amaryllis are spectacular in spring. Up to 5 blooms, from 5 to 10 inches across, open on each stem. There are miniature and full sized types, with stems from about 18 to 26 inches tall. The miniatures tend to have smaller flowers and more of them. Colors of amaryllis range through red, burgundy, orange, peach, pink, and white, with some bicolors and picotee edges. Monica used gorgeous white ones for her daughter's wedding flowers.

They are easy to grow outdoors in Florida, and multiply rapidly with proper conditions: well-drained, well-enriched, slightly acid soil in partial shade. A high phosphorus or bloom booster fertilizer will give the biggest and most numerous flowers.

The bulbs have been known to last for 75 years, passing down from generation to generation. Plants are also easy to start from seed. Or get your northern relatives to donate their amaryllis bulbs to you after the holidays.

amaryllis

Plant the bulbs half in and half out of the ground, like paperwhite narcissus. Plant a little deeper in northern Florida, more shallowly in southern Florida, using just enough soil to hold the plants up. When they get overcrowded, dig up the clump and separate the bulbs during their nearly dormant period in late summer or early fall. If given room to grow, the smaller offsets will eventually reach full size. Amaryllis bulbs can be left in the ground or else lifted in the fall and replanted at intervals from November to February for a succession of bloom. Fertilize when new growth begins and again after blooms end.

Cut flowers in the opening bud stage or after one or two of the flowers in a cluster have opened. Split stem ends. If conditioned in deep, cold water for several hours, amaryllis will last a day or two without water, or 4 to 7 days in a vase. Leave the foliage on the plant to make next year's blooms.

***Hyacinthus orientalis* var. *albulus* (Roman hyacinth).** The most popular hyacinths, tulips, and daffodils grown in northern states can only be grown in the northern and western parts of Florida, or farther south with 50 to 60 days of cold treatment prior to planting, for bloom one year only. However, these smaller, more graceful and slender hyacinths, which have several stems of flowers per bulb, grow well here without special treatment. They can be planted from October to December for bloom from February to April. With care, they may grow for several years outdoors, or they can be dug after the foliage dies down and stored in a dry place, then replanted. Plant 6 inches deep in full sun or under deciduous trees. Flowers last 3 to 6 days. Cut when nearly or fully open, and split stems. If they wilt, dip the stems in boiling water for a minute, then condition in deep, cold water overnight. Wrap like freesias during conditioning.

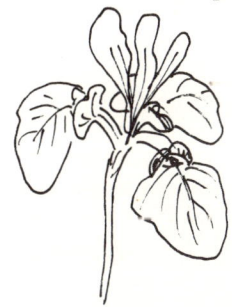

Iris, Dutch hybrids. Bearded iris can only be grown with much success in the hills of northwestern Florida. In other regions, Dutch iris can be planted in October through November for bloom in January and February. Plant 4 inches deep, 3 inches apart in sun in good soil. When foliage yellows in late spring, you can lift and store the bulbs, but do not be disappointed if they do not rebloom as well, or at all. They are not expensive to buy yearly.

***Ixia* species.** Stalks of bell-shaped white, greenish white, red, pink, or orange flowers with dark centers rise up to a foot above grasslike leaves. Plants like full sun but not wind, and are fairly drought tolerant. Average soil will do, and mulch is appreciated. Plant in fall for spring bloom. Florets last 2 to 3 days and keep opening up the stem for two weeks. Bring them in when the first two or three florets have opened.

***Leucojum aestivum* (giant snowflake).** For a taste of northern spring without much trouble, plant these. They have nodding bell-shaped white flowers, 4 to 8 on a half-inch stalk, with a green spot on the tip of each petal. Plant in fall for early spring bloom in full sun. Foliage will die down by June, but you can leave the bulbs in place for several years, until they are crowded. Divide in June if necessary. These grow in northern and central Florida, not in southern Florida.

A Cutting Garden for Florida

Lilium species and hybrids (lily).
Several of the true lilies, especially the Easter and Madonna lilies, do well in Florida, though you may need to dig and store them over the damp summer in most parts of the state. Madonna lilies tolerate very little frost. It is also wise to plant lilies in different spots each year to prevent soil-borne diseases. Give them full sun and fertile soil. Plant in fall for spring bloom. Lilies sold in market packs in late winter are good if fresh, but spoil quickly on the shelf. Formosan lily and several others bloom in the summer and tend to do best their first year. In sandy soil, plant them 25 percent deeper than directions say, to help keep bulbs cool  underground. Remove pollen-bearing anthers from lilies as they open to keep these from staining the petals or your fingers or furniture (use tweezers). Split stems slightly and stand in deep water for several hours to condition.

Lycoris species (Hurricane and spider lily). Yellow, rose, or red spider lilies thrive throughout Florida and can be left in the ground for several years in the northern half of the state. Divide after flowering, if they have become too crowded. In the southern half of Florida they may only last a few years. In either area, mark the spot, for they go dormant over the summer and you don't want to accidentally slice into the bulbs. Plant them in late spring in half shade for fall bloom, and give ample water during flowering. Add a bit of lime. They dislike acid soil.

Narcissus tazetta (paperwhite). It is easy to naturalize these lovely flowers in lightly wooded areas with sandy soil. Except in the northwesternmost part of the state, these very fragrant flowers are the only narcissus that do well here without special cold treatment (see also hyacinths). Plant in September for bloom from December to February, depending on variety, 2 to 4 inches apart, 6 to 8 inches deep. Give full sun or light shade and cut the flowers when half of the cluster is open. Feed after bloom and allow foliage to ripen, as it feeds next year's flowers. When leaves yellow about two months later you can remove them. Leave the bulbs in place to multiply if your soil is well drained, otherwise lift and store them in a dry place.

Oxalis species. These dainty flowers with clumps of cloverlike foliage are effortless to grow and seem to bloom better here than in northern states. Some varieties are definitely weeds and are best grown only in pots lest they spread. But others are well behaved and quite useful. Buy large-flowered types or those with purple leaves, and plant in early spring in full or partial shade in average soil. Water as needed. Leave tuberous roots in place until crowded. The main tuber becomes enormous. Separate offsets frequently.

Bulbs

Polianthes tuberosa **(tuberose).** These highly fragrant, waxy white flowers can be planted 8 inches apart in full sun in very fertile soil from January to March for bloom from late April until July. Each plant makes a succession of bloom stalks. Plant two inches deep and one foot or more apart. Where soil drainage is very good, you might leave them in the ground, but it is safer to lift them after foliage dies and store dry. Cut flowers last 7 to 12 days. Cut when half to three-fourths open, split stems, and condition overnight in cold water. Dwarf varieties have strong stems. Singles are more fragrant than doubles, but both are powerfully scented.

Ranunculus asiaticus. In all parts of Florida, you can grow these lovely but challenging florist flowers at home from tiny, clawlike tubers, which are sold dried. Soak them overnight in a cup of water. Then plant them 2 inches deep and 6 inches apart, with claws down. Choose good soil in a lightly shaded spot in fall for late winter and early spring bloom. It is easier to buy them in pots, in bloom. A trace of frost is no problem, but protect them from a hard freeze. They will not withstand hot weather either. In fact they love an air-conditioned, sunny room. Outdoors, they will not come back a second year if left in place, but are inexpensive to replace annually. You may be able to dig, dry, and store tubers indoors from late spring until planting time in fall. For cut flowers that last up to a week, sear stem ends briefly and condition in deep water.

Sparaxis tricolor **(Harlequin flower).** Spikes of charming, multicolored, star-shaped flowers in strong shades of red, purple, black, salmon, and yellow lend a slightly humorous touch to bouquets. They grow from corms and can usually be bought and planted in late winter, but it is even better to plant them in fall, in frost-free zones. Treat like gladiolus, providing full sun and evenly moist soil. Foliage is similar.

Sprekelia formosissima **(Jacobean lily).** This amaryllis relative has gorgeous red flowers in June, followed by straplike foliage. Water moderately and feed during the growth period.

Tritonia **species (montbretia).** These look like miniature red or orange gladioli with dainty, silky flowers on slender stems. Slender leaves form fan-shaped clumps a foot and a half tall. Plants prefer well-drained, rich soil in full sun. The corms should be treated like gladiolus, but *T. miniata*, the cinnabar-red variety, is sometimes left in the ground and will form large clumps. Divide when crowded.

A Cutting Garden for Florida

***Watsonia* species.** Here is another group of flowers resembling gladiolus in form and range of size, and needing the same culture. Flowers, often rose or red, are much narrower and more widely spaced on the stems than the glads. Plant corms a foot apart and leave them undisturbed to form large clumps, which usually bloom in early summer.

***Zantedeschia* species (calla lily).** Callas do well in Florida, but are reliably perennial only in the south, although you may be able to get them through the year in central Florida if you mulch them well or the weather is mild. They come in white (*Z. aethiopia* has a large white flower), yellow, red, or pink. Plant the tubers annually or grow in pots to avoid cold injury farther north. We recommend the Godfrey variety. Give full sun or light shade and rich soil. Keep the soil constantly moist during their growth, but not too wet, and much drier during their dormant period. Protect them from frost, but plant in fall or late winter for bloom from March to June. Then foliage yellows and dies. Plants that can be left in place in the garden or in pots will bloom more freely than ones that must be lifted and dried, but if your conditions are too moist and humid you may need to store the dormant tubers in dry sand. Submerge foliage for 1 to 2 hours to condition; stand flowers in deep water. Calla lilies are elegant in arrangements, but beware of juices that stain.

***Zephyranthes* species (zephyr, fairy, or rain lily).** This dainty pink or white lily, 1 to 4 inches wide on a stem up to a foot tall, is charming and easy. It is closely related to amaryllis. The grassy leaves are trim and straplike. There are many kinds, and they do well in all parts of Florida. *Z. atamasco, Z. treatiae,* and *Z. simpsoni* are native to Florida. *Z. grandiflora* has large pink flowers that are delightful in gardens or bouquets. For best growth, provide full sun or light shade, good drainage, and good soil. Plant large numbers in late fall for spring bloom. Fairy lilies can be left in the ground for years, until very crowded, then divide and replant them immediately. Feed in spring. Plant any extra bulbs in mixed planters for living bouquets.

Chapter Ten
CUT FLOWER CHOICES: TREES AND SHRUBS

Florida gardeners are especially lucky in their wide choice of beautiful flowering shrubs. Many are fragrant. Shrubs and trees form the backbone of the landscape, so a flower arranger should choose those that contribute the best foliage and flowers for bouquets. Using this method, limited growing space is more productive.

There are many flowering shrubs and trees that will thrive in all sections of the state, others that do best in the north or the south. Especially in southern Florida, tropical trees and shrubs grow to great size: hibiscus reaches tree size, for instance. In central and northern Florida, the same tropical shrubs may grow well, but their size is limited by the heavy frost damage which occurs most years. Sometimes it stays frost free for several years straight, and people get exaggerated ideas of what is hardy. Then along comes a frost and it is time to rethink and cut back.

Some types are grown for just one year's blooms, or else they can be grown in large pots and brought indoors for the few spells of freezing weather each year. Some, like allamanda, are easily grown from overwintered cuttings. Many tropical shrubs may be left in the ground even in central and northern parts of the state, for even if all the top growth freezes, they make a comeback from the roots. A broad group of cold-hardy types can safely remain in the ground all year.

If you are growing frost-sensitive shrubs in a borderline zone, protect the roots from frozen soil by mulching heavily. Use mulch year-round to keep soil in the root zone cool and moist, avoiding radical swings from hot to cold. Organic mulches such as bark chips and shredded leaves break down quickly, enriching the soil. Replenish them from above, leaving earlier applications of mulch in place for soil improvement.

Woody plants tend to be less work and more naturally suited to the predominating acidic soil types of Florida than annual or perennial flowers. Trees and shrubs are quite similar, except that shrubs usually have multiple trunks. Throughout the state, azalea, magnolia, beauty berry, datura, viburnum, buddleia (butterfly bush), crape myrtle, yucca, sweet bay, gardenia, jasmine, southern roses, hydrangea, and hibiscus are easy to grow and highly recommended. Choose flowering shrubs while they are in bloom because blossom colors and shapes vary widely. Keep your needs for indoor vases in mind as you decide, and do as much shopping around as you can.

In your garden plan, be sure to allow plenty of room for shrubs to grow. Do not plant too close to the foundation of the house. It is hard to imagine how large a small cutting or potted shrub will eventually become, so look at mature specimens in botanical gardens before you make your design. If your planting of new shrubs looks too sparse at first (and it will), fill in the spaces temporarily with annual and perennial flowers. Large annuals such as cleome, or large perennials such as *Pentas lanceolata* look very shrublike and are good placeholders until the shrubs mature. If your shrubs have been too closely planted, move them before they become so large that you need professional help for this.

A Cutting Garden for Florida

Research has found that, years after planting, roots of some woody shrubs were so contented in super-enriched planting holes that they never ventured beyond. So now the recommendation is to dig planting holes only a bit larger than the root area and enrich the soil in the hole only moderately, to encourage roots to branch out. Make sure the sides of the hole are rough and ready for penetration, not glazed and solid to resist it. Then mulch as needed. Add nutrients around the dripline of the tree or shrub. However, the guidelines above do not completely take care of those of us who happen to garden in extremely infertile sand. If you do, you should still make a large hole and add lots of compost or peatmoss, plus fertilizer, or the shrubs may become malnourished.

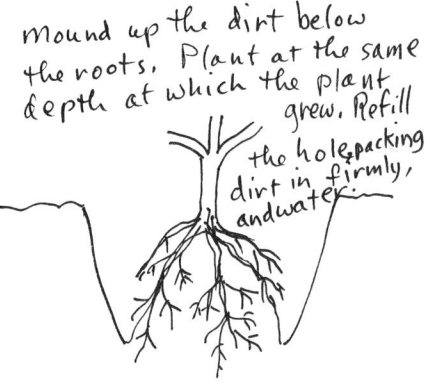

Mound up the dirt below the roots. Plant at the same depth at which the plant grew. Refill the hole, packing dirt in firmly, and water.

Plant bare-root stock at the same level as it was grown. If roots of potted plants have encircled the pot, break them apart so they are ready to head outward. Pack soil firmly against the roots as you fill the hole. Leave a doughnut-like depression two to three feet away from the trunk. A dishlike depression can lead to rotting of the trunk, especially in Florida's rainy season. Mulch the area under the dripline of the leaves well, but keep the mulch a few inches away from the trunk. Keep the plant watered until it becomes established, which may take two years.

MAINTENANCE AND PRUNING

Shrubs will need a little maintenance: feeding, pruning, and occasional renewal of the mulch. Fertilize under the drip line of the shrub's leaves several times each year, during the start and middle of the growing season, but not just before frost is expected. You can feed shrubs by mixing compost and composted manure with the mulch and applying it several times a year, or use any of the packaged shrub or all-purpose fertilizers. Spikes or beads of timed-release fertilizers permit long-term feeding with little effort.

Pruning is important. Check a pruning guide for more exact methods, but you will do well if you prune out deadwood and diseased stems, crossed branches, and interior growth that is too crowded. Make cuts with sharp clippers just above an outward-facing bud or branch. You can limit the outer size of the shrub with judicious pruning, and also let light and fresh air into the interior. Spring flowering shrubs that bloom on last-year's growth are pruned while they are in bloom (use the healthy pieces pruned off for bouquets) or just after blooming. Summer or fall-flowering shrubs that bloom on new growth are pruned in late

winter or early spring, well before they bloom. If frost damage occurs, leave it be unless it is too ugly or depressing to bear. In most cases it is best to wait at least until all danger of frost has passed before cleaning up the mess. Often, branches that appear dead may leaf out with new growth, months later.

UNUSUAL CHOICES

Edible Plants. Consider using edible plants for some of your cut flower material. Be sure to select low-chill varieties adapted to the Florida climate. Blooming branches of apple, blueberry (sensitive to salt!), peach, pear, nectarine, natal plum, plum, and feijoa are lovely in arrangements. You can stand them in warm water indoors to force them into early bloom, extending their season. Flowering branches of orange blossoms or fruited branches studded with orange kumquats or calamondin oranges will bring color and fragrance to bouquets or wreaths. The colorful seedpods of roselle make striking floral accents, either with the foliage left or stripped away.

Elderberry, a huge shrub whose blossoms recur throughout the year, can be used like Queen Anne's lace. Sprays of its dark, glossy berries are nice in bouquets, too. There is a form with attractive green and white variegated leaves. The Surinam cherry, with its dark green leaves, red when young, make excellent foliage, and the ridged cherries are nice as accents.

Foliage plants. Foliage plants for the landscape provide filler in bouquets. Consider using dracaena, podocarpus, ligustrum, pittosporum, sabal palm fronds, gray-leaved sage bushes, and other leafy shrubs this way. When Monica had a flower shop in Ohio, she bought boxloads of such foliage from a man in Orlando who provided most of it from his yard. It added great distinction to her work.

Some of these types of foliage will last up to three weeks in a vase and are lovely with flowers or by themselves in place of houseplants. Use them in your landscaping and prune them for bouquets.

Berried shrubs and trees. Pyracantha, callicarpa, nandina, castor bean, and more: Florida is rich in berried plants that are ornamental in the landscape and add richly to both fresh and dried bouquets. Firethorn or pyracantha has berries of yellow, orange, or red. If purple is in your interior color scheme, use the dramatically berried beautybush (*Callicarpa americana*). It grows like a weed in northern and central Florida with masses of small purple berries aligned on long stems. The seedpods of the crape myrtle or the hips of roses can add interest and be cut either green or dried.

Like flowers, berries have their ideal stages of development. Pick them while they are still firm, not overripe. For using fresh, treat like any woody branches. For dried use, they will last longer with a spray of anti-dessicant, clear plastic, or hair spray.

WOODIES FOR CUTTING

Here are some of the many woody plants to use for cutting in Florida:

***Abutilon* species (flowering maple).** There are many abutilon species and forms, ranging in cold-hardiness and size, up to 15 feet or so. Most are killed by frost, but in northern areas can be grown in tubs and brought indoors through cold snaps. Leaves have pointed lobes, like maples, and dangling flowers resemble those of partly opened mallow or hibiscus, with more complex coloration. The color range includes red, rose, purple, white, yellow and orange, and bicolors are common. They should have fertile, well-drained soil in partial shade or full sun. Stake if necessary, and prune to keep plants dense in shape. Take cuttings in summer or fall.

Flowering Trees and Shrubs for Bouquets

The shrubs and trees that form the backbone of your landscape can also be the ones from which you cut the foliage you need for bouquets. This makes limited growing space more productive, and the plants must be pruned anyway. Most of the choices listed here have flowers, but others have attractive or fragrant foliage, or colorful berries. Those marked with asterisks are grown mainly for foliage. N, C, and S refer to recommendations for Northern, Central, and Southern Florida.

- Allamanda (*Allamanda* spp.) CS
- Azaleas (*Rhododendron* hybrids) NCS
- Bauhinia, red (*Bauhinia*) CS
- Beautyberry (*Callicarpa americana*) NCS
- Butterfly bush (*Buddleia davidii* and others) NCS
- Camellia (*Camellia sasanqua*) NC
- Citrus (*Citrus* spp.) NCS
- Crape myrtle (*Lagerstroemia indica*) NCS
- Copper leaf, chenille plant (*Acalypha* spp.) CS*
- Coral plant (*Jatropha multifida*) CS
- Croton (*Codiaeum variegatum*) CS*
- Dogwood, flowering (*Cornus florida*) NC
- Dracaena (*Dracaena* spp.) CS*
- Elderberry (*Sambucus canadensis*) NCS
- Eucalyptus, especially Silver Dollar (*Eucalyptus* spp.) NCS*
- Firethorn (*Pyracantha* spp.) NCS
- Florida yew (*Podocarpus* spp.) NCS
- Flowering maple (*Abutilon* spp.) CS
- Gardenia (*Gardenia jasminoides*) CS
- Hibiscus (*Hibiscus* spp.) NCS
- Holly (*Ilex* spp.) NCS
- Hydrangea (*Hydrangea* spp.) NC
- Ixora (*Ixora* spp.) CS
- Magnolia, saucer (*Magnolia* x *soulangiana*) NC
- Magnolia, southern (*Magnolia grandiflora*) NCS
- Nandina, heavenly bamboo (*Nandina domestica*) NCS
- Natal plum (*Carissa macrocarpa*) CS
- Olive, tea or sweet (*Osmanthus fragrans*) NC*
- Orchid tree (*Bauhinia blakeana*) CS
- Pentas (*Pentas lanceolata*) CS
- Pineapple guava (*Feijoa sellowiana*) NCS
- Plum (*Prunus* spp.) NCS
- Poinsettia (*Euphorbia pulcherrima*) CS
- Quince, Japanese flowering (*Chaenomeles japonica*) N
- Rose (*Rosa* species) NCS
- Sweet gum (*Liquidamber styraciflua*) NC
- Sweet bay (*Magnolia virginiana*) NCS

Trees and Shrubs

***Acalypha wilkesiana* (copper leaf).** This showy, 10 to 15 foot shrub comes in many colors, variously mottled, including red, purple, green, and yellow, but the copper is most common. Flowers are rather inconspicuous. It grows best in full sun and average soil and does not like much salt. It is quite cold tender. Monica's has died back every winter but grows to six feet from the roots by the next fall. To condition, split stems and submerge the attractive foliage in cold water.

***Allamanda cathartica* (yellow allamanda).** Large, bright, waxy, yellow, tubular flowers about 4 inches wide are borne on scrambling plants with glossy, pointed green leaves. Each flower has a scalloped appearance, with 5 lobes. 'Hendersonii' is a favorite allamanda cultivar. Allamanda can be trained as either a shrub or a non-clinging vine; either way, it blooms for much of the year and can reach 15 feet in height. Don't prune too frequently for flowers are formed on the new growth. It loves full sun and soil that is not too moist. Fertilize in spring and summer. It is very poisonous, but mites and scale attack it anyway. Being cold tender, it is easily killed by frost, so keep a few cuttings rooting in water as frost insurance. Blooms continue opening on long stems for a few days or more. Sear stem ends for bouquets or before rooting cuttings.

***Bauhinia blakeana* (orchid tree).** This 20-foot relative of the redbud has large, rather coarse round, cleft leaves. It is deciduous, offering yellow autumn color, and sometimes many long, brown pods. It is lovely when in bloom, densely covered with 3- to 4-inch wide orchidlike flowers in purple, red, or white. Bloom season varies with species and weather. Some are very cold tender. Give plants full sun and average soil. They need much space but little care once established.

***Bougainvillea* species (bougainvillea).** This woody vine for southern Florida has arching branches which cascade over fences and walls, making any scene look tropical and flowery. It grows 8 to 20 feet tall or wide, but blooms best when trimmed back often, for flowers form on new growth. It can be grown in large pots or as a vine trained up a trellis or tree. Tie it onto supports if necessary. If allowed to form a bush, it becomes a thorny tangle. It will be nipped by frost, but plants do well even in the Tampa area, in protected places. There are many cultivars with showy, long-lasting bracts of purple, red, pink, white, orange, or lavender in flushes all year. Bougainvilleas like full sun and are highly drought and salt tolerant. Start with plants or cuttings. Cut flowers for bouquets when the bracts are in full color, split woody stem bases, remove most of the foliage, and submerge both stems and flowers in cold water until all parts are crisp, about an hour. Keep stems in cold water until arranged. They will last up to 8 days.

***Buddleia* species (butterfly bush).** Evergreen where freezes are rare, this 3- to over 6-foot hardy shrub is deciduous in cooler areas. Species and cultivars vary in frost tolerance. The elongated clusters of fragrant tiny purple, pink, or white flowers are graceful in bouquets and an excellent substitute for lilacs. *B. lindleyana* is quite hardy and has purple blooms all summer. *B. officinalis* is

A Cutting Garden for Florida

fairly hardy and bears lilac-pink spires in the winter. The white spikes of *B. asiatica* and orange-yellow flowers of *B. madagascariensis* both bloom in winter but are not hardy in northern Florida. The same is true in reverse of the most common northern variety, *B. davidii*, which does not grow well in southern Florida, below Zone 9. It is best to buy tried varieties from local sources rather than from northern catalogs.

Blooms attract birds and butterflies. Though large, plants can be pruned to the desired size as soon as danger of frost passes. Deadhead to keep the bush looking tidy. Prune an old, overgrown butterfly bush to the ground for a fresh start from new growth. Or start anew, for this shrub blooms in only a year or two from seed.

Set plants in full sun in poor to average soil with average water. They can be shorts lived due to nematodes. Some gardeners find they do best in large containers. Flower spikes should be cut when half open but before the first florets begin to fade or turn brown. Split stems and put in warm water to condition thoroughly. They last 5 to 8 days in the vase

Callicarpa americana **(beautyberry).** This native shrubs is evergreen in most of Florida and often grows wild. Pale lavender, fairly inconspicuous flowers circle the stems in spring and are followed by clusters of tiny sized berries of a bright purple that last into the winter. There is also a white-fruited variety, best used with the others for contrast. Many kinds of birds love these berries, so plant them were you can enjoy watching them feast. Plants grow 6 feet or more with arching branches. They fruit more in full sun, but do well in shade also.

Camellia **species.** Sometimes called japonica, named for the most common Florida species, *C. japonica*, camellias are wonderful evergreen shrubs with glossy green leaves. There is also a *C. sasanqua* that has smaller but numerous blooms in the fall and the *C. sinensis* that is the plant from whose leaves our tea is made. Although camellias stay compact and grow slowly, they are long lived and can reach small tree size. They bear exquisite flowers, often sold for corsages in northern flower shops, in abundance from early fall through winter and into spring, depending on variety.

All camellias plants are fully hardy throughout Florida, though the flowers and buds may be killed by an untimely freeze. But they do not thrive in Zones 10 and 11. They are also very sensitive to soil. Add acidic organic matter such as pine needles, peat moss, and oak leaves. Do not plant too deeply, but use mulch. In sandy soils and in hot areas they prefer broken shade; in the heavier soils of northern Florida, they grow in sun as well. Feed twice a year, late winter and early summer. Camellias cope with drought but dislike wind. Cut when flowers are just opening, and arrange stems in vases or float blooms in shallow containers. They last 3 to 8 days. Spray cut flowers and foliage daily with a fine mist of water.

Trees and Shrubs

***Citrus* species (orange, grapefruit, kumquat, etc.).** Citrus trees are easy to grow in the southern two-thirds of Florida, and some varieties such as kumquat, satsuma orange, and limequat are hardy farther north. Many are naturally small or can be kept small enough for containers with pruning. Trees may reach 25 feet if allowed to grow. It is best to start with grafted plants and give them as much sun as possible, though light shade works also. Do not mulch in summer or close to the trunk, for roots are subject to rot. Water once every 2 weeks. Citrus trees bloom for a month in February or March, but kumquats bloom in flushes all year. All are excellent landscape as well as fruit trees. Cut flowering branches when a third to a half open, split stem bases slightly, remove unneeded foliage, and condition overnight in warm water. Submerge non-flowering or fruiting stems (leafy stems and stems of small fruit are great in bouquets) in cold water for about an hour first, then split stem bases and condition in warm water. Flowers will last for 3 to 6 days and have wonderful fragrance.

***Coccolobis uvifera* (sea grape).** This is a distinctive evergreen shrub for southern Florida. Its leathery round leaves are great in bouquets, and clusters of grapelike fruit ripen to purple and make good jelly. Plants reach 20 feet and tolerate salty spray and sandy soil.

***Codiaeum variegatum* (croton).** This shrub with its bright, shiny foliage in many colors and forms is evergreen and often used in southern Florida. It is good in protected spots or in tubs central and northern Florida, but must be covered or taken in before frost. It grows easily from cuttings. Some varieties thrive in sun, others in shade, others in either but may be more brilliantly colored in the sun. Croton grows in average soil and is somewhat salt tolerant. Foliage will last three weeks in bouquets. Split stems. Wash and condition it in cold water. Large leaves may be rolled and tied to desired curves, submerged in cool water for one to two hours, drained, then used in long-lasting bouquets. Do not untie them until they dry.

***Cordyline terminalis* (ti plant).** This easily grown evergreen shrub has lush wide leaves in vibrant color combinations of red, green, pink, and yellow. There are many cultivars. Florist use them often. The plants are only hardy in southern Florida, but Monica's (near Tampa) have always come back after frost. They have never gotten mature enough to bloom, but that doesn't matter, for the foliage of this is much showier than the flowers. Cordyline will grow in full sun to considerable shade. Plants are sensitive to nematodes and leaf spot, but if you use them often, you will encourage new growth, which is the most colorful and least damaged. Condition in cold water. Any leaf damage can simply be cut away with scissors. These leaves are also strikingly sculptural when looped over and the stems put through slits in the leaf bases. In arrangements, they hold up for 5 days or more.

cordyline

A Cutting Garden for Florida

Cornus florida **(dogwood).** The flowering dogwood, a small deciduous tree, grows wild in northern hammocks and moderately well in gardens in central Florida. It does poorly in coastal areas and in southern Florida. Monica has seen it growing as far down as a bit south of Tampa.

In Florida, the beautiful white petal-like bracts sometimes begin to open in early winter while the dark red fall foliage persists, although it blooms in spring in northern states. Pink varieties thrive only in northwestern Florida.

Give plants light shade, ample water, and slightly acid soil. Guard against borer, especially on young or injured trees.

To harvest, cut branches before pollen appears on the flowers, "pruning" with the shape of the plant in mind. To condition, split woody stems and stand branches overnight in deep, warm water. This tree offers interest in the landscape or the vase all year round. Cut flowers will last seven to ten days, fruits and buds longer. Buds may be forced into early bloom.

Eucalyptus **species (silver dollar tree).** This plant, often used by florists, grows from seed, and is also available in pots of various sizes. It is very difficult from cuttings. It survives light but not heavy frost and can become a small tree in three years. Stake plants and train one branch as a central leader (trunk) for best growth. The foliage is aromatic and elegant when used alone or with flowers. Monica's first eucalyptus died out in a freeze but a new one is doing fine. Some types grow well as far north as Longwood and Orlando. Monica's neighbor has a striking indoor tree made from eucalyptus branches treated in glycerin and dried. Grow plants in average soil. Provide full sun to partial shade and average water. In the northern half of Florida, protect plants from frost or grow in containers.

Euphorbia pulcherrima **(poinsettia).** This traditional holiday plant grows to be a large shrub in southern Florida in good winters. Colorful bracts look like petals, blooming in red, pink, or cream. Frost hits it most years in central Florida, but sometimes not until after Christmas, when it is most in demand. If the plant is not too large, you can cover it with a cardboard box or a garbage can when frost threatens. It needs full sun for best flowering, and nights without any artificial light. Prune it back anytime until September to keep it in shape; later pruning will remove flowerbuds. Flowers bloom in winter and last 4 to 5 days if you recut stems and immediately singe the stem ends. If the plant is kept low (take cuttings about September), or is a new one, you can use it whole rather than cut its flowers. With proper disguise such as Spanish moss and holly, set it pot and all into an arrangement. Ordinary potted poinsettias used for holiday decor can be planted in the yard or moved into larger pots after they bloom.

Gardenia jasminoides **and other species (Cape jasmine).** These delicate, very fragrant white flowers, often sold as corsages by northern florists, bloom abundantly in spring on glossy-leaved evergreen shrubs that grow easily in Florida, even through frosts and freezes. They like full sun or light shade and deep, fertile, slightly acid soil with plenty of moisture and a thick layer of organic mulch. In southern Florida, buy plants grafted on *G. thunbergia* for nematode resistance. Spray each bush frequently during bloom with insecticidal soap if white flies or thrips are a problem. Cut just after buds open. Split woody stems and condition overnight in cold water. Handle with care. To keep gardenias fresh longer, try spraying them with ice water or turn flowers face down in the water each night.

***Hibiscus* species and hybrids.** These semitropical plants, mostly woody shrubs, offer a wide variety of color, shape, and size in their showy flowers. They also vary in hardiness, from types that are hardy in Pennsylvania to types that cannot withstand frost. Some, like the perennial 'Disco Belle', can be grown from seed, blooming the first year if started early.

Rose of Sharon *(H. syriacus)* is the hardiest hibiscus shrub. Tropical hibiscus (*H. rosa-sinensis*) is the most ornamental. In southern Florida, most hibiscus species thrive and bloom all year, quickly reaching tree size. From central to northern Florida, it is wise to plant hibiscus among evergreens, which cover temporary bare spots that result if the hibiscus tops freeze. Mulch or mound the base of the shrubs well for frost protection, for they will sprout again even if tops freeze. Go to specialists for amazing cultivars.

Hibiscus blooms on new shoots and will usually bloom again by late summer even when killed to the ground by frost. However, it's a shame to lose the old growth. Betty has seen gardeners tie quilts around their hibiscus plants to protect them from frost in central Florida.

Hibiscus needs full sun, moderate fertility and moisture, and protection from nematodes. Prune as desired in March. Most types have slight salt tolerance, but *Hibiscus tiliaceus* (mahoe) is quite tolerant of salt and sand.

Take cuttings of hibiscus species at any time during moist, warm weather. Plant the shrubs near the house so you can pick flowers daily. Most hibiscus blossoms last only one day, but a few last two, with or without water. A hibiscus holder containing a single bloom is lovely on a table. Or add 1 to 3 blooms as a focal point in a bouquet without having the short stems reach the water. To keep a bouquet appealing and fresh, discard closed blooms to avoid an empty looking vase. Or lay them among the leaves of a houseplant for added color for the day. A relative of okra, hibiscus is edible and can safely be used to garnish food. Refrigerate individual flowers during the day to keep them open in the evening.

***Hydrangea* species (hydrangea).** Hydrangeas are several feet wide and tall in Florida, and are not difficult once you find the right place for them. They will bloom in shade if it is not too deep. Although they are thirsty plants and wilt badly in a pot, they are surprisingly drought tolerant in the ground and only need occasional watering. Still, they will thrive in wet places if that is what you have. The oak leaf variety blooms with a spire of creamy flowers in early spring, and its leaves turn a rich burgundy in the fall. The lacecaps have flat heads with tiny flowers in the middle and showy bracts around the outside. French hydrangea's globe-shaped blooms come later from spring into summer, in shades of pink through blue and purple, depending on the acidity of the soil.

A Cutting Garden for Florida

Softwood and hardwood cuttings root easily. Cut flowers for bouquets when they reach full color. This "pruning" sometimes causes new blooms to form. For cutting, the flowers (really bracts) should be starting to become a bit leathery or more substantial. For fresh bouquets, split the stem bases and sear stem ends, remove lower foliage, and condition in cool water. Flowers dry easily and are great in wreaths, crafts, and bouquets. Make your wreath with freshly cut, more flexible branches, stripped of leaves, for an easier time weaving the stems into place. The flowers will dry in place.

Ilex **species (holly).** From low shrubs to huge trees, many varieties of holly thrive in northern and central Florida. They are useful for their glossy, leathery, evergreen foliage as well as for clusters of red berries on the female plants. East Palatka holly is a fine, small landscape tree. Each leaf has only one small spine, at the tip. Unless there is a male nearby, to get berries, plant both a male and a female plant, even if you must put them in the same hole to make enough space. One male can pollinate several females. Give plants full sun to light shade and slightly acid soil. Cut branches when fruits are well developed and in full color. Use foliage any time of year. Split bases of woody stems and submerge foliage in water to condition and get rid of dust. Condition overnight or longer. Do not use metal containers. Foliage will last for weeks, longer if sprayed with an anti-transpirant spray such as Wilt-Pruf.

Koelreuteria **species (golden rain or golden shower tree).** These trees can grow quickly and tall and can be invasive, so we don't recommend your planting them. But if you or a neighbor have one, you might as well use the sprays of yellow flowers or the clusters of colorful seedpods. Cut the flower clusters when about half are open. Split stems, remove unneeded foliage. Condition overnight in warm water to start. Flowers last 3 to 4 days. Cut the seedpods at an early stage when still light green and place in cold water. Or cut them when practically dried and hang to finish.

Lagerstroemia indica **(crape-myrtle).** This easy-to-grow, deciduous shrub or small tree is an excellent accent or border landscape plant. It provides fluffy sprays of lilac-like flowers for many weeks each summer in shades of white, pink, bright rose, magenta, dark red, and lavender. Some cultivars are delightfully fragrant, some not at all. In northern Florida, the foliage has lovely autumn color. With its black berries and mottled bark, crape myrtle adds winter interest to the landscape.

Plant crape myrtle in full sun with average soil and moisture. Buy potted plants or grow your own from cuttings or seeds; plants bloom while still small. There are dward types that remain small enough for pots. Tip cuttings are easy to root. Even large branches over an inch in diameter can be rooted as cuttings if conditions are just right.

Prune off dead flowers and seedpods for a second or third flush of flowers, and cut plants back severely after leaves fall. For bouquets, cut when some buds in the flower clusters show color. Remove all unnecessary foliage, split stems, and either condition in deep, warm water or submerge in cold water for two hours until petals are crisp. Cut flowers will last up to a week.

Lantana camara. A wildflower in Florida, shrublike lantanas grow in sunny fields. Balls of multi-colored florets bloom constantly, in combinations of white, pink, and lilac or yellow, orange, and red. Pure lavender, yellow, or white varieties and various named cultivars are also available. The foliage has an aromatic scent. Little or no care is needed for this well adapted perennial, and it is easy to start it from cuttings. However, it is considered a pest plant by farmers because its seeds are toxic to cattle and it can be invasive. Deadhead often to prevent seeds from forming and being spread by wildlife. Or plant *L. ovatifolia* var. *reclinata*, a dwarf variety with yellow flowers and very few seeds or *L. montevidensis*, trailing lantana, a dwarf with lavender or white flowers.

Cut for bouquets when the outer three rows of florets are fully open. Buds will continue to open for 6 days. Split woody stems and condition in warm water, 80 to 100 degrees F. You may need to replace the warm water to make foliage crisp little stars begin to drop.

Magnolia **species (saucer, star, and southern magnolia, and sweet bay)**. All of these magnolias, shrubs to large trees, have glossy, dark green, fairly leathery foliage that can be used fresh or treated with glycerin. Blooms are white or cream to pink with many stamens and can be 8 to 10 inches across, though size varies with the species. Saucer and star magnolias bloom from winter to spring. Southern magnolia blooms mainly in spring with additional blooms appearing throughout the rest of the year, and sweet bay blooms all summer. All except the saucer magnolia are very fragrant.

Plant in full sun and fertile, loamy soil for best flowering. Mulch with bark chips or similar material and fertilize several times per year. Older leaves turn yellow and drop periodically and are not a sign of trouble, as long as new growth is green and healthy.

For bouquets, cut the largest buds when well developed, split stem bases, scrape bark from base, and condition in cold water overnight or until buds unfold. Submerge flowers of southern magnolia in cold water until crisp. Handle with care. Blooms last 1 to 4 days.

Morus australis 'Unryu' **(contorted mulberry)**. This fast-growing small deciduous tree has striking twisted branches and large shiny leaves. It is mostly used dried, without the leaves. It tends to be a much larger tree, on the high side of 25 feet, than the corkscrew willow, but it also produces some fruit and serves birds and wildlife. Plant only where dropped fruit will not matter. Mulberries root easy from cuttings. Cut branches for the shape wanted and prune the tree as you cut. Remove foliage, and use the twisted bare branches in arrangements, fresh or dry.

A Cutting Garden for Florida

***Musa abysinnica* (banana, edible or ornamental).** Bananas grow in much of Florida, but need protection from frost for two years in order to bloom and set fruit. There are dwarf and tall types ranging from a few to over 20 feet. Not all of them produce edible fruit. In freezing weather, the tops of banana plants die but the roots send up new growth, eventually. Plants spread by way of suckers and need thinning and division when they become crowded. Bananas prefer moist, enriched soil in full sun or bright partial shade. For arrangements, cut the smallest new banana leaves or trim larger ones as needed, applying lemon juice to cut edges to prevent their turning brown. Condition by submerging in cold water until crisp, then put stems in water. They will last up to a week and are very dramatic.

***Nandina domestica* (heavenly bamboo).** This medium sized evergreen shrub from China is a graceful addition to the Florida landscape. It also serves as a constant source of forest-green, fernlike leaves with a bit of red on the stems, plus plumes of white flowers and red berries for bouquets. It tolerates frost and grows in all parts of Florida. Plant it in good soil, in sun or bright partial shade. Mulch to keep soil moist, so leaves will keep their fresh look. Prune off older stems if they start to look ragged. Condition leaves and flowers in cool water. They will last several days or more in arrangements.

***Nerium oleander* (oleander).** Oleander is a lovely shrub that grows throughout the state. It grows in sun and average soil, and is very popular for landscaping. It is sold in specific sizes: miniature, a foot or two tall; petite, 2 to 5 feet; dwarf, 5 to 8 feet; intermediate, 8 to 12 feet; and large, 12 to 20 feet. Colors range from white and yellow to salmon, many shades of pink, and bright to deep red. Flowers come in clusters and can be single, double, or semi-double. Some varieties are fragrant. They have insect problems in some areas. All parts of oleander are very poisonous, but they are not likely to be dangerous because they have a terrible taste, and none of their parts are particularly attractive to children. This is one of Florida's most popular plants, for it stands up to drenching rain and high heat. It blooms from spring to fall. Cut branches when half the flowers in the cluster have opened, early in the morning or late in the evening. Split stem ends and sear them to prevent the milky fluid from leaking out. Immerse the stems in deep warm (not hot) water to dondition. A floral preservative can be effective in extending the life of cut flowers. Don't use softened water. Keep the flowers in the refrigerator or in a cool place until you arrange them. They can last for up to 7 days, as more flowers open on the stems. The single-flowered forms tend to remain fresh longer than the doubles.

Pittosporum tobira (**Japanese pittosporum**). This staple Florida landscape plant is used by northern florists as filler in bouquets. Variegated types are preferred for their lovely, oblong, Williamsburg-green leaves touched with cream markings. This useful shrub is evergreen and has fairly good salt tolerance. It has small, fragrant flowers if it is not pruned before its summer blooming season. Start from seeds or cuttings or buy plants at almost any nursery. This one likes well-drained, sandy soil in partial shade, and grows well in all parts of the state. Cut or prune it after bloom to keep the size within bounds or prune as needed and grow it only as a foliage plant. Tall forms can be as high as 15 or 20 feet. Mulch with bark chips and feed plants several times a year. For bouquets, condition cut branches by slitting stem ends and standing them in deep water for several hours.

Plumeria species (**frangipani**). These shrubs or small trees are hardy wherever they can be protected from frost. They are the flowers from which the Hawaiian leis are made and each species has a separate, wonderful fragrance. Blooms come in white, pink, yellow, and deep red. A plant grows slowly in full sun and some can get 15 to 20 feet tall. They have high drought and salt tolerance and start easily from cuttings, but start with good cultivars, for many seedlings and cuttings are inferior. Each flower last only 1 to 2 days, but buds keep opening for several more days. Float individual flowers in a bowl. Cut stems when flowers are half open. Sear stem ends in a flame for 15 seconds. Then condition overnight in cool water. Dip flowers in cold water just before arranging.

Rhododendron **species (azalea and rhododendron).** Azaleas love Florida. Be sure to drive through Orlando in late winter when azaleas light up the city. Plentiful blooms are borne separately or in clusters, depending on the type. Some azaleas begin blooming in fall and continue all winter. February and March bring the climax, and mountains of flowers are glorious at the same time as dogwood in central Florida. They like well-drained, loamy, slightly acid soil, and partial shade. Hardiness varies with species, but most azaleas take cold and hot weather well. Most are evergreen and in the red, white, or pink to lavender color range. Flowers may be large or small, double or single.

Select special cultivars marked "sun azalea" if planting in the sun. Bushes are usually sold in small sizes, but some types are dwarf while others grow very large, so check before buying. You can keep the size of yours in check for a while by harvesting flowers for bouquets each year. Do not prune after July. Plants are not deeply rooted, so when they outgrow their locations, they are relatively easy to move if you do it while soil is moist and weather is cool. For unusual or native types, shop the catalogs and attend plant sales given by your local rhododendron society. Cut them when 3 or 4 flowers are completely open on the stem. Shape the plant as you cut. Split woody stems and condition overnight in cold water. Mist foliage and flowers with cold water. Clusters will last 5 to 10 days while buds continue to open.

A Cutting Garden for Florida

***Rosa* species (rose).** Roses have symbolized love and beauty throughout history. It is not hard to grow excellent roses in any part of Florida, if you are growing varieties suited to your area. Purchase Number 1 grade plants from reputable area nurseries, making sure they have been grafted onto vigorous, nematode-resistant rootstock such as Fortuniana (also known as Double Cherokee) and Dr. Huey. You can expect these roses to grow for 5 to 20 years. In addition, fragrant antique roses of Mediterranean origin grow fairly well, and usually need no spraying for black spot or mildew. Miniatures do well also. When choosing roses for arrangements, consider ease of growth, color, size, shape, and scent. Some roses have fiercer thorns than others. You'll enjoy having wonderful fresh roses for winter holidays!

Roses need sunshine, but can do with less here in Florida than they require in cooler climates. If they can only get half a day of sun, it it better if it is morning sun, to dry the dew and prevent disease. Roses prefer deep, rich, well-drained soil, and a cover of mulch to keep the roots cool and moist. Improve soil with lots of dried manure, peat moss, and compost. A layer of additives several inches deep can work wonders. Some rosarians add nitrogen by incorporating alfalfa pellets from the feed store into the soil. Specially packaged rose food fertilizers are excellent. Use timed release fertilizer, or fertilize once a month, all through the year. Water frequently (twice a week if it is dry) and deeply during hot weather. To minimize mildew, water in the morning so leaves dry quickly.

Plant bare-root roses in late winter, potted ones at any time. The graft joint should be just above the soil surface. Firmly pack soil around roots.

Roses grow a little larger here than in the north, and are not pruned as severely. In February, prune tea roses to 3 feet high, leaving 3 or 4 main canes. Let climbers and species finish their main flowering before pruning them, and then take out only old or small, twiggy canes. Train the fat new shoots of climbers as they grow. Do not cut strong, new canes.

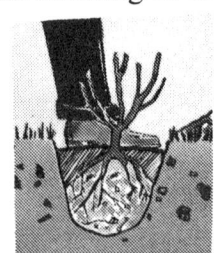

AARS

Fill the hole with water and allow it to soak in. Trim canes back. Water again and add more soil to protect canes.

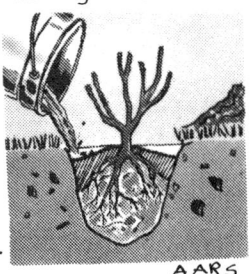

← Work the soil mixture around the roots to eliminate any air pockets. Firm the soil around the roots and add more soil until nearly full.

AARS

***Salix matsudana* 'Tortuosa' (corkscrew Hankow willow).** This willow is a small deciduous tree, under 25 feet. It tends to be shrubby, which is ideal for taking some of the contorted stems for arrangements. It is also more drought tolerant than other willows. The leaves are bright green and turn darker green and yellow-green in the fall. Like most willows, it is easy to start from cuttings. For arranging, cut branches for the shape wanted and prune the tree as you cut. Use fresh or dry. For fresh arrangements, slit stem bases and condition in deep water. To dry, remove foliage and hang in an airy place. The variety 'Golden Curls' has golden bark. It isn't easy to find, but is available from Forest Farm.

Trees and Shrubs

***Serenoa repens* (*Sabal* palmetto, saw palmetto).** This native grows well in all parts of Florida in sun or partial shade. It is shrublike, several feet tall and wide. The plentiful big green fan-shaped leaves, sometimes silvery or blueish, can be trimmed and shaped for bouquets. Condition by submerging in deep, cool water for several hours. Native Americans used the leaves for brooms and the seeds for medicine.

Stephanotis floribunda. This fragrant white tubular flower is a favorite for bridal bouquets. It is a woody tropical vine with handsome leaves, and does well outdoors in south Florida or as a pot plant farther north. Vines may be trained on topiary forms and also can be used for excellent hanging baskets. plant.. Frost will kill stephanotis, so bring it inside during cold spells if you can. Give it rich, loamy soil, frequent feedings, and partial shade. Like most other vines, it grows easily from cuttings.

***Vitex agnus-castus* (chaste-tree).** This herbal shrub grows to 10 feet and has a wonderful fountain shape in full sun. In shade it will grow in whatever shape it needs to find the sun. The leaves are finely cut and palmately compound and look a bit like marijuana, but are a gray green and fragrant. Plants start easily from seeds or cuttings. Flowers bloom in spires of lavender all summer and fall and are followed by many small, round fruits that dry well if picked when green and firm and hung to dry. Cut the spires when only a few buds are showing color. Remove all foliage but dry it for potpourri. Split stem bases and condition overnight in warm water. Cut non-flowering stems for foliage and condition the same way. Flowers will last 5 to 7 days in bouquets.

***Yucca* species (Adam's needle, Spanish bayonet).** There are several types of the semi-evergreen shrubs that grow from 3 to 25 feet tall. All have rosettes or branches of gray-green or variegated green and ivory, daggerlike leaves. The individual leaves may be over a foot long and dangerously serrated on the edges. Huge panicles of nodding creamy white flowers bloom on stems several feet tall in spring or early summer. They are striking with modern or Spanish architecture and ideal for seaside plantings in full sun and almost any soil. In some areas weevils are a big problem. Though the full stems are too large for most settings, you can use side blooms or shoots in arrangements. For a massive bouquet for a major event, you can use the whole spike. It will only last a few days. Cut flowers in the advanced bud stage; splits stems at the base and soak in deep, cool water to condition. Or open the buds and submerge them in cold water until crisp. Since the flowers are edible, they make a lovely garnish for festive foods.

Yucca filamentosa

A Cutting Garden for Florida

Chapter Eleven
BEAUTY FROM EVERLASTINGS

If you want really crisp, bright looking dried flowers, grow your own at home. Any flower, leaf, or pod can be dried, but some varieties dry and last better than others. We like naturally air-dried, straw-textured everlasting flowers, grasses, and pods best, for they hold their shape well even during humid spells, which cause other dried materials to wilt. Collect and dry them throughout the year, and you will have fine material for arrangements for your home plus gifts for friends. Dried arrangements and decorations can be made well in advance for special occasions.

Sometimes delicate garden flowers dried in silica gel in the microwave, freeze-dried, or dried using other special drying methods reabsorb humidity and lose their shape after they have been arranged. Then they droop. However, this is less of a problem in air-conditioned homes.

CHOICES FOR DRIED BOUQUETS

The most successful flowers for drying, for instance strawflower, statice, and globe amaranth, have naturally firm textures. Many of them originated in harsh climates—that's why they developed strawlike textures in the first place. Other plants developed leathery or felted leaves for protection. Many plants, including grasses, have long-lasting plumes or pods to keep seeds off the ground until the right time of year for germination. This also gives them a long decorative life indoors. In Florida, the extended growing season allows time for everlastings to develop fully and achieve peak quality.

Ferns, dusty miller, nandina leaves, and palm fronds can be dried flat between layers of newspaper, weighted down with telephone books. If they are too brittle when dried, spray them with acrylic varnish to give them greater flexibility. Spanish moss can be collected and used for wreaths, baskets, and arrangements. You may want to zap it in the microwave to rid it of invisible pests. You wouldn't believe the price it sells for in garden shops in the rest of the country! Seed cluster sheaths from palm trees, pieces of bark, driftwood, and other natural materials can be used as holders for or elements in arrangements.

Here are some of the many good plants to grow and air-dry at home. Other plants with attractive pods or flowers for drying can be found all around us. They lend themselves to use in wreaths, bouquets, and other everlasting arrangements. Some are also popular as fresh flowers. If you cannot find the plants at nurseries, grow them from seed. Try a packet of mixed everlastings plus a packet or two of essential types such as strawflowers. Seeds of the most popular flowers for drying are available in either mixed or single colors. White or pale flowers are effective in arrangements and sell out quickly in the stores, so grow your own to be sure of a supply.

ORNMENTAL GRASSES

If you have space in the sun, try some of these grasses. There are many annual and perennial types. Some perennials such as pampas grass are over 8 feet tall while in bloom. Container-grown perennial grasses are available in the nurseries. Hardy annuals such as quaking grass, hare's tail grass, and spelt wheat are easy to grow from seed (available from Park Seed, Thompson & Morgan, Johnny's, and many others). Plant seeds in fall where frost is light or rare, in early spring elsewhere or if the species is not hardy.

Hardy Grasses

Avena sterilis **(animated oats).** Branched spikes of long-haired oats on 3-foot stems.

Briza maxima, Briza minor. **Large and small quaking grass.** Airy clusters on branched, wiry stems, 1 to 2 feet.

Hordeum jubatum **(squirrel's tail grass).** Feathery gray seedheads on 18-inch stems.

Lagurus ovatus **(hare's tail grass).** Furlike, one-inch heads in a pretty beige, on 18-inch stems.

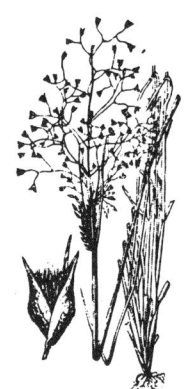

Panicum violaceum. 6-inch, silky purple tassels arch gracefully on 3-foot plants.

Pennisetum villosum **(fountain grass).** Ivory or purple plumes on two-foot stems. Protect from frost. Can be perennial.

Setaria glauca **(foxtail grass).** Thick, red-brown "tails" 5 inches long on 18-inch stems. Protect from frost.

Triticum spelta **(spelt wheat).** Spikes of long haired wheat, 2 feet tall. Golden beige kernels, black or beige beards (awns).

FAVORITES FOR DRYING

Achillea **species (yarrow, milfoil).** This perennial usually does not live through summer in Florida. Fortunately, it can be planted in fall and grown as a biennial. The popular All-America selection 'Summer Pastels' is quickly grown from seed, taking only 4 or 5 months from seed to bloom. It likes sun with average soil and water. Colors are white, cream, yellow, pink, red, and lavender. Hang to dry in small bunches. Other achillea species and cultivars are more likely to expire from the heat before they bloom. See also page 60.

Ammobium alatum **(winged everlasting).** Small, pearly white strawflowers an inch or two wide have broad yellow centers. They grow in big bunches on well-branched, 1- to 3-foot plants. Give them full sun and average soil and moisture. In frost-free areas, plant seeds in fall or winter for bloom in spring; elsewhere start indoors in January or February and transplant outdoors after the danger of frost passes. Perennial in mild climates, this is usually grown as an annual or biennial, but is hard to find except as seed.

Everlastings

Cecropia palmata **(snakewood)**. Collect the large, palmate leaves from this tropical tree after they have fallen. Use as bouquet filler and in crafts. If you can find it growing in a nearby park, you won't have to plant this somewhat messy tree.

Celosia cristata (see page 39). Both the cockscomb and plume types are used. Dwarf types sold for bedding are not the best choice: look for taller types (3 or 4 foot) with large heads. `Big Chief' and `Kurume' are of the long-stemmed, cockscomb type. Hang to dry. The colors tend to darken. To use in smaller arrangements, break heads into wedges or plumes and tape to wires.

Cocos nucifera **(coconut palm and many other palms)**. We have not tried this but have read of using the dried calyx and sheath from flower clusters. They resemble boats and can be used as containers for dried arrangements.

Driftwood, easily collected on a trip to the beach, also makes an execellent container itself, or an addition to dried bouquets

Gomphrena globosa **(globe amaranth)**. Short types are often used for summer bedding in Florida; both short and tall types are fine for drying. This tender annual plant is easy, drought and heat-tolerant, and useful. Colors are white, pink, purple, or rusty orange. Plant in full sun after danger of frost passes. Let flowers to be dried mature on the plants to their maximum size and color before picking them, but harvest before they fade. Hang to dry. These may be used on their own firm stems in arrangements, or taped together in clusters of several flowers, then inserted. See page 40.

Gypsophila paniculata **(perennial babysbreath.** Perennial gypsophila is best for dried bouquets, but grows only in central Florida and northward, and is difficult in hot areas. It likes a gritty, alkaline, well-drained soil and dislikes excessive heat. Give it full sun in winter, bright partial shade in summer. Adding terra cotta or rinsed seashell chips to the soil will probably help with its texture and pH. Double-flowered white cultivars such as 'Bristol Fairy' dry most successfully. Annual babysbreath (*G. elegans*, p. 53) is not quite as attractive when dried. However, it's a lot easier to grow.

Helichrysum bracteatum **(strawflower)**. See page 54. Everyone's favorite, this daisylike plant with the texture and shine of straw is easy to grow, withstanding wet, dry, hot, or cold weather. For best results, buy bedding plants or start the small seeds indoors.

helipterum (acroclinium)

Helipterum roseum **(syn. *Acroclinium roseum*)**. These daisylike hardy annual flowers are similar to but more delicate than strawflowers (*Helichrysum*). Blooms are half an inch to an inch wide. The 2-foot plants bear salmon, pink, rose, white, and cream strawlike flowers with golden or black centers. Seedlings are quite hardy through light frost, but plants are killed by prolonged heat in the nineties. They like cool temperatures, average soil, full sun to partial shade, and ample moisture. In central Florida and below, where frosts are rare, sow in late fall; elsewhere sow outdoors four weeks before the last expected frost, or earlier indoors. Hang to dry.

A Cutting Garden for Florida

Limonium sinuatum **(statice).** See page 55. Statice grows in sandy soil, and takes drought well. Check the seed catalogs for strains that feature paler colors. Start seeds in fall for spring bloom.

Lunaria annua **(money plant, honesty).** In northern Florida only, plant this biennial in summer or fall for bloom the next year. In other parts of the state, it grows but never blooms. After blooming, circular pods form—the silvery "coin" is a shiny membrane under the husk. When ripe, the husk and seeds come off, leaving the everlasting coins on the stem. Save the seeds for the next crop.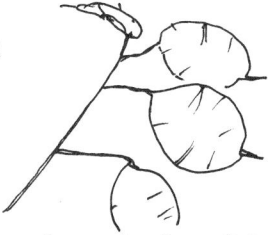

Merremia tuberosa **(wood rose).** A tender perennial morning glory, the "rose" is the dried seed pod, which looks like a blossom carved from wood. To grow this, soak seed overnight and plant indoors in February, then set outside near a sturdy trellis or other support. This one takes lots of space and is easily killed by frost. In frost-free areas, it can become invasive.

Molucella laevis **(bells of Ireland).** These bells of greenish hue are interesting in dried arrangements. For longest lasting dried flowers, cut after most of the soft white flowers in the papery green bells have opened. Remove the leaves and hang to dry.

Nigella damascena **(love-in-a-mist).** See page 56. The beautiful 2-inch green and purple striped pods are easily dried, but the flowers are not.

Physalis alkekengii **(Chinese lantern).** Seed pods are two-inch, red, papery lanterns to hang to dry for everlasting bouquets. Plants grow two to three feet tall in sun or partial shade. Though perennial, they bloom the first year in warm weather. They tolerate cold weather and any soil, and are invasive in the cooler half of the state. Because they need some winter chilling, you may have to replant each year in the warmer half of the state.

Salvia farinacea **(blue sage, mealycup sage)** See page 76. Slim blue or white spires are highly valued in dried bouquets. Plants are perennial where frost is rare. Hang to dry.

Solidago **species (goldenrod).** This underestimated hardy native perennial plant is a great addition to dried bouquets. Pick the flower heads before the blossoms open but after the buds fill out. Then hang them to dry, and you'll get non-shattering, colorful yellow flowers.

HARVESTING

Grow everlastings like other plants but harvest them differently. Pick flowers for drying before they open fully, for they will continue to open as they dry. Babysbreath should be picked about when the first third of the flowers on the stem open. Strawflowers should be nearly closed, with only a few bracts open. All flowers, pods, and grasses should be picked in their prime, and only unflawed specimens should be used. Poppy pods should be picked when mature but still green in color. Grasses should be picked before they are weathered, if possible, and all kinds of pods before they split open. The plumes of grasses should be silky and fully formed, but not yet fluffy and dry. Grasses like spelt wheat and quaking grass should still be pale green, not tan. They will age and change color as they dry.

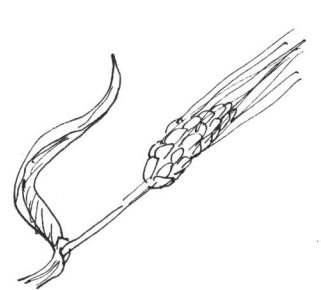

If you gather seedheads of meadow grasses, go on collecting trips in different seasons, for variety. Venture into the field only with permission of the property owner, of course. Wear boots and gloves, and watch out for snakes and spiders. DON'T collect sea oats or anything rare. Do not walk on dunes or collect plants near the seashore, for this makes the sand less stable, more likely to wash away.

If a grass or pod has matured and weathered in the field, and still is good looking, consider it a finished product. If the stems are fully dry, you probably can use it right away, without hanging it to dry first. Beware of plants like thistle with silky threads attached to the seeds. The threads catch the wind and will carry the seeds all over the place unless you squirt them with hairspray or fixative first.

WAYS TO DRY EVERLASTINGS

It has been said that drying flowers is like making wine, for there are good and bad years. Growing and drying conditions affect the color and texture of your plants.

Air Drying. This the simplest, best technique, especially if you dry large amounts. Choose a shady, airy, warm place, not too hot or cold—an attic in summer may be too warm and cause color to fade, but a ventilated garage may be fine. Small amounts can be dried in the house, if it is not too humid, even in a closet (leave the door open and don't crowd the plants). The more bunches you dry, the more humidity you release, so fans and ventilation may be vital for those of you drying plentiful supplies.

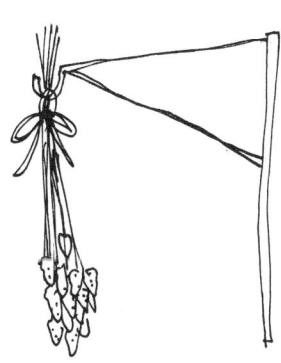

Hang the flowers to be dried in small bunches, heads down, ten to twenty pieces per bunch. They can be tied with string, or, better yet, bound in rubber bands that contract as stems shrivel. Betty's friend, Heather Lovett, uses a drying rack in her livingroom and slips hooks made from bent paperclips into the rubber bands on the bunches. The colorful, neat bunches are decorative as they dry. After one to three weeks, she crowds the fully dried bunches, heads up and wrapped in tissue, into wicker and wood baskets on an unused hearth. They stay there until the growing season ends, and then they are arranged.

Freshly picked strawflowers and also small rosebuds may be wired instead. Discard the stem below the flower head and immediately insert a piece of florist's wire 3/8 inch deep into the flower so that it does not show through. The green stem will seal itself to the wire as it dries. Dry the wired flowers upright in vases or hang in bunches. As they dry, they continue to open. If you don't need the flexibility of the wire, you can dry them on slim bamboo skewers or even toothpicks instead.

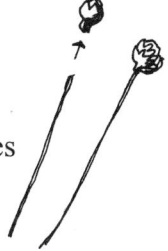

Glycerine and Water. Branches of azalea leaves, holly, privet, nandina, ivy, pittosporum, eucalyptus, and individual magnolia leaves and palm fronds, may be preserved by setting their stems in a solution of two parts glycerine (available at drug stores) to one part water. Choose only fresh, mature leaves or they will wilt. Flowers do not work well. The leaves will darken and turn leathery in the glycerine; magnolia leaves become nearly black. Holly takes only a few days, but the others take several weeks.

First prepare the mixture. Then pick leaves fresh (on stems about a foot long), slit the woody stem ends, and put them in a vase containing three or four inches of the mixture. The plants will draw it up and become preserved, changing color as the process works. Don't put them into water first or they will draw up less of the glycerine. Check plants daily and add more liquid if necessary. As soon as the leaves finish changing color (approximately 1 to 3 weeks), they are ready to use. The glycerine may be re-used.

Holly is faster!

Pressing. You can dry leaves, ferns, and flowers by pressing them between sheets of newspaper and weighting them down, or in an old telephone book. If you use a telephone book, start in back and work toward the front to protect the first plants you dry from wear and tear. The plants will dry flat in the position you place them. Be sure not to let leaves or petals fold or overlap. Take apart thick, multipetalled flowers like zinnia, and dry the loose petals in a single flat layer. Reassemble the flower when you make your project. Pressed flowers will be too flat for bouquets, in most cases, but are good in other crafts such as making notecards and decorating candles. The leaves and ferns will be fine. If you like, curve stems of ferns slightly for a more natural look. Let pieces dry for two to four weeks, then store them flat in labelled covered cardboard boxes until you need them. Keep in mind that some flowers hold their color longer than others, after being pressed. We recommend violas and pansies, zinnias, gaillardia, coreopsis, orange California poppies, and cosmos.

Being flat, pansies are easy to press, and hold their color.

Scanning. If you are computer savvy and have a flat-bed scanner (the kind with a big, flat glass panel that does not move and a cover to lay over the item being scanned, **not** an upright slot that pulls paper through for copying), you can put the flowers or leaves (fresh or dry) right on the glass bed of the scanner. Lay a white or colored piece of paper or cloth over the top, for a background. Cover, scan and crop, and you'll have photo-type files with very real looking results. You can make artwork or notecards with the scans.

Scan of real grass

Drying compounds. You can dry soft, less papery types of leaves and flowers in **silica gel** (sold in craft stores), in clean sand, or in a homemade mixture of two parts white cornmeal to one part laundry borax. They need less dusting off if dried in silica gel. Roses, zinnias, dahlias, hollyhocks, larkspur, marigolds, orchids, and many other flowers can be dried this way without their losing shape or color. As mentioned, there can be problems with the flowers sagging during humid spells, but the technique adds many plants to the list of those to be dried. The use of spray sealants helps to keep humidity from wilting dried flowers. Use commercially prepared drying compounds according to directions. Get the blue kind of silica gel, which loses its color as it absorbs moisture, and turns blue again when dry. You can redry it in the oven (its instructions will explain this).

To dry flowers, put a one-inch layer of the compound into a sealed, air-tight container such as a cookie tin. Different flower shapes are handled differently. Lay flowers which grow in spires, like larkspur, on their side. Place flat, daisylike flowers face down, and frilled double flowers like zinnias face up. Cover the blossoms with the compound, being sure to fill in any hollow portions so they don't flatten out. Leave short stems on single flowers, and attach wires later. Check on the flowers in about two weeks. If they are not dry yet, seal the tin and check again a week or two later. When the flowers are dry, dust them off gently with a paintbrush and use them right away.

You can use your microwave to dry flowers in silica gel almost instantly. Be sure to use a microwavable container such as a cardboard box, not a metal one. Pack the flowers as described, supported with gel so they keep their shape, but do not cover the container. Microwave on high for short periods (30 seconds at a time) and test flowers for dryness each time. Cooking time depends on the dampness of the petals, the amount of silica gel, and the quirks of the individual microwave, so experiment as much as possible before trying to do an important project. Pansies are perfect for trying out this technique. When finished, microwaved flowers and leaves are papery in texture. If overdried, they may shatter. If you are in a hurry, you can even microwave everlasting flowers that you would normally air dry, and you do not need the silica gel for this.

Sand. Sylvester Rose, agricultural extension agent in Brevard County, supplied us with a recipe for quickly drying flowers in **sand**. He says to start by sifting clean, dry sand to remove all coarse particles. Remove the leaves from the stems of flowers you are planning to dry. Pour two inches of sand into a shallow cardboard box, then place the flowers face down. Pour more sand over each flower to the depth of about an inch. The stems need not be covered. Space flowers so that they do not touch.

Place the box of sand holding the flowers in the sun to bake. If the weather is dry and hot, 2 or 3 days will be enough. Carefully pour the sand off the flowers, and, if necessary, use a small pint brush to remove particles sticking to the flowers. You can re-use the sand. Then use the flowers for dried arrangements or crafts, or store them until needed in clean boxes along with a little silica gel.

ARRANGING DRIED FLOWERS

The same dried flowers are prepared differently for various styles of arrangements. For natural looking, airy, country-style bouquets, generous bunches of flowers or grasses are used on their own long stems, sometimes in transparent vases. For more formal, modern compositions, select several pods, flowers, and twisted branches, and stand them in a neat, flat ceramic container, using mechanics such as oasis or pin holders to keep them in place.

Plan your color combinations carefully. Unless you are very experienced, do not use too many colors in the same arrangement, but choose two or three that are compatible with your interior decor. Remember that some dried materials, especially green

Wrap small bunches onto wires with tape

leaves, stems, and grasses, change color as they age. The pink and green arrangement may become pink and yellowish brown! Blues, whites, and grays are more stable.

Colonial style bouquet. In baskets or bowls, densely filled Colonial style bouquets are appropriate and charming. In these, the stems are mostly hidden.

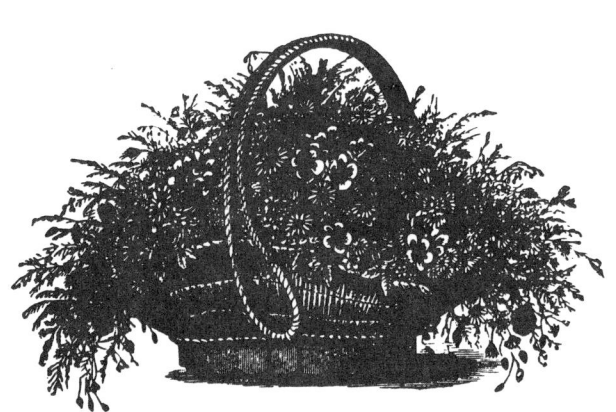

To make one of these full, rounded arrangements you will need to work when you have several hours of uninterrupted time. Supplies include florist's tape, preferably brown, Oasis (florist's) foam, 12-gauge wire, wire clippers, scissors, and some craft glue. It takes a generous amount of flowers to make even a small bouquet in this style.

Choose a small container the first time you try this. Fill it completely with Oasis—flush with or even half an inch above the top of your container. To get a full look, tape small bunches of flowers together on a wire, as shown, tightly wrapping the stretchy tape around the cluster of stem ends and the wire. There should be three to nine flowers or plumes of flowers per wire. You can combine flowers in the bunches, or not. Break large heads or plumes of celosia or hydrangea into several pieces and wire them separately.

Arrange the flowers in logical order as you build the bouquet. Put some of the filler such as babysbreath, statice and the heavier flowers in first, sticking the stems or wires deeply into the oasis. These will define the shape of the bouquet and help cover the oasis. They will be partially covered as you continue to add pieces. Place flowers at the bottom to cover the rim of the container.

Use small and light colored flowers near the top of the arrangement, large and dark or bright ones near the bottom. Watch your heights and the angle of insertion of the parts of the bouquet. Keep adding to it, repeating various elements evenly around the bouquet if it is to be viewed from all sides. This style is usually easier to succeed with if you use many light or white flowers— they keep it from looking too heavy. Keep to your color scheme, but try to include an interesting variety of shapes and textures.

A DRIED FLOWER TOPIARY TREE

With your supply of dried garden flowers, perhaps you would enjoy making a dried topiary tree. It is modeled after a formal standard, a shrub or small tree trained to grow with a globe of foliage atop a straight trunk, usually in an attractive flowerpot. The dried flower topiary is actually a globe of Oasis studded with flowers, leaves, and pods. A dried branch makes a good trunk. It must be firmly anchored in a cachepot or flowerpot filled with dry sand and stones.

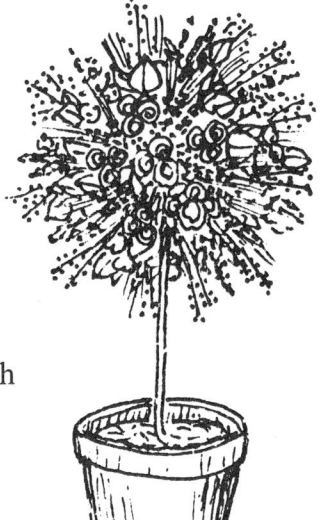

Materials needed. For this project, you will need:

⇛ One flowerpot or container about 6 inches wide, 6 to 8 inches tall.

⇛ One fairly straight tree branch about 1 1/2 inches in diameter and 2 to 2 1/2 feet tall.

⇛ One globe of Oasis at least 6 inches in diameter, up to 8 inches. This can be made by gluing two blocks of oasis together and carving them into a ball. Or you may be able to find a ball of Oasis at a craft shop.

⇛ Spanish moss, microwaved (if gathered from your yard) for a few seconds to kill any invisible pests, enough to cover the top of pot 1 inch deep.

⇛ A small hammer and several 1-inch nails.

⇛ A 1-foot wooden ruler or similarly shaped piece of wood, to anchor treetrunk.

⇛ Dry sand and stones, for use as "soil," enough to fill the pot.

⇛ About 6 dozen wired bunches of flowers, pods, and leaves, made of 12-gauge wire cut into 4 inch lengths, florist's tape, and dried floral materials. We suggest strawflowers, babysbreath, globe amaranth, statice, winged everlasting, rose hips, quaking grass, and others that are not too large. Make at least a dozen wired clumps of each different plant type. 6 types should make a good arrangement. Follow your preferences, using varied shapes and textures.

Assemble your materials. Cut the wooden ruler into two pieces, each 5 inches long. Make a tree stand by crossing them and nailing them into the base of the branch you are using for the trunk. Then stand your branch upright in the flowerpot, and fill the pot with sand and stones up to 2 inches from the rim. Push the oasis globe firmly, deeply onto the top of the branch. Now you are ready to arrange the flowers for the topiary arrangement. Select your dried flowers and foliage, in your choice of colors, and wire them into several dozen little bunches. Each bunch should be 3 to 5 inches long and have 3 large, 5 to 9 medium, or several sprays of tiny flowers (or pods or leaves).

Make the topiary. Working all around the globe of oasis, set the shape and size by inserting the strongest, most flexible materials in first. Space them evenly around the arrangement, aiming for the center with each insertion (as in the Colonial bouquet). Keep on inserting the wires of bunches of dried flowers and fillers, adding the most delicate materials last so they won't get broken. Be sure that the oasis is densely, evenly covered on all sides. Continue adding material if the topiary top looks too sparse. Replace broken materials, add special accents if they are needed, and it is finished.

Many other kinds of dried arrangements can be made. Use this book for help in growing the materials in Florida, and find wonderful suggestions for dried floral designs in specialized books on this topic from your library or bookstore.

A Cutting Garden for Florida

Chapter Twelve
ARRANGING THE BOUNTY

Flower arranging is like painting: there are materials, techniques, styles, tips, and guidelines, but no hard and fast rules. Creating great looking arrangements is a matter of finding a balance between making the flowers go into the bouquet your way, and respecting their natural shapes, colors, sizes, and stem directions as they are. An overly forced looking bouquet may be charmless, but a tangled one is messy. Arranging takes a light, deft touch. It's both an art and a skill, so practice makes a difference. After you develop the knack for it, the flowers will seem to fall into the bouquet just where you want them to (though you might not know where that is until they do it). Before you arrive at that stage, however, these tips may help:

CHOOSING THE FLOWERS

What should you cut for a bouquet today? What is in season? Which flowers are out in the garden showing off? In a bouquet, you can sometimes spotlight flowers that no one would notice in the open garden. Choose flowers in their early prime, or before they open fully, for longer vase life. Or choose flowers in several stages of development for an interesting look. Avoid picking imperfect blooms. They'll be more useful holding color in the garden than indoors in bouquets, where their defects would be obvious.

Plan your color scheme before you cut the flowers: it's tricky to work with too many colors at once. Palm fronds, whole or trimmed, look great in bouquets, and so do leaves and ferns. Ordinary ivy combines gracefully with any type of flower. What can your garden spare? What needs pruning? Use the pieces you prune off in your arrangements. Do you need flowers for a special event or party? What colors, what degree of formality do you want? If you find your garden lacking in your favorite flowers, make a note to plant more of them in the needed quantities and colors. Plan ahead so that you will have a garden well-stocked with flowers for holidays, birthdays, and special events. On your calendar or in your diary, jot down what blooms each week, for future reference.

HARVESTING

With the right handling, your homegrown flowers will last longer than flowers from the florist, for they are fresher and have not been shipped. Picked with care, conditioned, and arranged, they make a worthy gift or lasting spot of beauty in your home.

Harvest flowers and foliage for bouquets in the morning or evening. During hot weather, morning is better, for plants are well-filled with water. Evening is also good if the weather is not too hot, and flowers are not wilted, for at that time of day they contain the most stored food. Avoid harvesting at midday, when plants are stressed from lack of water, and may not recover in the vase.

Before you go out, get a pruning knife or sharp clippers and a clean bucket half filled with tepid water (100 degrees

A Cutting Garden for Florida

F). Warm water has fewer bubbles to clog the thin, tubelike veins in the stems, and less oxygen. Cut flowers so that stems are as long as possible. However, some flowers may be cut and used even though their stems are quite short. Short-stemmed choices for floating in a bowl are water lilies, camellias, gardenias, roses, tuberous begonias, stephanotis, hibiscus, and lilies.

Whatever their length, cut stems slantwise and plunge them into water immediately. This way the flowers won't wilt before you bring them inside. Try to cut all the flowers and leaves you will need for your bouquets in one trip. Strip unneeded foliage off outdoors, for less clutter in your work area later. Bring in your harvest and fill the bucket, adding floral preservative (see below). Remove any remaining unwanted leaves from the lower portion of the stem, wherever they will be submerged in water after being arranged. If you don't, they are likely to rot and cloud the water. And keep them away from ripening fruit. It gives off ethylene gas which causes flowers to age and wilt faster.

EDIBLE FLOWERS AND FLORAL GARNISHES

One of the benefits of growing your own flowers is that you know how they were grown. Certain flowers are edible, and if they are used in or near food, it's comforting to know that they have not been exposed to toxic pesticides. Nasturtiums and chives add sparkle to a platter and a tasty tang to salads.

Calendulas, pansies, and roses add color and interesting flavor. With some flowers, especially roses, different varieties have different flavors or strength of flavor. Taste and decide which you prefer. Tuberous begonias have a piquant, citrusy taste, and are lovely as decorations for food. Citrus flowers add a lovely aroma. You can mince edible flowers and add them to cheese spreads, butters, and pancake batter. Large squash blossoms can be stuffed and fried. Yucca flowers are an edible marvel. Daylilies and hibiscus lend a festive air to plates and platters, but watch out that they don't close before they are needed. After picking, keep them chilled in the refrigerator until serving time.

CONDITIONING

Condition your freshly cut flowers by setting them in tepid (or in some cases, cool) water up to their necks for several hours or overnight. This firms them up for arranging and is called hardening off. Do not crowd them. Mist them and keep them in a cool, dark, or dimly lit place. When conditioned, they are crisp from having absorbed the maximum amount of water, and will stay fresh much longer. Add floral preservative to the water to kill germs and provide nutrients. It's especially important to pre-condition flowers that will be used in arrangements set in floral foam or shallow water, or that are for gifts or special events.

Add floral preservative to both the conditioning and arranging water. Use a commercial product according to directions on the packet, or make your own by adding sugar and bleach to the water:

- ➤ 1 teaspoon of sugar (to feed flowers), and
- ➤ 2 teaspoons of bleach (to kill germs), and
- ➤ 4 cups tepid water.

slit woody stems at the base.

EDIBLE FLOWERS

HERB	COLOR
anise hyssop	dark blue
bachelor's button	blue, white, pink, burgundy
beebalm	red, white, lavender, pink
borage	blue edged with pink
calendula petals	yellow, orange, cream
carnations	pink, white, red, yellow, orange
chamomile	white and yellow
chive	lavender, pink
chrysanthemum petals	yellow, bronze, white, lavender, red
citrus blossoms	white
coriander	white
dandelion petals	bright yellow
daylily	yellow, orange, red, violet, pink, cream
elderflowers	white
garlic chive	white
geranium (*Pelargonium* species)	pink, red, white
gladiolus	white, pink, yellow, lavender, red
hibiscus	yellow, orange, white, pink, lavender
honeysuckle	white, yellow, pink
hyssop	white, pink, blue
impatiens	pink, white, red, purple, orange
lavender	lavender
lemon thyme	pale lavender
marigold	yellow, orange, reddish bronze
mint	white, pink
myrtle	white (remove green part)
nasturtium	cream, yellow, orange, red
pansy	white, pink, yellow, purple, blue
pink	pink, purple, red, white
pineapple sage	red
portulaca or purslane	yellow, orange, pink, white
redbud	lavender
rose	all colors but blue
snapdragon	all colors but blue
squash and pumpkin	yellow (avoid white)
sunflower (petals)	yellow, gold, orange, cream, rust
violas (violets and pansies)	lavender, white, yellow
winter savory	white
yucca	cream

* Blooms of all culinary herbs are edible. The flowers listed above are also edible, but others may be unappetizing or even poisonous.

* As with any edibles, try new types cautiously, in small amounts, in case you are allergic to them or find the taste disagreeable.

Put a little clorox, about a tablespoon or so to a pint of water, in an old dish soap container and label it "Bleach for Bouquets." Then squirt just a bit of this into the water when you bring flowers indoors. It will retard the development of bacteria in the water and keep the flowers fresh longer.

Foliage for arrangements, for instance fern, nandina, ivy, and caladium, should be completely immersed in the conditioning water for a few hours. Leathery, mature leaves will last longer than soft, new ones.

INSTANT BOUQUETS

My mother had a hibiscus holder, a cornucopia-like ceramic vase that looks nice on a table even when it is empty, but hers was always filled. The hole in the center allows you to insert the stem of a hibiscus blossom. It isn't necessary to add water. These blooms will last as long dry as they will wet.

You don't have to have a hibiscus holder to enjoy these blossoms indoors. They look nice in a saucer or among the foliage of your favorite house plant or in a dried or fresh bouquet. Most types of hibiscus last only a single day. If you want party decorations, check the variety beforehand to see what time of day they naturally close, for some types close in the evening but others in the morning. You can refrigerate the flowers during the day to keep them open later.

I was pruning the *Quiaqualis* (Rangoon Creeper vine) when I found the last bloom of the season. I put it into a small pitcher where the cluster of flowers hung gracefully for two days, a good return of beauty for minimal effort. I am now planting nasturtiums for my favorite winter-spring nosegays. It is easy to gather some, surround them with a few of their round leaves, and plop them into a small vase where their jewel-like colors light up a room. They have a special fragrance that you only notice if you get close. Try them on a bedside table.

It is easy to cut a rose or three for a bud vase. Even my husband has been known to do it. The best time to cut roses is in the bud stage after the sepals, the little green points that hold the bud, have turned downward. If you cut it before that, the bud will not open. If you cut it too late, you could lose the fragrance and much of the beauty of its unfolding.

The blooms of pinecone gingers are heavy with scented, lanolin-like lotion. You have to look under the forest of ginger leaves to find the pinecone-shaped flower heads on their stout stems. From these the small true flowers first protrude and fall off, but the cone part turns from lime green to red and stays decorative from the Fourth of July until New Year's Eve. I am always gently squeezing these when I'm working in the yard to enjoy the lotion and the fragrance. As long as there is rain, the lotion is constantly renewed. One very dry year I squeezed and got nothing, but other years some of the heads are bent over with the weight of the water within. Those are the ones we might as well cut, to bring indoors and enjoy. If they are dirty, a careful washing will remove the debris on the outside. I wash them off in the rainbarrel.

Bring in a piece of their own foliage or any other you favor. Put the cone and foliage in a bud vase, and you can squeeze the cone indoors for two weeks. I change the water every few days. When my last cone goes dry, I cut another and add it to the same vase. The first is still attractive, but out of lotion. Cones of pinecone ginger will dry right in the vase if you keep them long enough.

The cones gradually turn to bright red with orange tints. I combine them with orange and yellow zinnias and red pentas in bouquets. As a focal point in a vase, the pinecone gives added interest and lotion and usually outlasts the rest of the bouquet. The green cones blend well with purple and pink flowers.

I constantly discover new ways to bring the beauty that is often unseen in the jungle of my garden to the spotlight of a bouquet. Remember how much fun it was to pick a handful of violets or dandelions when we were little and how happy they made our mothers? It's still fun to bring in a handful of flowers.

—Monica Brandies

Some flowers need special treatment during conditioning. Yarrow, begonias, and coreopsis like a teaspoon of salt in addition to the bleach/sugar/water recipe above. Most flowers can be chilled, but lilies prefer warm conditions. Chilled hibiscus and daylily flowers last several hours without water.

Several types of plants, including poppies, allamanda, and poinsettia, contain a white, milky juice which can leak into the water and quickly spoil the flowers. Sear the cut end of their stems by scorching them with a small flame. Just light a match or candle and use it to blacken the bottom quarter inch of the stem. Or sear the stem ends in boiling water. If you recut the stem later when arranging it, scorch or sear it again. Do not use these plants in pin-holders, which pierce the sealed end.

At their base, slit stems of woody plants or flowers with thick stems before conditioning them. Though some authorities say to mash woody stem ends, we have experimented and found that making a few half-inch cuts at the bottom, parallel to the stem, works better to keep the stems unclogged.

When arranging flowers, recut stems and make new slits in the bases of woody stems. Cutting stems under water prevents bubbles of air from getting into them. A clean, slanted cut is best, for it keeps the base of the stem from being blocked by resting tightly against the bottom of the container. With woodies, peel away a ring of bark or outer skin near the stem base for better water uptake.

A cleanly snapped end is good, too, if plant cells are not crushed, especially for carnations (but not at the stem joints). All these methods help keep the small veins in the stems from becoming blocked. As long as they are open, the stems can drink water from the vase to keep blossoms and leaves fresh and alive.

For the same reason, it's a good practice to change the water and recut the stem ends every day or every other day. If your flowers wilt in a few hours, recut the stems an inch or two above the old cuts and provide fresh water. Drooping roses often revive if recut and put in deep, hot water, but protect the flowerheads from steam. When you are bringing flowers and foliage indoors, use your scissors to cut off brown ends of stems such as gingers and ti plant, or simply to shape them to suit the vase.

The clear, sticky juice from paperwhite narcissus is bad for other flowers, so wash it off under a faucet for several minutes, then presoak the flowers upright in a bucket for several hours. Then use them in a mixed bouquet, in fresh water or, better yet, arrange them by themselves.

Dianthus

No matter how well you condition the flowers or leaves, some types last only a day or two but others last more than two weeks. The individual plant listings in the earlier chapters are a good guide. Keep longevity in mind as you select what to grow, what to cut, and what to give as a gift.

After you condition flowers, recut the stems as you arrange them. Remember that cut flowers are still alive: new buds will open, and mature flowers will fold up after a few days indoors. To keep flowers fresh longer, keep the water level in the vases up, change the water often, recut stems, and clip off spent blooms.

A Cutting Garden for Florida

MAKING THE ARRANGEMENTS

Flowers fit in everywhere; there are styles and colors for any location. If the room or setting has a strong period style (Colonial, Victorian, Art Deco, Post-modern) you'll probably want the bouquet and its container to blend in harmoniously, matching the period and degree of formality. An angled bouquet of lobster claw heliconia, anthurium, and driftwood is not a natural partner for a frilly Victorian room. Of course, contrast can be effective, but takes an exceptionally knowing hand.

You can develop your eye for period style by studying arrangements found in florist and decorator shops, garden club flower shows, museums, paintings, and books on arranging. The style of the bouquet is partly determined by its container. As an arranger, you'll want to collect vases and containers that go with your setting. The less decoration on the containers, the better, for it detracts from the flowers. There's still plenty of range of color, shape, texture, and size among unembellished glass, metal, or pottery vases. Ordinary pitchers, glasses, jars, bowls, cups, and baskets make good containers if they are in keeping with the setting. Green containers harmonize with the leaves and make a visual substitute for the flower stems. Neutral colors don't detract from flowers.

Garage sales, thrift shops, and Goodwill stores are excellent places to pick up vases, lined baskets, and sometimes pin holders, at so little expense that you don't mind giving them away when you give a gift of cut flowers. Be sure you wash any container sparkling clean before you use them. A glass container should be clean enough for a person to drink from.

By the way, those expandable cup holders for the car make it very easy to transport bouquets of flowers.

In many cases you will want to recut the stems of your flowers differently before you use them, especially if they have branched stems, but it depends on the kind of arrangement you make. Low bowls indicate that the flowers should be more widely separated and have shorter stems. Chrysanthemum clusters, for instance, can be broken into several pieces. The flowers have better access to water if their internal circulation is more direct: fewer stem joints between the vase and the flower. For the sake of circulation, break or cut stems above the joints, not below.

In a transparent glass container, the stems of the flowers are a conspicuous part of the arrangement. They should not visibly be held in place by any device inside the vase such as wire mesh or a metal frog (weighted cluster of pins for holding stems). If there must be extra support, use clear glass marbles. But it is better to match the flowers to the vase so well that nothing is needed. The flowers in a clear glass vase should look as if they were casually stuck into the water, though it might take a few tries to get them just right. Even the water is important, visually. It should be crystal clear, not clouded by flower preservatives (some brands make the water look a little milky) or decaying foliage.

Arranging the Bounty

EQUIPMENT AND MECHANICS

For lined baskets, copper pots, pottery bowls, and other containers you can't see through, you may want to use something to anchor the flowers in place, especially if the bouquet is a gift. Fill the container with flowers densely enough to cover the mechanics. There are several popular aids:

Florist's Foam (Oasis). As mentioned in the chapter on everlastings, this lightweight green foam is a favorite for holding fresh flowers, especially flowers in densely packed bouquets. The brown foam is for artificial or dried flowers. Use a kitchen knife to cut a fitted piece for your container and then put it in. Half-fill the foam-filled container with warm water that has been mixed with floral preservative.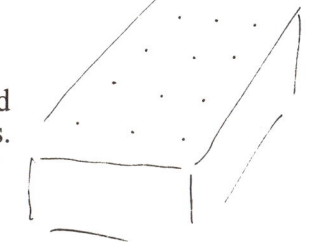
The preservative will help to counteract the acidity of the foam. Let the water soak into the foam: poke a few holes in it with a pencil to help. Then add more water until the foam is well saturated before you put in leaves and flowers.

A block of Oasis is large enough to use for several bouquets. It has the advantage of holding both water and the stems without the water spilling or the stems moving, which is great for bouquets that must travel. You can also let it extend up to an inch above the lip of the vase and put some stems in at angles or even upside down and they will still get enough water. For a container like a basket that will not hold water, or an arrangement without a container in driftwood or a fruit basket, wrap the wet oasis in foil, stick in the stems, and add a cone-shaped pick-tube (available from florists) with the bottom end cut off, to use as a funnel for adding more water as needed.

Vermiculite. Available in garden centers, this can be used in place of oasis in bouquets around your home, and is less expensive. Monica finds that a bagful containing four cubic feet does not cost much and lasts her a year, and she uses lots of flowers. It also goes into soil mixes and is used for rooting cuttings. To use vermiculite with cut flowers, fill the container with it to within an inch of the top. Add enough water so that the vermiculite is damp but not soggy before you make the arrangement. Afterward, add as much water as the vase will hold. The only disadvantage of this material is that it is messy if spilled.

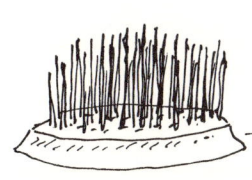
Pin Holders (Frogs). These weighted clusters of pins are set at the base of your container to hold stems in place. They come in many sizes and may be round or rectangular. If necessary, hold the frog in place with a wad of florist's clay or similar substances. It is easier if you put only a third of the water in at first, while you make the arrangement. Then fill the container the rest of the way.

Wire Mesh. A small piece of chickenwire mesh fencing with two-inch holes makes a good fitted flower holder. Cut the chickenwire with strong clippers or stub scissors (sometimes sold by florists). The piece should be about three times as large as the upper surface area of your container. The sheet of mesh, crumpled slightly, should fill the space moderately, but not so densely that you can't get the flower stems in.

A Cutting Garden for Florida

Evergreen branches. If you don't have anything else handy, you can anchor a bouquet by packing the vase with a few pieces or a loose roll of evergreen branches from landscape shrubs such as podocarpus. With these, don't worry about spoiling the water. The leaves decompose so slowly that they stay fresh longer than the flowers in the bouquet.

Florist cones, funnels, and orchid tubes. Sometimes called water picks, this family of useful small, insertable containers can be used to add height to a bouquet, transport stems of orchids, or add a few cut flowers to dish gardens. Usually they are green and somewhat like test tubes, with or without covers.

Florist's tape. This narrow, crepelike, waxy tape comes in green or brown, in rolls. Its stretchiness makes it easy to use to attach flowers to wires or false stems, or bind them together in many ways, and to conceal messy ends. You can use it to attach candle holders or orchid tubes to picks which are then inserted into the oasis or anchoring device used.

Stub wires. Straight lengths of wire, usually coated with a thin layer of green plastic to prevent rust. They are used in combination with florist's tape for false stems, and inside hollow stems of certain weak stemmed, top-heavy tall flowers to keep them upright.

SCALE AND PROPORTION

Cut flowers should be in scale with their containers, but of course judgments about this are matters of opinion. Arrangements should look balanced, and as a practical matter, actually be balanced so that they do not tip over. If you are using few enough flowers to count, odd numbers seem to be more artistic than even ones. Three lovely flowers and appropriate foliage can make a striking arrangement.

The vantage point of the viewer affects the shape of the bouquet. A table centerpiece should be equally attractive from all sides, and should not block the view of diners seated at the table. That usually means a low bowl filled with flowers. The tallest stem should be no longer than the length of the bowl. Alternatively, you can use just one or a few long-stemmed blossoms in a tall, narrow vase: a spray of orchids in a glass, for instance. Other sites for flowers have other vantage points. A bouquet on a small table next to a wall is seen from only three sides, and has a definite back and front. A fan-shaped background of leaves sets off the flowers nicely. However, if there is a mirror behind the arrangement, all four sides may be visible.

When making an arrangement, look at it from the same angles while working as it will be viewed from, when it is finished. Look down at a coffee table bouquet, up at one for a mantle.

Arranging the Bounty

Usually, short-stemmed, large, wide flowers such as hibiscus and gardenia will look great when floated in low bowl or saucer. Short-stemmed, medium sized flowers such as pansies look nice in low bowls and small containers. Short-stemmed, linear, tiny flowers such as violas and linaria are nice in small, narrow cups and vases. Long stems of tiny flowers in airy clusters such as babysbreath can be used by themselves in masses (ten or more stems together) for country-style bouquets. Or they can be used as accents or fillers in mixed bouquets.

Long, linear plumes or stems of flowers such as snapdragons can be arranged by themselves or combined with other flowers in many ways. If you have only one long-stemmed cluster, it can go in a tall, slender bud vase. Stick a dozen in a glass pitcher or arrange them in a formal mixed bouquet. Having a lot of small or narrow vases lets you put flowers all around the house quite easily, without stripping the garden.

Large rounded blossoms with long stems such as calendulas and asters can be used in almost any kind of bouquet, alone or in combination with others. Since they look heavier than spires or sprays, they are usually used near the base in mixed arrangements. Taller and heavier vases require more and longer-stemmed flowers. Select your vase according to the size and kind of plant material you have.

To make bow-like loops near the focal point, fold the leaf down, make a slit just far enough back from the end to have solid leaf to work with, and loop this over the stem before you insert the stem into the vase. This is a quick and easy florist's trick to make a bouquet look professional.

bow-like rolled leaf

STYLES OF ARRANGING

Country-style bouquets fit nearly any setting. The easiest ones to make contain only one or two kinds of plants. For most flowers, the container should be approximately as wide as it is deep, so it will hold lots of water and support the stems. The flowers and leaves should be about three times as tall as the container (before they are arranged). When the stems are put in, the parts showing should be a little greater in height than the height of the vase, but not so tall that they dwarf or unbalance it. One and a half times is usually the right proportion. They should spill out evenly in all directions, giving you a gentle mushroom shape overall. Fill the container with water. Bunch the flowers in your hand, as illustrated, trim the stems, and set them into place.

In a mixed country bouquet, a filler such as baby's breath or leaves is used all around to lightly sketch in the outer shape of the bouquet. The filler is there to make the composition harmonious, not to fill every little gap. The uniformity of the filler sets off the individuality of the various kinds of blossoms, leaves, and berries you put in. Again, you may find it helpful to bunch and trim the flowers before setting them into place.

TRADITIONAL SHAPES

Here are the most traditional shapes for massed bouquets:

A crescent shaped
B asymetric
C triangular
D S-shaped
E dome-shaped

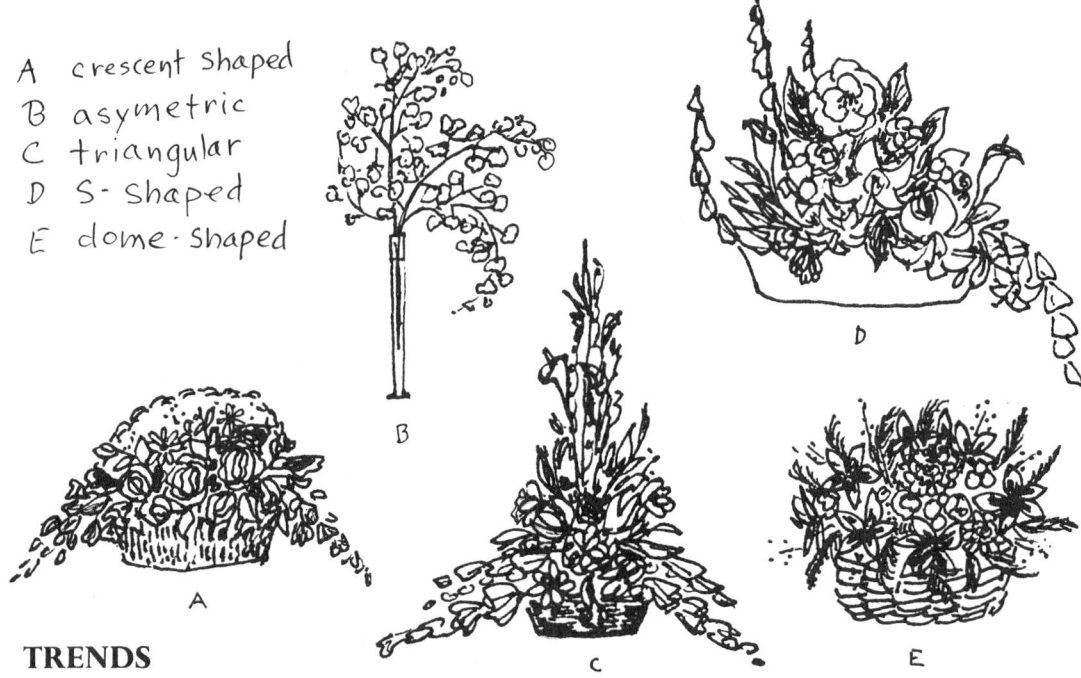

TRENDS

Newer styles of bouquets can be exciting. They are more relaxed, and employ natural looking elements, combined imaginatively. Here are a few ideas.

Vegetative style. This form of arrangement copies nature, using materials taken directly from a particular natural setting. The items used, both living and non-living, are in harmony with one another, for instance from the waterside or from the forest. They are set on a flat base such as a shallow saucer or container. Materials that were obviously cultivated are inappropriate here. You might use driftwood, sand, shells, sea grapes, and prickly pear for a seashore-themed arrangement. Landscape style is similar, but materials have been arranged as if growing naturally, using small stones and moss to set off the plants: perhaps a "lawn" of baby tears or moss with a "flower garden" of miniature African violets, growing in a wide, low bowl filled with soil.

Biedermeier style. This "nosegay" style is also called pillowing or tufting, and describes a compact, rather formal arrangement. Tussy-mussies are generally made in this style. In these mannered arrangements, the flowers are firmly set by type in concentric rings, in a low, round container or square boxlike one. Or they may be

Arranging the Bounty

spirals up a cone instead. The flowers tend to lose their individuality, while their contrasting colors and textures are emphasized. The modern version is less dense and has more texture. Limit the number of kinds of plants you use, so people can admire the combinations you have chosen.

Linear style. The linear arrangement is created with a few controlled lines: vertical, horizontal, or diagonal. Restrained use of superb materials is the key. Form, rhythm, and proportion are the essential elements here. For drama, create an asymmetric design emphasizing the few individual flowers or leaves.

Parallel style. Flowers are arranged in close, parallel groups (usually three groups), each including several bunched or tied specimens of the same species. There are open spaces between the groups. Containers are flat and do not distract from the arrangement. Form may be rectangular, square, round, or triangular. All materials are kept within the rim of the container. Interest must be added near the base to balance the strong vertical lines, and to camouflage the mechanics.

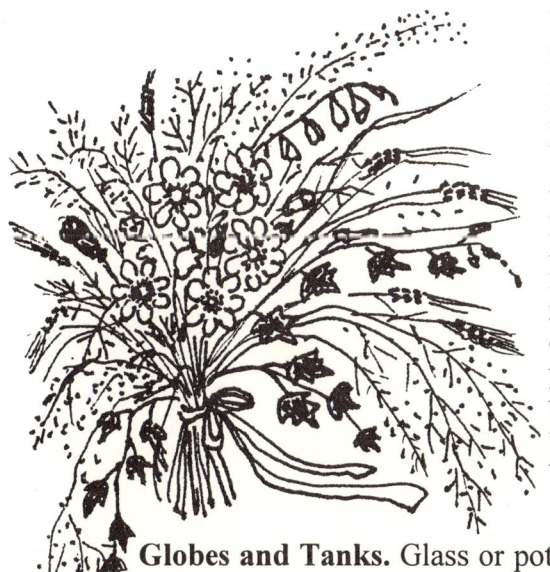

Waterfall style. In this, flowing foliage and linear sprays of accent flowers and grasses are layered by holding the bunch with one hand while adding material with the other. All the lines should flow out and trail down from the center, where they are held. It is best not to use large flowers. The bouquet may be tied near the base with a decorative cord or ribbon. You can stroll through your garden gathering and bunching the material. After it is tied and the uneven stems at the base trimmed, set the bouquet in a raised container.

Globes and Tanks. Glass or pottery vases that are nearly round or nearly square are easy to fill. Crystal tanks can be stylish anywhere. One successful look is to use identical flowers, bunched densely, or just two types, with high contrast, meticulously arranged in two separate layers. Alternatively, you can feature a single perfect flower. When using a transparent glass vase, some designers add nonfloral objects such as stones, lemons, and eggs to the water, or to the setting. You can use colorful or textured leaves, submerged and pressed against the glass. They alone *are* the arrangement.

A Cutting Garden for Florida

Wrapped containers. Any container can be given a new look with a bit of wrapping. Take a straight sided glass and arrange magnolia leaves all around, trimmed to fit, and tied with a cord. Cover the container before making the arrangement, using a rubber band to hold the leaves tightly in place. After the leaves are trimmed evenly at top and bottom, and the cord or string is in place, cut through the the rubber band to remove it. The flowers and water can then go inside the glass.

For winter holidays, wrap a round container with red velvet and fill it with leatherleaf fern leaves and white roses. In summer, wrap it in layers of airy tulle, tie it with a ribbon, and fill it with daisies or baby'sbreath. White on white always lends a cool and refreshing look.

OTHER IDEAS:

⇒ The look of Provence, a hot-colored, 'Thirties kind of look with "gardeny" sun-loving flowers like zinnias and dahlias

⇒ Fruit mixed into the arrangement, or that IS the arrangement, or that adds color inside the water in clear vases

⇒ Paired bouquets, large and with many flowers, but all of a single color and type, symmetrically placed to set off a formal, symmetrical room

⇒ Blue and white pottery vases

⇒ Garlands

⇒ A row of glasses, five or more, on a table, in line, with poppylike flowers in each, or roses or orchids

⇒ An urn, with three stems of blooming amaryllis standing upright (in oasis), tied together with a sheer green ribbon. Hide the oasis under a layer of moss

⇒ Green flowers in green vases

⇒ Bunched clusters of flowers, not dotted about, for example five pink roses next to five white ones next to five more pink ones, and so on

⇒ Woody branches of magnolia, rambling rose, or whatever is in bloom, long and rangy, and very dramatic

⇒ Unusual containers, such as an old lantern or metal bucket

⇒ Lots of hydrangeas, densely packed

⇒ Planters used as vases, especially block-shaped ones

⇒ Urns on pedestals, where a formal look is desired

Arranging the Bounty

LIVING ARRANGEMENTS OF POTTED PLANTS

Flowers do not have to be cut to be featured in arrangements. African violets, mums, gloxinias, azaleas, and many other plants in their prime make lovely, long-lasting indoor plants, the right size for a tabletop. But have you thought of buying bedding plants with a living bouquet in mind? Pots with combination plantings of blooming petunias, pansies, geraniums, globe amaranths, dianthus, or even pentas can be used for a party decoration or a few weeks of indoor enjoyment, and then be planted in the garden. You can also take a potted vine and train it onto a hoop, using it indoors or out.

Living arrangements are basically dish gardens, and can be made in many ways. Choose plants suit a party theme, or that harmonize with the room where they will be used, or flowers with colors that will fit into the garden, later. You might like red pentas in the center and white alyssum around the edges for a winter holiday arrangement, or red geraniums with white petunias.

Freesias are sold blooming in pots. Sometimes they have been specially treated to keep them from becoming too tall. In central and northern Florida, they will grow outdoors, to rebloom each year (see page 83). But first, why not use them in a tabletop arrangement? You could take one potful, planting it in a plastic lined basket or a ceramic planter, filling any crevices with moistened potting medium, and topping the soil with a silky layer of green moss or a coating of gray Spanish moss. Then water occasionally as for any potted plant.

Or take the idea a step farther by choosing a very large basket or container, and buying 3 or 5 pots of freesias. Set them into the lined or waterproof container. If some are straighter than others, they belong near the center, with the others leaning outward. If the plants are all the same height, set a stone or an upside down dish under the center or back plant to elevate it, and then cover all this with moss, straw, dry grass clippings, stones or any other material that blends with harmony. Then water. You could treat potted begonias, African violets, liriope, orchids, and other plants in similar fashion.

Monica recently made up a pretty basket filled with deep lavender impatiens that was low and spreading and full of blooms. Around it she put three pots of white pansies. The basket graced the dining table with living color for a week, then moved to the shelf of the arbor just outside and visible from the front door, where sun and cool, moist air allowed several more weeks of bloom.

Pots are easier to water outdoors, and in Florida, it is possible to move such container arrangements in and out as needed for as much as a month. Eventually the plants will go into the ground. This is also a good idea during the winter when you have blooming plants such as the impatiens, begonias, coleus, and miniature roses that might get nipped by frost. Well ahead of time, in early November, take cuttings, pot them up in 4-inch pots, pinch to make them bushy, and they should be in full bloom and usable in indoor dish gardens when frost threatens. After the weather warms up, they are ready for the outdoors.

It is possible to root cuttings of some plants while you use them as bouquets. Moist vermiculite or perlite in the container work well for this. You can make an arrangement of foliages of different colors and textures, begonias of different colors and shapes, crotons, podocarpus, and scented geraniums.

Or make a dish garden of house plants or cactus or succulents or both. Monica uses the various kalenchoes in her yard, some silver clusters of Echeveria, and some donkey's tail to cascade over the edge. This combination is long-lasting and easy-to-care for.

If you don't have any of these in your garden, buy such a dish garden ready made. When it outgrows its dish, separate the plants and plant them in a dry sunny spot in the garden, or combine them in a larger pot for the balcony or terrace. Then take more cuttings and make smaller arrangements to use indoors or give as gifts.

FREEDOM WITH FLOWERS

You may be old enough to remember, as we do, when some people were terrified of arranging flowers for fear they would somehow do it wrong. The recommended placement of flowers in a bouquet was fairly stiff and rigid, as were the mechanics such as wires and foam. All this was backed up by authoritative flower show judges. One could feel very foolish.

There are still flower show judges, but, along with the floral arts in general, they have changed and become more free-wheeling. There's a fresh, natural, and nature-loving trend with bouquets, and it starts in your own house and garden.

Floral arranging may be handled casually or taken quite seriously as an art form, but above all it should be enjoyable. Look around outside and discover something that is interesting or beautiful, and use it. With an unending bounty of materials at hand from your cutting garden, you are free to try anything without worrying about the cost. Trust your own impulses and preferences. Let your arrangements follow natural forms, and they will always be attractive.

ABOUT THE AUTHORS

Monica Moran Brandies

Monica Moran Brandies lives near Tampa where she is well known as a garden writer, lecturer, photographer, and newspaper columnist. She grew up in the Dayton area and lived on a farm in Xenia, Ohio for most of her childhood. She attended a small Catholic school before studying at the Pennsylvania School of Horticulture (now part of Temple University). She returned to Xenia and married David Brandies. Over the next two decades, their nine children were born, and Monica helped feed the family by growing all their vegetables and flowers and working in a greenhouse. She studied floral design under Bill Hixson in her greenhouse days and has been learning about growing plants in Florida since moving there in 1987.

Her articles have appeared in such magazines as *Family Circle, Woman's Day, Midwest Living, Family Digest, Catholic Digest, Mature Outlook, House and Garden, Flower and Garden, Lutheran Digest, Women's Circle,* and *Organic Gardening.* In Iowa, she wrote a garden column for the *Des Moines Register.* Then came a job change for David and a readjustment to Florida gardening for Monica. Since then, she has written or contributed to many books, some just for Florida, others nationally distributed, including *Florida Gardening: The Newcomer's Survival Manual, Xeriscaping for Florida Homes* (an award-winner)*, Herbs and Spices for Florida Gardens, Bless You For The Gifts, Ortho's Guide to Herbs, The Florida Gardener's Book of Lists, Better Homes' New Garden Book,* and *Better Homes' Step-by-Step Landscaping.* Her current book project is about shade gardening in Florida.

Betty Barr Mackey

Betty Mackey grew up in Kingsville and Lutherville, Maryland. After living in several states, including Florida, with husband Tom and sons Ed and Al, she became interested in regional gardening. She is a garden writer, lecturer, photographer, and independent press publisher and editor living in Wayne, near Philadelphia. She has contributed articles to *Organic Gardening, Horticulture, Flower and Garden,* and *Green Scene.* She is the main author of *The Gardener's Home Companion,* an award-winning general guide to gardening published by Macmillan, and is coauthor of *Cutting Gardens* (Simon & Schuster), a main selection of the Garden Book Club.

Betty started B. B. Mackey Books (then called Longwood Cottage Publishing) in 1986, while living in Longwood, Florida. She was a frequent contributor to the Orlando Sentinel. Her first title was the first edition of this book, to provide information on cut flowers for Florida gardeners. She then installed a cutting garden at Leu Botanical Gardens in Orlando. After Tom's job transfer moved them from Florida, she teamed up with Florida writer Monica Brandies for the second edition. The partnership worked out so well that the two have worked together for more than ten years. Monica's other books with B. B. Mackey Books are *Florida Gardening: The Newcomer's Survival Manual, Herbs and Spices for Florida Gardens,* and *Bless You For The Gifts.*

Betty also designed and publishes *Garden Notes Through the Years, The Plant Collector's Notebook,* and *The Herb Collector's Notebook,* three unique blank journals for keeping structured garden notes. She designs and makes horticultural notecards using her photographs and scans of flowers. Her recent publication, *Creating and Planting Garden Troughs,* by expert rock gardeners Joyce Fingerut and Rex Murfitt, won a Book of the Year 2000 award from the American Horticultural Society.

BIBLIOGRAPHY

Armitage, Allan. *Specialty Cut Flowers.* Varsity Press/Timber Press: Portland, OR, 1993.

Balfour, A. P. *Annual and Biennial Flowers.* Geoffrey Bles: London, 1963.

Broschat, Timothy, and Meerow, Alan, *Betrock's Reference Guide to Florida Landscape Plants.* Betrock's Information Services, Hollywood, Florida, 1991.

Bell, C. Ritchie, and Taylor, Bryan J. *Florida Wild Flowers and Roadside Plants.* Laurel Hill Press: Chapel Hill, 1982.

Bond, Rick, and Paterson, Allen. *Successful Flower Gardening.* Ortho Books: San Ramon, CA, 1990.

Brandies, Monica Moran. *Florida Gardening: the Newcomer's Survival Manual.* B.B.Mackey Books, Wayne, PA, 1992.

Brandies, Monica Moran. *Herbs and Spices for Florida Gardens.* B. B. Mackey Books, Wayne, PA, 1996.

Byczinski, Lynn. *The Flower Farmer: An Organic Grower's Guide to Raising and Selling Cut Flowers.* Ball Publishing: Batavia, IL, 1997.

Cathey, H. Marc. *Heat Zone Gardening.* Time-Life Books: VA. 1998.

Chaplin, Lois Trigg, and Brandies, Monica Moran. *The Florida Gardener's Book of Lists.* Taylor Publishing Co., Dallas, 1998.

Creasy, Rosalind. *The Complete Book of Edible Landscaping.* San Francisco: Sierra Club, 1982.

de Bray, Lys. *Manual of Old-Fashioned Flowers.* The Oxford Illustrated Press: Somerset, England, 1984.

Dirr, Michael. *Manual of Woody Landscape Plants*, Stipes Publishing Co.: Champaign, IL, 1990.

Embertson, Jane. *Pods: Wildflowers and Weeds in their Final Beauty.* Charles Scribner's Sons: New York, 1979.

Fell, Derek. *Annuals: How to Select, Grow, and Enjoy.* HP Books: Tucson, Arizona, 1983.

Fell, Derek. *The Easiest Flowers to Grow.* Ortho Books: San Ramon, CA, 1990.

Gattrell, Anthony. *Dictionary of Floristry and Flower Arranging.* B. T. Batsford, Ltd.: London, 1988.

Gardiner, Allan. *Modern Plant Propagation.* Lothian Publishing, Australia, 1988.

Haehle, Robert G., and Brookwell, Joan. *Native Florida Plants.* Gulf Publishing: Houston, 1999.

Halpin, Anne Moyer. *Foolproof Planting.* Rodale Press: Emmaus, PA, 1990.

Halpin, Anne Moyer, and Betty Mackey. *Cutting Gardens.* Simon and Schuster: New York, NY, 1993

Harper, Pamela, and McGourty, Frederick. *Perennials: How to Select, Grow, and Enjoy.* HP Books: Los Angeles, 1985.

Hill, Lewis. *Secrets of Plant Propagation.* Storey Communications: Pownal, VT, 1985.

Hillier, Malcolm. *Flower Arranging.* Reader's Digest Association: Pleasantville, NY, 1990.

Horton, Alvin. *Arranging Cut Flowers.* Ortho Books, San Ramon, CA, 1985.

Kasperski, V. R. *How to Make Cut Flowers Last.* New York: William Morrow & Co, Inc., 1975.

Kieft Bloemzaden B.V., Staff. *Kieft's Growing Manual.* Blokker, Holland 1989.

MacCubbin, Thomas. *Florida Home Grown: Landscaping.* Sentinel Communications: Orlando, 1987.

Mackey, Betty, and Kite, Pat. *A Cutting Garden for California.* Wayne, Pennsylvania, 1990.

Mackey, Betty, et. al. *The Gardener's Home Companion.* Macmillan: NY, 1991.

Maxwell, Lewis S. and Betty M. *Florida Flowers.* Tampa, Florida, 1984.

McSwain, Mary Jane. *Florida Gardening by the Sea.* University Press of Florida: Gainesville, 1997.

Nehrling, Arno and Irene. *Gardening for Flower Arrangement.* Dover Publications: N.Y., 1976. Other editions are available.

Rice, Graham. *Discovering Annuals.* Timber Press: Portland, OR, 1999.

Taylor's Guide to Annuals, Bulbs, Perennials, Shrubs. Houghton Mifflin Co., Boston, 1986.

Thompson & Morgan, Staff. *Successful Seed Raising,* Suffolk, England, 1991. (Pamphlet).

Watkins, John V. and Wolfe, Herbert S. *Your Florida Garden.* Gainesville: University of Florida Press, 1968.

Watkins, J. V. and Sheehan, T. J. *Florida Landscape Plants.* Gainesville: U. of Florida Press, 1975.

SOURCES AND RESOURCES

We are familiar with many of the resources listed here, and the others have a good reputation. This selection is not our endorsement, just a helpful guide. Please note that data changes frequently.

American Camellia Society, Massee Lane Gardens, 100 Massee Lane, Fort Valley, GA 31030. www.camellias-acs.com

American Hibiscus Society, P.O.Box 321540W, Cocoa Beach, FL 32932-2576. Telephone 407-783-2576. www.americanhibiscus.org

American Horticultural Society, 7931 East Boulevard Drive, Alexandria VA 22308. Telephone 703.768.5700. www.ahs.org

Association of Specialty Cut Flower Growers, MPO Box 268, Oberlin, OH 44074. Telephone 440-774-2887. www.ascfg.org

Banana Tree, The, 715 Northampton Street, Easton, PA 18042.

Better Lawns and Gardens. Radio show with Tom MacCubbin. 7-9 Saturday mornings in Florida. Telephone 888-45LAWNS.

Brent and Becky's Bulbs, 7463 Heath Trail, Gloucester, VA 23061, 804-693-3966. Bulbs for all seasons and climates.

Bromeliad Society International, Membership Secretary, Mrs. Carolyn Schoenau, P. O. Box 12981, Gainesville FL 32604-0981.

Brown's Edgewood Gardens, 2611 Corrine Drive, Orlando, FL 32803. Telephone 407-896-3203. Catalog $3. Nursery open, plants, seeds, bulbs, and supplies.

Brudy's Exotics, P. O. Box 820874, Houston, TX 77282-0874. Telephone 800-926-7333. Ginger, tropical plants.

Burpee Seeds, 300 Park Avenue, Warminster, PA 18974-4818. www.burpee.com

Fancy Hibiscus, 1142 SW First Ave., Pompano Beach, FL 33060. 250 varieties. www.fancyhibiscus.com.

Florida Federation of Garden Clubs, Inc., State Headquarters, 1400 South Denning Drive, Winter Park, FL 32789-5662. Telephone 407-647-7016. This is the parent group of 280 active garden clubs. www.ffgc.org

Florida Gardening (Magazine), P. O. Box 500678, Malabar, FL 32950-9902. Just for us, a magazine dedicated to gardening in Florida. (1 year, $19.00).

Florida Nurseryman and Growers Association, 1533 Park Center Drive, Orlando, FL 32835. Telephone 407-295-7994. For professionals. www.fnga.org

Florida State Horticultural Society, P. O. Box 2247, Goldenrod, FL 32733-2247 Telephone 407-673-7595.

The Fragrant Path, P. O. Box 328, Ft. Calhoun, NE 68023. Fragrant plants, seeds.

Gardener's Supply Company, 128 Intervale Road, Burlington, VT 05401. Tools and supplies. www.gardeners.com

Gilberg Farms, 3209 Bouquet Road, Pacific, MO 63069. Telephone 314-458-4717. Large selection of hibiscus. www.hibiscuscentral.com

Harris Seeds, P.O. Box 24966 Rochester, NY 14624-0966.

Hartley's Herbs and Everlastings, 6391 NW 150th Street, Chiefland, FL 32626. Phone/Fax 1-352-490-6977 Info@hartleysherbs.com www.hartleysherbs.com

Heliconia Haus, 12691 SW 104th Street, Miami, FL 23186.

A Cutting Garden for Florida

Heliconia Society International, c/o Fairchild Tropical Gardens, 10901 Old Cutler Road, Miami, FL 33156-4296.

Horticulture Society of South Florida, 464 Fern Street, West Palm Beach, FL 33401. Telephone 561-655-5522.

J. L. Hudson, Star Route 2, Box 337, La Honda, CA 94020. Just about any seed you can think of!

Johnny's Selected Seeds, Foss Hill Road, Albion, ME 04910-9731. Telephone 207-437-4301. Lots of special flowers for cuts. **www.johnnyseeds.com**

J. W. Jung Seed Company, 335 S. High Street Randolph, WI 53957-0001

Kinsman Company, P. O. Box 428, Pipersville, PA 18947. Telephone 215-766-5613. Tools and supplies.

Le Jardin du Gourmet, P. O. Box 75, St. Johnsbury Ctr., VT, 05863-0075. Famous tiny packets of international seeds, 30 cents each, larger quantities too.

Mellinger's, Inc., 2310 W. South Range Rd., North Lima OH, 44452-9731. Seeds and supplies for the garden.

Michael's, The Arts and Crafts Store. 850 North Lake Dr., Suite 500, Coppell, TX 75019. Floristry and craft supplies. **www.michaels.com**

Park Seed Company, 1 Parkton Ave., Greenwood, SC 29647-0001. Wonderful flowers, veggies, and more. Informative free catalog. **www.parkseed.com**

Pinetree Garden Seeds, Box 300, New Gloucester, ME 04260. Telephone 207-926-3400. Great variety, low cost, small or large seed packets. **www.superseeds.com**

Planet Begonia, 6329 Alaska Ave., New Port Richey, FL 34653. Free catalog. Visits by appointment only. **PlanetBegonia@cs.com (email).**

Renee's Garden, 7389 W. Zayante Rd. Felton, CA 95018.

R. H. Shumway's, P. O. Box 1 Graniteville, SC 29829-0001.

Roses of Yesterday and Today, 803 Brown's Valley Road, Corralitos-Watsonville, CA 95076. Telephone 831-728-1901. **www.rosesofyesterday.com**

Seedman.com (www.seedman.com). Jim Johnson, Seedman, 3421 Bream Street, Gaultier, MS, 39553. Seeds from around the world.

Seeds of Change, P. O. Box 15700, Santa Fe, NM 87506-5700. Organic flower and vegetable seeds. **www.seedsofchange.com**

Select Seeds, 180 Stickney Hill Road, Union, CT 06076-4617. Wonderful antique flower seeds. Catalog $1.00. **www.selectseeds.com**

Southern Exposure Seed Exchange, P. O. Box 170, Earlysville, VA 22936. Heirloom flowers for southern gardens. Catalog $2, refundable with order.

Stokes Tropicals, P. O. Box 9868, New Iberia, LA 70562. Color catalog of gingers, bananas, frangipani, and more. 800-624-9706. **www.stokestropicals.com**

Stokes Seeds, Inc., Box 548, Buffalo, NY 14240-0548. Telephone 800-263-7233. Seeds for growers and others, since 1881. **www.stokeseeds.com**

Territorial Seed Company, P. O. Box 158, Cottage Grove, OR 97424-0061. Telephone 541-942-9547. **www.territorial-seed.com**

Thompson & Morgan, Inc., Box 1308, Jackson, NJ 08527-0308. Fine flower seeds, more. **www.thompson-morgan.com**

University of Florida Cooperative Extension Service. Branches in every county, for help with all aspects of Florida gardening.

Tropiflora, 3530 Tallevast Rd., Sarasota, FL. Bromeliads.

Van Bourgondien & Sons, Inc., 245 Route 109, Box 1000, Babylon, NY 11702-9004 Bulbs, wholesale and retail. 800-552-9916.

Sources and Resources

Van Engelen, Inc., 23 Tulip Drive, Bantam, CT 06750. Telephone 860-567-8734. Bulbs, wholesale and retail.

Walt Disney World Nursery, Lake Buena Vista, FL 32830. AAS Flower Trial Gardens.

Wayside Gardens, One Garden Lane, Hodges, SC, 29695-0001. Telephone 800-845-1124. Shrubs and perennials. www.waysidegardens.com

We-Du Nurseries, Route 5, Polly Spout Rd., Marion, NC 28752. Rare plants.

Woodlanders, Inc., 1128 Colleton Ave., Aiken, SC 29801. Phone 803-648-7522

MORE WEBSITES

www.afloral.com. Website for complete array of supplies for florists, wholesale.

www.betterlawns.com. Website for "Better Lawns and Gardens" radio show.

www.discovering annuals.com. Esthetics and data for endless investigations.

www.FloridaGardener.com. Plenty of info here! All designed for the community of Florida gardeners.

www.google.com. Search engine. Find any plant, or anything else, for that matter.

www.ifas.ufl.edu/www/extension/index.htm. Link to all the IFAS county extension agency homepages, for urban horticulture and agricultural information.

www.jo-anns.com. Floral craft supplies, fabrics.

www.lusterleaf.com. Plant supports, soil test meters, labels, more.

www.NationalGardening.com. Clearinghouse of horticultural information.

www.plantcare.com. Expert info on greenhouse and indoor plants, huge database.

www.provenwinners.com. Sturdy plants, tested for performance.

GARDEN VISITS

If you are interested in visiting Florida gardens with conditions similar to yours, there are many possibilities. Check first with your county agricultural extension service (it's in the phone book). Many have display gardens that are both inspiration and explanation. Visit them often to see how plants change and seasons vary. Also watch for notices on the garden page of your newspaper for classes, garden tours, special displays, sales, and other events. Listed below, in alphabetical order, are just some of the many gardens open to the public. Phone first for current visiting hours and prices. On your visits, you may be able to watch plants develop through the seasons, attend classes, see demonstrations, use libraries, browse through the horticultural bookstore or giftshop, or question experts. Many places combine special plantings with other attractions that non-gardening members of the family can enjoy. Some offer annual or senior passes at reduced prices.

Alfred B. Maclay State Gardens, 3540 Thomasville Road, Tallahassee, FL 32308. Telephone 850-487-4115. 300 acres of trees, fine camellias and azaleas.

Arboretum, University of Central Florida, c/o Dept. of Biology, Orlando, FL 32816-2368. Telephone 407-823-2978.

Audubon House & Tropical Gardens, 205 Whitehead Street, Key West, FL 33040. Telephone 305-294-2116. www.audubon@flakeysol.com

A Cutting Garden for Florida

Nearly an acre of vibrantly colored tropical gardens featuring bromeliads, orchids, other exotics, native plants, a herb garden, and an unusual, 1840-style nursery. Trees and plants are labeled with their common names, Latin names, and country of origin.

Bok Tower Gardens 1151 Tower Blvd., Lake Wales, FL 33853-3412. Telephone 941-676-1408. Designed by Frederick Law Olmsted. Camellias, azaleas, Florida plants. Bell tower.

Botanical Garden, Inc. 3584 Exchange Avenue, Suite C, Naples, FL 34104. Telephone 941-643-7275.

Butterfly World Ltd. 3600 W. Sample Road, Coconut Creek, FL 33073. Telephone 954-977-4400. Rainforest trees, tropical plants, flowers, and butterflies.

City of St. Petersburg Sunken Gardens, 1825 Fourth Street N., St. Petersburg, FL 33704.

Conservancy of Southwest Florida, 1450 Merrihue Drive, Naples, FL 34102. Telephone 941-403-4239.

Cummer Museum of Art & Gardens, 829 Riverside Avenue, Jacksonville, FL 32204. Telephone 904-356-6857. The gardens reflect the blooming cycle and seasonal variety of their climate. Fall blooming plants include cannas, roses, and dahlias. Winter features azaleas, jasmine, sweet peas, pansies and camellias.

Cypress Gardens, 2641 S. Lake Summit Dr., Winter Haven, FL 33884. Telephone 863-324-2111. A wonderful old theme park with wide walks and boat rides through botanic and rose gardens. Chrysanthemum festival each October.

Disney's Horticultural Library and Resource Center, WDW Nursery SSA, P.O. Box 10000, Lake Buena Vista, FL 32830-1000. Telephone 407-938-3909.

Fairchild Tropical Garden, 10901 Old Cutler Road, Miami, FL 33156-4299. Telephone 305-667-1651. Allow plenty of time to tour this world class botanical garden and bird sanctuary. Important collections of tropical flowering trees, palms, ferns, orchids, and bromeliads. Events and educational activities.

Flamingo Gardens, 3750 Flamingo Road, Fort Lauderdale, FL 33330, 954-473-2955.

Flamingo Groves Botanic Garden, 3501 Federal Highway, Fort Myers, FL 33302. Tropical fruit and flowering trees, shrubs, and vines cover 12 acres.

Florida Botanical Gardens, 12175 125th Street North, Largo, FL 33774. Telephone 727-582-2100.

Gifford Arboretum, University of Miami, Dept. of Biology, Cox Science Center, Room 215, 1301 Memorial Drive, Coral Gables, FL 33146. Telephone 305-284-5364.

Goodwood Museum and Gardens, 1600 Miccosukee Road, Tallahassee, FL 32308. Telephone 850-877-9887.

Harry P. Leu Botanical Gardens, 1920 N. Forest Avenue, Orlando, FL 32803-1537. Telephone 407-246-2620. World-famous camellias, display and rose gardens, classes and lectures.

Heathcote Botanical Gardens, 210 Savannah Road, Fort Pierce, FL 34982, Telephone 561-464-4672.

Hialeah Park, East Fourth Avenue and 25th St., Hialeah, FL. Tropical gardens along with the racetrack from mid-January. through mid-March.

Sources and Resources

Horticultural Arts & Park Design Institute, 8700 SW 99th Street Road, Ocala, FL 34481. Telephone 352-854-0805.

Kanapaha Botanical Gardens, 4700 S.W. 58th Drive, Gainesville, FL 32608. Telephone 352-372-4981. Butterfly, rock, herb, bamboo, cycad, hummingbird, spring flower, sunken, wildflower, and other gardens (on SR 24 one mile west of I-75/exit #75). **http://hammock.ifas.ufl.edu/kanapaha/**

Marie Selby Botanical Gardens, 811 S. Palm Avenue, Sarasota, FL 34236. Telephone 941-366-5731. World Orchid Center, tropical plants, bromeliads, conservatory, and display gardens. Classes and special exhibits. Book and plant shop. Library open to members.

Marjorie Kinnan Rawlings State Historic Site, Route 3, Box 92, Hawthorne, FL 32640. Telephone 352-466-3672. Site of Cross Creek. Home, grove, and vegetable garden of the author of *The Yearling.*

McKee Botanical Garden, 350 U.S. Hwy. 1, Vero Beach, FL 32962-2905. Telephone 561-794-0701.

Mounts Botanical Garden, 559 North Military Trail, West Palm Beach, FL 33415. Telephone 561-233-1749. All America Selections Display Garden. This is Palm Beach County's oldest and largest public garden, displaying tropical and subtropical plants including natives, exotic trees, tropical fruit, herbs, citrus, palms, flowers, herbs, and much more.

Palma Sola Botanical Park Foundation, P.O. Box 14214, Bradenton, FL 34280. Telephone 941-722-2966.

Redland Tropical Gardens Botanical Foundation, Inc. P. O. Box 924785, Homestead, FL 33092. Telephone 305-258-5545.

Thomas Edison Home, McGregor Boulevard, Fort Myers, FL 33901. Many plants collected and used by Edison as well as orchids, trees, bougainvillea. 13-acre waterfront park.

Unbelievable Acres Botanic Gardens, Inc., P. O. Box 2695, Palm Beach, FL 33480. Telephone 561-655-7116.

University of South Florida, 4202 E. Fowler Avenue, SCA238, Tampa, FL 33620. Telephone 813-974-2739. (Southwest corner of campus.)

Vizcaya Museum and Gardens, 3251 South Miami Avenue, Miami, FL 33129. 305-250-9133. 70-room Italianate palace with ten acres of formal gardens. Gondola rides too!

INDEX

Abelmoschus hybrids, 60
Abutilon species, 91,92
Acalypha species, 92,93
Acanthus species, 60
Achillea species, 60,106
Achimines species, 79,80
acroclinium, 107
Adam's needle. See *Yucca.*
Aechmea species, 63
Agapanthus africanus, 7,21,80,81
Ageratum houstonianum, 36,37
ageratum, hardy, 25
air plant, 25. See also *Kalanchoe.*
Alcea rosea, 48,49. See also hollyhock.
Allamanda species, 7,92,93,119
Allium species, 80,81
aloe, 25,34,61
Aloe barbadensis, 61
Alstroemeria species, 80,81
alyssum, 22
amaranth, globe, 105. See also gomphrena.
Amaranthus species, 25,36,37,38
amaryllis, 7,19,21,22,25,79,80,84
Ammi majus, 48,49
Ammi visagna, 49
Ammobium alatum, 106
Ananas comosus, 63
Anemone species, 80,81
Angelonia grandiflora, 61
anise hyssop, 117
annuals, 7,8,20,22,35-58. See also by name.
 hardy, 35,36,47-58
 tender, 35-46
Anthemis tinctoria, 61
anthurium, 7,61
Antirrhinum majus, 48,50. See also snapdragon.
apple, 91
arrangements, floral, making of, 120
 of dried flowers, 111,112
 of fresh flowers, 115-128
 of living plants, 127,128
Asclepias species, 25,62. See also butterfly weed.
asparagus fern, 8,62
Aster, china, 36,38
 stokes, 77
authors, about, 129
Avena sterilis, 106.

azalea, 9,21,89,92,101,109
Aztec lily, 21
babysbreath, 7,9,20,22,48,53,112,123
 perennial, 107
bachelor's button, 48,51,117
Bacillus thuringiensis, 17
banana, 100
 flowering, 69. See also *Heliconia.*
basil, 21
 African blue, 73
baskets, 121
Bauhinia blakeana, 92,93
bay, sweet, 89
bean, runner, 22
beautyberry, 89,91,92,93
beebalm, 117
begonia, 116,119,128
Belamcanda chinensis, 25,62
bells of Ireland, 55,108
berries, 91. See plants by name.
Biedermeier style, 124
biennials, 7,8,47-58
Billbergia species, 63
bird-of-paradise, 7,33,77
bishop's flower, 49. See also *Ammi majus.*
blackberry lily, 25,62
black-eyed susan, 57. See also Rudbeckia.
blanket flower, 25,47,48,53
blueberry, 91
bluebonnet (lupine), 8,22,73
borage, 117
Bougainvillea species, 7,8,22,93,94
bouquet, colonial style, 112
 dried, 105-113
 fresh, 115-128
 instant, 118
Brassica, 48,50
Briza species, 106
Bromeliad species, 63
Buddleia species, 9,92,93
bulbs, 19,20,21,34,79-88
butterfly bush, 29,89,92,93,94
butterfly lily, 21
butterfly weed, 25,62
Cabbage, ornamental, 48,50
Caladium x *hortulanum*, 19,21,80,82,117
calendula, 19,22,48,50,116,117
calla lily, 7,33
Callicarpa americana, 91,92,94. See also beautyberry.
Callistephus chinensis, 36,38

Camellia species, 9,21,92,94
campanula, 47
candytuft, 19,54
Canna x *generalis*, 21,33,80,82
Capsicum annuum, 36,38
Carissa macrocarpa, 92
carnation, 7,65,117,119. See also dianthus.
castor bean, 91
cat whiskers, 74
Catharanthus rosea, 36,38
Cattleya species, 73
Cecropia palmata, 107
Celosia species, 21,36,39,107
Centaurea species, 48,51. See also bachelor's button.
Centratherum intermedium, 64
Chaenomeles japonica, 92
chamomile, 117
Chasmanthium latifolium, 25
chaste tree, 103
chenille plant, 92
chive, 117
chrysanthemum, arranging of, 120
Chrysanthemum species, 7,21,22,33,117
 C. frutescens, 64
 C. leucanthemum, 25
Citrus species, 92,95,116,117
Cleome hasslerana, 20,25,36,39,89
climate, of Florida, 7,8,19-22
clivia, 21
Coccolobis uvifera, 95
Cocos nucifera, 107
Codiaeum variegatum, 92,95
cold frame, 23,24
coleus, 21,36,43
Color, and garden design, 11
columbine, 7
Conditioning, of cut flowers, 35,119
 of tender annuals, 37
Coneflower, purple, 25,66
cones, floral, 121,122
Consolida ambigua, 25,48,51. See also larkspur.
containers, for cuttings, 30
 for floral arrangements, 120
 wrapped in cloth, 126
 for seeds, 26
copper leaf, 92,93
coral plant, 92
Cordyline terminalis, 25,95
coreopsis, 110,119
Coreopsis grandiflora, 64
 C. tinctoria, 25,48,52
 C. verticillata, 64

138

Index

coriander, 117
corms, 34,79
cornflower (Centaurea), 22,48,51
Cornus florida, 92,96
Cosmos species, 9,21,36,39,40,110
crape myrtle, 9,19,20,89,91,92,98
Crinum species, 19,21,80,82
Crocosmia species, 80,83
Crossandra infundibuliformis, 65
Croton, 92,95
Cryptanthus species, 63
cutting, of flowers, 115,116
cuttings, rooting of, 21,29-33,127
dahlia, 19,21,22,36,40,80,83
daisy, 25,47
    African (Transvaal) 7,9,33,48,52,67
    gloriosa, 8
    shasta, 7,72
dandelion, 117
daylily, 7,21,33,69,116,117,119
deadheading, 18,79
Delphinium hybrids, 65
Dendrathema species, 64
design, of floral arrangements, 122-128
design, of garden, 9-11,22
dianthus, 9,19,20,21,22,47,48,52
Dianthus caryophyllus, 65
Dietes vegata, 65,71. See also iris, African.
Digitalis species, 48,52,66. See also foxglove
Dimorphotheca species, 48,52. See also daisy, African.
dividing, of perennials, 33-34
dogwood, flowering, 19,92,96
Dracaena species, 8,91,92
dragonhead, false, 75
driftwood, 107
drying, of floral materials, 105-113
drying compounds, 110,111
dusty miller, 105
Dychorisandra thyrsiflora, 68
Dyckia brevifolia, 63
Echinacea purpurea, 25,66
elderberry, 91,92,117
Emilia flammea, 25,48,52
Erigeron hybrids, 66
Eschscholzia species, 48,53. See also poppy, California
Eucalyptus species, 8,25,92,96,109
Eucharis grandiflora, 80,83
Eupatorium coelestinum, 25
Euphorbia pulcherrima, 92,96

Eustoma grandiflorum, 53. See also lisianthus.
everlasting, winged, 106
everlastings, 22,105-113
    and glycerine,109,110
Feijoa sellowiana, 91,92
fern, 21,33,105,110,115,117
    leatherleaf, 8,9,76
fertilizer, 12,13,14,21
filler, for arrangements, 123
Firethorn, 92
flag. See *Iris.*
fleabane, 66
floral arrangements, design of, 122-128
    equipment for, 120-122
Florida, climate of, 7,8,19-22
Floss flower (ageratum), 36,37
flowers, conditioning of, 116,117
    dried,105-113
    edible, 116,117
Four o'clock, 25
foxglove, 8,22,47,48,52
frangipani, 7,101
Freesia hybrids, 19,80,83
    living arrangement of, 127
frogs, 121
frost, damage from, and pruning, 90
frost, protection from, 16,19
fungicide, 18
Gaillardia grandiflora, 66
    G. pulchella, 7,21,25,48, 53,110. See also blanket flower.
garden, dish,127,128
Gardenia jasminoides, 9,89,92,96,123
Garlic, society,21
Gaura lindheimeri, 25,66
Gazania species, 67
gels, water-retaining,16
geranium,32,75,117
Gerbera jamesonii, 67. See also daisy, African.
germination, of seeds, 26
ginger, 8,33,67,68
    blue, 68
    pinecone, 25,68,118
Gladiolus acidanthera,84
    G. hybrids, 7,21,22,34,80, 83,84,117
globes, (vases), 125
gloriosa (glory) lily, 19,84
Gloriosa rothschildiana, 19,84
glycerine, 109
Golden rain (shower) tree, 98
Goldenrod, 25,77,108
Gomphrena globosa, 21,36,40,107

grape, sea, 95
grass, 105,106,108,109,112
    fountain, 106
    foxtail, 106
    quaking, 106,108
    squirrel's tail, 106
groundcover, 9
growing conditions, 10
Guzmania lingulata, 63
Gypsophila elegans, 48,53. See also babysbreath.
Gypsophila paniculata, 107
hare's tail grass, 106
Harlequin flower. See *Sparaxis tricolor.*
harvesting, of everlastings, 108
    of flowers, 115,116
heavenly bamboo, 92. See also *Nandina domestica.*
Hedychium species, 67
Helianthus species, 36,41,68. See also sunflower.
    H. maximilianii, 68
Helichrysum bracteatum, 48,54,107. See also strawflower.
Heliconia caribaea, 69.
Heliotropium arborescens, 36,41
Helipterum roseum, 107
Hemerocallis species, 69. See also daylily.
Hibiscus moscheutos, 70
    H. species, 8,9,21,22,70,89,92, 97,116,117,119,123
hibiscus holder, 118
Hippeastrum species, 80,84. See also amaryllis.
holly, 92,98,109
    East Palatka, 8,98
hollyhock, 47,48,49
honesty. See *Lunaria.*
honeysuckle, 117
Hordeum jubatum, 106
Hosta species, 7,70
humus, 14,15
Hyacinthus species, 22,80,85
Hydrangea species, 9,89,92,97,98
Iberis umbellata, 48,54. See also candytuft.
Ilex species, 92,98. See also holly.
impatiens, 7,8,21,36,117,127
insects, beneficial, 17
Ipomoea batatas, 70
iris, African, 33,71. See also *Dietes vegata.*
Iris species, 7,33,70,71,80,85
ivy, 9,109,117
Ixia species, 80,84
Ixora species, 92
jasmine, 89

A Cutting Garden for Florida

Jatropha multifida, 92
jewels of opar, 25,78
Joseph's coat, 38. See also *Amaranthus.*
Justicia species, 71
Kalanchoe species, 7,25,71,72
Koelreuteria species, 98
kumquat, 95
ladybug, 17
Lagerstroemia indica, 92,98. See also crape myrtle
Lagurus ovatus, 106
landscaping, Florida, 7,8,9,10,11
lanolin, 118
Lantana camara, 99
lantern, chinese, 108
larkspur, 22,25,47,48,51,111
Lathyrus odorata, 48,54. See also sweet pea.
Lavatera trimestris, 48,54
lavender, 117
    sea, 55
lawns, 21
layering, 32,33
leaves, 115
Leucanthemum x superbum, 72
Leucojum aestivum, 80,85
Lifting, of perennials, 34
light, and seedlings, 23
ligustrum, 91
Lillium species and hybrids, 80,86
lily
    blackberry, 74
    candy, 74
    crinum, 19,21,82
    fairy. See *Zephyranthes* species.
    gloriosa, 19,80,84
    Jacobean, 87
    Madonna, 86
    milk-and-wine (crinum), 19,21,82
    of Peru, 81. See also *Alstroemeria.*
    of the Nile, 81. See also *Agapanthus.*
    rain. See *Zephyranthes* species.
    spider, 21
limequat, 95
Limonium sinuatum, 48,55,108. See also statice.
Linaria marrocana, 48,55. See also toadflax.
linear style, 125
Liquidambar styraciflua, 92
Liriope muscari, 33,72
lisianthus, 20,53
Lobelia cardinalis, 72

love-in-a-mist, 48,56,108
love-lies-bleeding, 37
Lunaria annua, 47,108
Lupinus species, 8,73
Lycoris species, 80,86
Macleaya microcarpa, 25,73. See also poppy, plume.
Magnolia species, 8,10,89,92,99
maintenance, garden, 18,21
    of shrubs, 90
mallow, 48,54,70
Manaos beauty, 64
maple, flowering, 91,92
marguerite, golden, 61
marigold, 20,21,26,43,44,117
Matthiola incana, 48,55. See also stock.
Merremia tuberosa, 108
mesh, wire, 121
microclimates, 20
mildew, and roses, 102
milfoil, 60
mint, 21,117
Mirabilis jalapa, 25
mites, 21
Molucella laevis, 55,108
money plant. See *Lunaria.*
Montbretia. See *Tritonia* species.
mordica, 8
Morus australis, 99
moss, Spanish, 105,113
mound layering, 32,33
mulch, 14,15,18
Musa abysinnica, 100
myrtle, 117
Nandina domestica, 8,9,91,92,100,105,109,117
narcissus, 20,22,79,80,86,119
nasturtium, 7,13,20,25,26,36,45, 47,58,117
natal plum, 92
nectarine, 91
nematodes, 13,14
Neomaria species, 71
Nerium oleander, 100
newspaper, mulching with, 15
Nicandra physalodes, 48,56. See also shoo-fly plant.
Nicotiana alata, 36,42
Nigella damascena, 48,56,108. See also love-in-a-mist.
nonfloral materials, and arrangements, 125
Oasis, 112,113,121
oats, animated, 106
obedient plant, 75
Ocimum kilimanscharium x *basilicum purpureum,* 73
oleander, 100

olive, tea or sweet, 92
onion, ornamental, 81
orange, 91,95
orchid, 7,73
orchid tree, 92,93
oregano, 21
Orthospiphon stamenis, 74
Osmanthus fragrans, 92
Oxalis species, 7,80,86
palm, 8,105,109,115
    coconut, 107
    sabal, 91,103
palmetto, 103
Panicum violaceum, 106
pansy, 19,20,22,47,110,111,116,117
Papaver rhoeas, 48,56. See also poppy, shirley.
parallel style, 125
Pardancanda norissii, 74
Passiflora species, 21,74
passion flower, 21,74
peach, 91
pear, 91
Pelargonium species and hybrids, 75
Pennisetum villosum, 106
Pentas lanceolata, 7,21,25,75,89,92
peonies, 7
Pepper, ornamental, 36,38
perennials, 7,8,59-78
    and regions, 59
    division of, 33-34
    short-lived, 49,59
Perilla frutescens, 25,36,42
periwinkle, 21,36,38
pests, control of, 17
petunia, 19,20,22,48,56
pH, 14
phlox, 7,22,47,48,57
Physalis alkegengii, 108
Physostegia virginiana, 75
pin holders, 121
pineapple, 63
Pineapple guava, 92
pink, 117. See *Dianthus.*
Pittosporum tobira, 8,9,91,101,109
planning, of cutting gardens, 7,8,9,10
plantain, wild, 69. See also *Heliconia.*
planting, and seasons, 7,8,12,19,20,21,22
    of shrubs, 90
planting medium, for cuttings, 31,32
    for seeds, 26
Plants, for bedding, 35
plum, 91,92
Plumeria species, 101
Podocarpus species, 8,91,92
pods, 105,109

Index

poinsettia, 7,21,92,96,105,109,119
Polianthes tuberosa, 80,87
poppy, 19,20,22,119
    California, 48,110
    Iceland, 47
    plume, 25,33,73
    pods of, 108
    shirley, 7,8,22,47,48,56
portulaca, 21,117
potato, sweet, 34,70
prairie gentian, 53. See also
    Eustoma species.
preservative, floral, 116
pressing, of flowers and leaves, 110
privet, 109,
propagation, from seed, 23-28
    with cuttings, 21,29-33
    with divisions, 33-34
proportion, for floral arrangements, 122,123
pruning, 90
    of roses, 102
Pyracantha species, 91,92
Quince, Japanese flowering, 92
Ranunculus asiaticus, 87
regions, of florida, 7
remedies, for pests, 17,18
rhizomes, 79
Rhododendron hybrids, 92,101. See also azalea.
Rosa species, 92,102. See also rose.
rose, 6,19,20,22,89,92,102,109, 116,117,118
Rose, Sylvester, 111
rose, wood, 108
Rudbeckia species, 22,25,33,48,57,76
Rumohra adiantiformis, 76. See also fern, leatherleaf.
sage, 91
    mealycup (blue), 76,108
    Mexican, 76
    pineapple, 117
    scarlet, 36,43,76
Salix matsudana, 102
salt, and conditioning, 119
Salvia coccinea, 25
    S. farinacea, 76,108
    S. leucantha, 76,108
    S. species, 20,25,57,76,108
    S. splendens, 36,43
Sambucus canadensis, 92
sand, as drying compound, 111
Scabiosa atropurpurea, 47,48
scanning, of flowers and leaves, 110
screening, and seedlings, 23
sea grape, 95
Sea oats, northern, 25

searing, of stem ends, 119
seeds, 9,18,23-28
    of hardy annuals, chart, 48
    of tender annuals, chart, 36
    saving of, 27,28
Serenoa repens, 103
Setaria glauca, 106
shade, 20
    and seedlings, 23
shoo-fly plant, 48,56
shrimp plant, 25
shrubs, 89-103
    and conditioning, 119
Silene species, 47,48,57
silica gel, 110,111
site, for cutting garden, 12
slits, in stem ends, 119
snakewood, 107
snapdragon, 9,19,20,22,47, 50,117,123
sod, removal of, 13,14
soil, 7,10,13,14
    for cuttings, 30,31
Solenostemon species, 36,43. See also coleus.
Solidago species, 25,77,108
Spanish bayonet. See *Yucca.*
Sparaxis tricolor, 80,87
Spider flower. See cleome.
spiderwort, 25,78
Sprekelia formosissima, 87
squash, 117
star-of-Bethlehem, 21
statice, 48,55,105,108,112
Stephanotis floribunda, 103.
stock, 19,22,47,48,55
Stokesia laevis, 77
strawflower, 54,105,107,109
Strelitzia species, 77. See also bird-of-paradise.
Strobilanthes, 21
styles, of floral arrangements, 122-128
sunflower, 9,20,22,36,41,47,117
    Mexican. See Tithonia
    prairie, 68
sweet bay, 92
sweet gum, 92
sweet pea, 7,22,26,48,54
sweet william, 47
Tagetes species, 36,43,44. See also marigold.
Talinum paniculatum, 25, 78
tanks, 125
tape, florist's, 122
tassel flower, 48,52
thistle, 109
ti plant, 21,95

tickseed, 25,48,52. See also coreopsis.
Tillandsia species, 63
Tithonia species, 20,36,44
toadflax, 48,55. See also *Linaria.*
Tobacco flower, 36,42. See also *Nicotiana.*
topiary, of dried flowers, 112,113
torenia, 21,36,44
Tradescantia ohioensis, 25,78
treasure flower, 67
trees, 89-103
    and conditioning, 119
trinity flower, 78
Triticum spelta, 106
Tritonia species, 80,87
Tropaeolum species, 36,45,58. See also nasturtium.
tubers, 79
tubes, orchid, 122
tulip, 22
vases, 120
vegetative style, 124
verbena, 22,36,45,47
vermiculite, 121
vervain, 45
viburnum, 9,89
vinca, 36,38
vines. See by name.
viola, 22,47,48,110,117
Virginia creeper, 8
Vitex agnus-castus, 103
Vriesa splendens, 63
wandering jew, 9
water, and cut flowers, 119,120
waterfall style, 125
Watsonia species, 88
wheat, spelt, 106,108
willow, corkscrew, 102
windflower. See *Anemone.*
wire, 109,122
woody plants, and conditioning, 119
yarrow, 60,119. See also *Achillea.*
Yucca species, 7,19,89,103,116
Zantedeschia species, 80,88. See also calla lily.
Zephyranthes species, 34,80,88
Zingiber species, 68. See also ginger.
Zinnia species, 20,21,36,46,110,111
zones (climate), 7,19-22

141

A Cutting Garden for Florida

BOOKLIST

B. B. Mackey Books, Publisher · Box 475 · Wayne, PA 19087
bbmackey@prodigy.net   www.mackeybooks.com

Books may be ordered from any full service bookstore or by mail from B. B. Mackey Books. Or order on the web from **www.Amazon.com**.

$15.50. HERBS AND SPICES FOR FLORIDA GARDENS, by Monica Moran Brandies. This wonderful book contains full instructions for growing and using herbs for flavor, health, beauty, crafts, scent, and garden color, in Florida's unique conditions. Also, Monica takes you to visit growers in Northern, Central, and Southern Florida. There's hard-to-find info on neem, ginger, and other tropicals. The extensive plant directory is a delight unto itself. 250 pages, paperbound, indexes and supplements. Rave reviews! Recommended by many herbalists and herb stores. ISBN 09616338-6-7.

9.95. FLORIDA GARDENING: THE NEWCOMER'S SURVIVAL MANUAL, by Monica Moran Brandies. Help is here! Laugh off the garden perils and grow a wonderful new landscape. Here's the inside information on Florida lawns, flowers, veggies, fruits, terrace gardens, trees, and shrubs. Organic methods are emphasized. Indexed and illustrated. Loads of resources listed. Paperbound. 8 1/2 by 11 inches, 86 packed pages. Very popular, reprinted many times. ISBN 09616338-3-2. 1993.

15.95. A CUTTING GARDEN FOR FLORIDA, THIRD EDITION, by Betty Barr Mackey and Monica Moran Brandies. Revised 2001. Grow marvelous flowers for bouquets in your Florida landscape. This new edition of a well-loved book tells how to grow the best cut flowers for Florida, and how to harvest, condition, and arrange them. The month-by-month Florida calendar is a special feature. Here is wonderful information on many annuals, biennials, perennials, shrubs, and bulbs, including plant-by-plant conditioning information. 144 pages, paperbound, indexed, resource list, public garden directory. ISBN 9616338-9-1.

11.95. GARDEN NOTES THROUGH THE YEARS. Organize your garden records. This cleverly designed four-year blank journal by Betty Mackey prompts you to record tasks done, weather observations, and plants in bloom or fruit. On each page spread, you can see four years of notes at a glance for that week of the year. Comb-bound to lay flat, with a laminated cover. Printed on heavy cream-colored paper and illustrated with pen and ink drawings and lithographs. Designed in 1994, revised in 2000. ISBN 9616338-4-0.

BOOKLIST

$7.95. PLANT NOTES: THE PLANT COLLECTOR'S NOTEBOOK. Name that cultivar! Here is the perfect little notebook for tracking garden plants, designed by Betty Mackey, with a space for your illustration or plant tag on each page. Record the genus, species, cultivar, source, etc. There's a whole page per plant, with room for a hundred plants, and a table of contents you fill in as you go. The cover depicts blue *Campanula rotundifolia* in bloom. This is a nice gift for a dedicated plant person, or someone beginning a garden. Don't you wish you still had all those name tags? Comb-bound to open flat. ISBN 09616338-3-5

8.00. A CUTTING GARDEN FOR CALIFORNIA, by Pat Kite and Betty Mackey. 1990. How to grow flowers for bouquets at home in your California landscape. Wonderful information for all zones of California. Not many copies left. $8.00, paperbound. ISBN 9616338-1-6.

$21.00. CREATING AND PLANTING GARDEN TROUGHS, by Joyce Fingerut and Rex Murfitt. Photos by Jane Grushow. This book is the complete guide to creating and planting wonderful, lighter-weight garden troughs, and a **winner of the American Horticultural Society's Year 2000 Book Award.** Troughs, those elegant antique stone containers so treasured by alpine gardeners, can now be made at home with a lightweight cement-based material called hypertufa, formed with simple molds. Troughs make the perfect environment for evocative miniature gardens, each with the perfect size, soil type, rock forms, mulch, and siting for the desired plants. Also includes hundreds of photographs, drawings, plant discussions, sample planting plans, resource lists, bibliography, subject index and plant index. Praise-filled reviews abound for this much-needed title. Hardcover, 7 x 10 inches. Color photos, 170 pages, index, extensive resource list. 1999. ISBN 1-893443-00-0.

10.95. BLESS YOU FOR THE GIFTS, by Monica Moran Brandies. Humorous true stories of life in a large, rural family, including schooldays, cows, babies, parents, and gardens. In Monica's classic style, a delightful reading experience! "Extraordinary tales that demonstrate the faith, humor, and wisdom of ordinary people," says *Midwest Book Review*. If you enjoy Monica's garden books, this is a special treat. Paperbound, 200 pages. 1997. ISBN 09616338-7-5.

--------------------------- **TO ORDER BY MAIL** ---------------------------

Postage is free on any two or more books going to the same address. Add $2.00 on single orders. Pennsylvania residents (only), please add 6 percent for state sales tax. Send your check and order to:

B. B. Mackey Books
P. O. Box 475
Wayne, PA 19087-0475

Be sure to include your mailing address and phone number.

▲▲▲▲▲▲▲

Bookstores and libraries, call Great Outdoors Publishing in St. Petersburg, Florida (800-869-6609) to order from our distributor and fellow publisher. Ask for their catalog of nature, cookbook, garden, and Florida books.

epicurious.com
Infusing Oil w/ Herbs

Wash & dry herbs
Rosemary & Thyme
Heat in oil over medium heat
for 5 min until bubbly
Cool completely
Bottle.
If you put herbs in bottle
oil will be slightly cloudy.
Store in refrigerator for 1 mo

Rosemary + Thyme Infused Oil
Keep Refrigerated · Exp - 1-25-15
Shelf life - 1 mo.
Let sit At Rm Temp for 20min Before each use.

Use on Salads! - for Dipping, ~~Add Sap~~ stir frying or sauteing
or Drizzle over Pasta or Seafood.